THE ENGLISH

DRAMATIC LYRIC, 1603-42

A STUDY IN

STUART DRAMATIC TECHNIQUE

WILLIAM R. BOWDEN

ARCHON BOOKS
1969

[Yale Studies in English, Vol. 118]

SBN: 208 00776 8
Library of Congress Catalog Card Number: 69-15680
Printed in the United States of America

PREFACE

OUR CONTINUING ENJOYMENT of the many incidental lyrics contained in English plays, particularly of the Tudor and Stuart periods, is attested by a long line of anthologies of these lyrics, the most distinguished being that by Edward Bliss Reed.[1] It is, in a way, unfortunate that this anthologizing of the songs, the acknowledgment of an intrinsic value undiminished by the passage of three centuries since their composition, has tended to make us forget that originally they were not isolated poems but parts of plays which were written for the professional stage. Everyone is familiar with Suckling's "Why so pale and wan, fond lover," but a poll of professional scholars will reveal surprisingly few who know anything about the play of which it is a part, fewer who can describe its setting or purpose. This situation is unfortunate in much the same way as it is unfortunate for a city child not to know where milk comes from, even though his ignorance in no way diminishes the nutritional value of his noontime glass.

Scholars have concerned themselves with special problems related to the songs—the musical settings, the use of music as entr'acte entertainment, the authorship of certain lyrics—but they have never quite agreed on just what the songs are doing in the plays. There is disagreement even on such a fundamental question as whether the Stuart dramatists regarded the lyric as mere spit and polish to make their product more attractive or whether they sought and achieved more significant ends by its use. One small but articulate group has held the incidental song to be extraneous entertainment and little more.[2] The spokesmen of the opposing school have published little, and their contributions have been, in the main, essays at classifying and cataloguing the situations in which song is likely to be used.[3] Now, the fact that about 70 per cent of the plays of

1. Edward Bliss Reed, *Songs from the British Drama* (New Haven, Yale University Press, 1925). The notes, which supply the setting of each song, and an appended essay, "Some Aspects of Song in the Drama," make this the most valuable book available on the dramatic lyric.

2. The most emphatic statement of this position is that of Louis B. Wright, "Extraneous Song in Elizabethan Drama after the Advent of Shakespeare," *Studies in Philology*, 24 (April, 1927), 261–74. Somewhat similar views are expressed by G. H. Cowling, *Music on the Shakespearian Stage* (Cambridge, Cambridge University Press, 1913), 97–8, and elsewhere.

3. Reed's essay in *Songs from the British Drama* is excellent, but very brief. See also John Robert Moore, "The Song in the English Drama to 1642" (Ph.D. dissertation, Harvard University, 1917; much of this material has been published in the form of articles—see below, notes and Bibliography); Andrew Jackson Walker, "Popular Songs and Broadside Ballads in the English Drama, 1559–1642" (Ph.D. dissertation, Harvard University, 1934); and Warren Welles Wood, "A Comparison between Shakespeare and His Contemporaries in Their Use of Music and Sound Effects" (Ph.D. dissertation, Northwestern University, 1944).

the Stuart period contain anywhere from one to twenty songs suggests that, whether the dramatic lyric was decorative or functional, the playwrights considered it one of the most important devices at their disposal. But even those scholars who have made special studies of the dramatic technique of individual playwrights have had little or nothing to say in interpretation of their subjects' use of song.

Shakespeare is, of course, an exception to this observation. But although the published work on the dramatic functionalism of his songs has its value, it has been prejudicial to our understanding of the general contemporary attitude toward the use of song in the early seventeenth-century drama. For one reason, an orthodox but uncritical idolatry of Shakespeare is likely to lead to unfairness to his contemporaries. For another, a good part of his work was produced during years when the technique of the song was still being perfected; new and effective techniques were developed after his own practice had become relatively set. Finally, the canon of his plays is not large enough to justify broad generalizations. Disregard of these facts may lead to false conclusions or may result in failure to reach sound conclusions which are not demonstrable from Shakespeare alone, but for which there is sufficient evidence in the plays of his contemporaries. It is better to interpret Shakespeare's techniques through a study of the period as a whole than to generalize about the period as a whole from a reading of Shakespeare.

The aim of this study is to answer, as fully as the evidence will permit, the double question of how the song is used in the Stuart drama and why it is used as it is. The conclusions presented have been reached by inductive methods; they are based on an examination of over 475 plays —virtually all that have survived from the period under consideration. In deference to the amount of material already published on Shakespeare's songs, I shall have little to say about them other than to mention some of the more familiar as illustrations of principles based on the work of other authors. This fact, however, is not to be interpreted as an indication that I agree with everything that has been printed about Shakespeare's use of song.

I have set the years 1603 and 1642 as the limiting dates for this investigation. The arbitrary limitation is possible because this is not a historical study; it is an analysis of fully developed techniques and, as such, is concerned only with the maturity of the English Renaissance drama. The early limit of 1603 has been extended, however, to allow the inclusion of the complete canons of authors like Heywood, Dekker, and Chapman, who, although they flourished in Jacobean times, began writing in the 1590's.

This investigation is further limited, naturally, to the legitimate drama. Such forms as the court masque, the royal entertainment, and the civic pageant in no sense attempt to create an illusion of life. Their appeal is spectacular rather than dramatic, and they have their own highly formal sets of rules, based on principles very different from those governing the offerings of the professional theater.

A few more explanatory comments are necessary; two relate to critical assumptions, and two to mechanical procedure. In the first place, the plays under examination are (and, I think, must be) considered as living drama, planned and written for the theater, and not as dramatic poems, collections of significant metaphors, or allegorical puzzles. This approach will make possible the illustration or clarification of occasional points by reference to the dramas of other times and countries. The analogy with the modern cinema is particularly rewarding. Both it and the Stuart plays represent a drama in its vigorous youth, one sufficiently detached from the critical standards of the past to have to make up its own rules as it goes along, and appealing to a wide and not very selective audience. Each allows the dramatist almost boundless freedom. The motion picture carries the audience beyond the theater walls by the realistic nature of its visual effects; the bare stage depended on the imaginative cooperation of the audience for release from limitations of place and time, but the result was substantially the same—a drama fluid in movement, unrestricted in scope, laying primary stress on plot, and relying on the simplest and most basic emotional values. The permanent organization of the Stuart acting company resulted in the development of somewhat stereotyped "lines" of characterization, much as the star system has done in the cinema. There are other correspondences. The corroboration of one's interpretation of certain phenomena in the Stuart drama, then, sometimes can be found in the fact that very similar phenomena have occurred in the cinema within one's own memory.

Second, it must be admitted that the period 1603–42 did not bring forth 475 good plays. But for two reasons a study of dramatic technique justifies the bringing of any dusty playbook from its perhaps deserved obscurity. The greater the dramatist, the more his art conceals his artfulness; the second-rate writer produces a work which, though inferior as literature, can be analyzed with more ease and less ambiguity. Moreover, an imitative author, because he can be counted on to repeat the devices which have proved most successful in the work of the major figures, presents what amounts to a digest of material worthy of attention.

If one were to be diverted into weighing all the incidental problems of authorship, date, and details of production that arise in connection with any study of the Stuart drama, neither time nor space would be left for the study itself. The solution is to transfer to some single authority the responsibility for all such factual information. Harbage's *Annals of Eng-*

lish Drama, 975–1700,[4] is my authority. This book is ideal for the purpose because of its completeness and the convenience of its arrangement
of data. Since my investigation is not primarily historical or comparative,
the effect on my conclusions of possible minor errors in ascriptions of
date and authorship will be negligible.

A second mechanical problem is that of finding a uniform system of
reference for locating songs or quotations in the plays. The most exact
reference would be to the volume and page of a standard edition; but its
disadvantage is that the reader who does not have access to that edition
is left at a loss. My notes, therefore, locate passages by act and scene.
In the event that an author himself begins a new scene at every entrance
or exit of a major character, as Jonson does, I follow his example;[5]
otherwise I accept the modern system of division according to actual
change of place. When the acts of a play are not separated into scenes,
as is frequently the case in the second folio edition of Beaumont and
Fletcher, for example, I make the obvious divisions. When a play is not
divided into acts, however, I have thought it best to cite the page of a
particular edition.

In the following chapters I shall begin by examining the concept of an
interrelationship between music and the emotions which was current in
the popular psychology of the early seventeenth century. I shall illustrate
the effect of this concept on the dramatic lyric by examining in detail one
phase of it, the connection between music and love, and then devote two
chapters to a more general demonstration of how the dramatists put the
emotional values of the lyric to work in their writing of compact and effective plays. Chapter v will deal with those functions of the song which
are dependent on its accidental qualities of duration and text rather than
on its psychological meaning; Chapter vi will examine briefly the per-
sistent idea that the dramatic lyric is designed for extraneous entertainment and nothing more. The question of extraneousness leads into a
consideration of the possibility that certain extant songs were late interpolations rather than integral to the original plan of the plays in which
they appear, and justifies a study of the relation of some of the songs to
the early printed copies or manuscript texts of these plays. The final
chapter will consider the more important ways in which the human element was likely to influence the amount of song in the drama.

The unifying principle underlying this entire study is my attempt to
give a definitive picture of exactly what the dramatic lyric meant to
everyone whom it concerned—the dramatist and the theater audience
first of all, but also the actor, the book-seller, and the reading public. The

4. Alfred Harbage, *Annals of English Drama, 975–1700* (Philadelphia, University
of Pennsylvania Press, 1940).

5. Marston is an exception. For the specific texts used for citation and scene division, see Bibliography, sec. i.

research involved has made possible, and the evidence discovered has necessitated, a re-evaluation of many of the more confidently expressed theories which have been promulgated about the place of song in the drama. From my work I have gained a better understanding of the artistic craftsmanship of the Stuart dramatists and a sense of comradeship with the Stuart public as fellow playgoers. These gains I hope I shall be able to share.

In its original form, this work was submitted to the Graduate School of Yale University in candidacy for the doctoral degree. The general subject of the investigation was suggested to me by the late Robert J. Menner. I am indebted to O. J. Campbell for assistance during the early stages of research. The bulk of the work was done under Charles T. Prouty, in whom I found not only a wise and patient adviser but a good friend; Ruth Prouty also gave me valuable help. Eugene M. Waith and Eric W. Barnes have read my manuscript, and I have profited from their competent criticism. I am very grateful to these people, to the staff of the Yale University Library, and to my wife, without whom the job could hardly have been done at all.

CONTENTS

I

The Meaning of Song in the Seventeenth Century

ONE OF THE STOCK COMMENTS on the lyrics scattered throughout the Tudor and Stuart plays is that "Music was popular in the drama because it was popular everywhere."[1] The danger in this as in any other truism is that it inhibits further thinking: it seems to explain the presence of the songs without actually doing so. Moreover, in its implication that the incidental lyrics were either part of a photographic reproduction of contemporary life or else a supine surrender to a public taste which demanded song in plays even to the detriment of their dramatic interest, it disregards the vitality of these plays. A first-rate drama such as that of the English Renaissance cannot be undiscriminating in its choice of materials for creating the illusion of life nor can it endanger that illusion by the irresponsible incorporation of extraneous matter. The dramatic use of song, then, can hardly be wholly without meaning.

What is that meaning? A logical attempt to discover it might be based on the assumption that the employment of song in the drama is related to the concept of song held in undramatic everyday life—that is, to the interpretation of song in the light of seventeenth-century psychology. The word "psychology" has come, of late, to have an unfortunate ring to students of the English Renaissance.[2] It is used here in a nonclinical sense: the interpretation of behavior through principles which formed part of the aggregate information not only of scholars and philosophers but of every seventeenth-century Englishman. Specifically, if certain ideas were current as to what made people sing, what their singing meant, what music was good for, then those ideas would certainly be reflected in the drama. A dramatist of insight might be expected to use song purposively to suggest those ideas to his audience and so to achieve dramatic effects which it would be slower and more difficult for him to achieve otherwise.

The dramatic effects achieved through the use of song depend in varying proportions, as we shall see, on both the musical setting and the text

1. G. H. Cowling, *Music on the Shakespearian Stage* (Cambridge, Cambridge University Press, 1913), p. 92.
2. See Louise C. Turner Forest, "A Caveat for Critics against Invoking Elizabethan Psychology," *PMLA*, 61 (September, 1946), 651–72. The psychology of this study would not offend the author of the "Caveat," being based not on technical writings but on the average man's furniture of ideas.

of any lyric. Now, although much may be learned from an analysis of the sort of music that was composed to attain a given emotional effect or, conversely, from a minute examination of the semantic implications of the texts of the songs, a reconstructive study must attempt to look at its subject through seventeenth-century eyes. In the eyes of the great English composers of the period, words and music were aimed at a conjoint effect.[3] Therefore, when we speak in this study of particular lyrics, we must try to think of their words and music as forming a single effective unit.

It should be remembered, however, that unless the dramatists had been deeply concerned with the emotional overtones produced by the melodic line, they would have found no particular functional advantage in the use of song as opposed to spoken words. For this reason the distinction between the meanings of "song" and "music" is not always observed in the following pages. The difference, so far as the plays are concerned, is in fact one of degree rather than of kind. It has long been recognized that the early English dramatists were aware of the value of music for emotional effect;[4] song simply offered them certain advantages over instruments. It was the natural way of making music: whereas the ability to play an instrument acceptably was not a universal acquirement, any actor could sing, well or ill—and that without the necessity of lugging a lute or viol about the stage with him. In the seventeenth century vocal music had attained a higher degree of perfection than had instrumental music.[5] Most important of all, song afforded the extra communicative medium of words. There was a disadvantage, of course, in that although pantomimic action could continue through a song, dialogue could not; whereas the psychological development of a particular scene might be intensified by a formal song, the chronological action was, except in rare cases, virtually suspended. Consequently, it was when a mood or emotion momentarily assumed primary dramatic importance that the playwright sought the maximum emotional effect from music by employing voices rather than instruments; for instruments, though they might induce the same moods as voices, could not compete with voices in emotional power. The philosophic concepts held by the dramatists

3. Thomas Morley, laying down "Rules to be observed in dittying" in *A Plaine and Easie Introduction to Practicall Musicke* (1597), stresses the fidelity with which the music must follow the sense, rhythm, and emotional intention of the words. The passage is too long for reproduction here but is easily available in M. C. Boyd, *Elizabethan Music and Musical Criticism* (Philadelphia, University of Pennsylvania Press, 1940), pp. 234 ff. Boyd also quotes Robert Jones and Thomas Campion on the importance of coupling "Words and Notes lovingly together"; in fact, Boyd's entire chaps. v ("Songs") and ix ("Musical Theory") are relevant here.

4. E.g., Cowling, *op. cit.*, pp. 71–2. But the dramatists themselves sometimes point out their awareness of this power of music; see below, pp. 49–50.

5. See, for example, Charles Villiers Stanford and Cecil Forsyth, "The Palace of Greenwich. January 26, 1595," *A History of Music* (New York, Macmillan, 1917), chap. ix.

and audiences of Stuart England apply to music in general. The dramatic lyric is simply music in the spotlight. When a Stuart writer generalizes on *music,* then, whatever he says of it must be understood as applying even more directly to *song.*

In 1614 the musician Thomas Ravenscroft wrote,

> I have heard it said that Love teaches a man Musick, who ne're before knew what pertayned thereto: And the Philosophers three Principall Causes of Musick, 1. Doulour, 2. Joy, 3. Enthusiasme or ravishing of the Spirit, are all found by him within Loves Territories. Besides, we see the Soveraignty of Musicke in this Affection, by the Cure and Remedy it affoords the Dispassionate, and Infortunate Sonnes of Love, thereby to asswage the turmoyles, and quiet the tempests that were raised in them.[6]

This quotation makes a good text, not because it sets up a rigid, authoritative system but simply because it shows that there *was* a philosophical interpretation of music (or song) and either names or suggests all the important ideas traditionally connected with song. It names the emotions commonly associated with singing, and in connection with one of them it suggests a very important aspect of music, its dynamic power over man's feelings and actions. This dynamic power had been discussed earlier by John Case, who illustrated it in *The Praise of Musick* by telling the familiar story of Alexander and Timotheus which is retold by Dryden in his second ode for St. Cecilia's Day, "Alexander's Feast."[7] A celebrated layman in music, Bishop Hooker, had written even more positively of the influence of harmony over the emotions, adding his opinion that it had the moral power to sway men to righteousness or to sin.[8] Not many years later Robert Burton was to reiterate the traditional beliefs about music, with special emphasis on its therapeutic value in cases of mental or even physical disorder.[9]

One must recognize, then, as a philosophical axiom in the seventeenth-century mind the belief that whereas music is normally the result, expression, and symptom of one or a combination of the "Principall Causes," it may be employed to induce, by a homeopathic effect, any of those basic states of mind or a number of others.

6. Thomas Ravenscroft, *A Briefe Discourse of the true (but neglected) use of Charact'ring the Degrees by their Perfection, Imperfection, and Diminution in Measurable Musicke* . . . (1614), quoted by Boyd, *op. cit.,* p. 35.

7. John Case, *The Praise of Musick* (1586). Boyd, *op. cit.,* gives copious extracts from this work in his Appendix C (pp. 292–300) and quotes Case's version of the story of Alexander and Timotheus on p. 30.

8. Richard Hooker, *Of the Laws of Ecclesiastical Politie* (1594–97), quoted in Boyd, *op. cit.,* pp. 35–6.

9. Robert Burton, `The Anatomy of Melancholy* (1621), *passim;* see especially part. 2, sec. 2, mem. 6, subsec. 3.

Such are the opinions of musicians and of scholars. The man in the Jacobean street, especially the man high enough in the intellectual scale to attend the theater, was more closely in touch with advanced thought than his equivalent in the overspecialized twentieth century—partly, no doubt, because advanced thought was founded on classical material which, in the form of tradition, had become a common heritage. The man in the street was not very considerate about summing up in writing his philosophical credo and leaving it for future scholars to analyze. It seems reasonable, however, that the beliefs of the everyday citizen should be reflected in the ideas expressed by the characters in the drama he enjoyed—not in introspective soliloquies and philosophical debates but in ordinary conversation. In other words, no practical playwright working toward an immediate dramatic end would have risked distracting his audience by voicing, as obiter dicta, concepts which would clash violently with their background of reading, traditional beliefs, and experience.

It therefore becomes important to consider what the plays say about music and the song. It would be easy to point out any number of dramatic lyrics whose functions demonstrate a general acceptance of the principles under discussion. But to do so would be to establish the principles by the very examples that later must be presented as growing out of these principles. Therefore illustrations in the following discussion will be restricted to words actually spoken in the Stuart plays, sometimes in the introduction to a song, sometimes in passages where no song is performed. Such comments seem to be acceptable evidence that the dramatist and his auditors shared the concepts thus expressed.

1. "Doulour"

In the Stuart drama the idea of "singing for sorrow," though stated occasionally as paradox,[1] is fairly common in both figurative and literal usage. Thus an unhappy lover may lament the fact that his romance is hindered by his lady's father,

> whose words like charmes, do hunt me from these thresholds,
> & make mee sing my griefe to philomell.[2]

Or the keeper of a captive king may describe with admiration the noble conduct of his royal prisoner:

> Then will he Sing, wooe his afflictions,
> And court 'em in sad airs, as if he wou'd wed 'em.[3]

In many cases of sad singing, especially when the singer believes or knows that death is imminent, the Stuart audience would have thought

---

1. E.g., Heywood, *The Rape of Lucrece*, II, i.   2. Neale, *The Ward*, I, ii.
3. Fletcher, *The Island Princess*, II, i.

immediately of the fabled song of the dying swan. Occasionally the play-wrights assured themselves the benefit of this connotation by deliberately reminding their audiences of it.[4] The connection between song and sorrow is, in general, so widely accepted that Holyday has Musica marry Melancholico in *Technogamia,* and Nabbes, seeking a real-life occupation for his personification of Melancholy, makes him a musician and an amorist.[5]

Perhaps underlying this concept of dolorous song is the idea that music may furnish a vent to emotion otherwise inexpressible; this may be true even though the actual singing is done vicariously, as for a frustrated suitor:

> But I doe feele a pouerty of words
> Begin to ceize mee. Good *Endimyon,*
> Where is my boy *Luscinio?* Call him in,
> That hee may touch a string which may dissolue mee
> Into a flood of teares——come on my boy,
> O teach that hollow pensiue Instrument
> To giue a true relation of my woes
> Whilst I lye here, and with my sighes keepe time.[6]

Moreover, as we have seen, Renaissance philosophy attributed to music the power of creating almost any emotion that could be expressed by music. Accordingly, although "doulour" is hardly a state of mind to be desired in oneself or in anyone else, the power of music to induce it is recognized on a few occasions in the plays. Marston's thoroughgoing villain Piero, after reducing Antonio to bewildered grief by arranging evidence to indicate Mellida guilty of unchastity, attempts to improve his handiwork by demanding

> Some plaining dittie to augment despaire.[7]

An example of the purposive use of song by a character to cause a mood of sadness in other characters will be described later.[8] The Duke of

4. E.g., D'Avenant, *Love and Honor,* v, ii; Fisher, *Fuimus Troes,* v, iii; Massinger, *The Emperor of the East,* v, iii; Middleton, *A Chaste Maid in Cheapside,* v, ii; Peaps, *Love in Its Ecstasy,* v, i. Note that all these examples come from the fifth act, when the dramatist is working toward a climactic emotional effect.

5. Nabbes, *Microcosmos,* "The Persons figur'd." In the absence of real agreement among Tudor and Stuart writers on the precise meaning of "melancholy," it seems justifiable to employ quotations using the word to illustrate the connection between song and either low spirits or madness, the context of each quotation determining in which sense melancholy is understood.

6. Hausted, *The Rival Friends,* I, iii. The most extravagant statement of this same idea is found in Marston, *Antonio and Mellida,* IV, i; cf. also a comment by Andrugio earlier in the same play (III, i). Other references to song as an expression of sorrow occur in Anonymous, *The Fair Maid of Bristow,* x (C3v); Chapman, *The Revenge of Bussy D'Ambois,* I, ii; Fletcher, *Monsieur Thomas,* v, iv (v, iii, in F2); Marston, *The Dutch Courtezan,* introduction of act music after II and III.

7. Marston, *Antonio's Revenge,* II, ii.

8. Fletcher (and another?), *The Captain,* III, iv; see below, pp. 49-50.

Illyria, of course, employs music to induce a pleasing melancholy,[9] and Jessica says,

> I am never merry when I hear sweet music.[1]

Some of their contemporaries also find music saddening even when it is not intended to be so.[2]

Under other circumstances, however, song might have exactly the opposite effect. Barten Holyday, in a tongue-in-cheek passage, reports,

> Musicke then at the first was found out as an antidote against griefe.[3]

Facetious though he is in the pseudohistorical explanation that follows (that song originated from the grieved man's cry of "oh" and "hey-ho"), he is in no sense ridiculing the faith of every Stuart Englishman in the ability of music to alleviate sadness; he is merely inventing a whimsical derivation for an accepted idea. Many dramatic lyrics reflect this idea. Usually they are prefaced by a word of explanation:

> . . . I am full of melancholy thoughts,
> Against which I have heard with reason Musick
> To be the speediest cure, 'pray you apply it.[4]

> Sing but a strain or two; thou wilt not think
> How 'twill revive thy spirits.[5]

But the song to combat grief or sadness is, obviously, one aspect of the song to induce joy or happiness.

2. Joy

Detailed documentation of the connection between song and joy is unnecessary, since their relationship is unquestioned even today. No modern audience would be perplexed by a character who chortled,

> . . . all fine, unreasonablie fine, me sing vor joy; by gor me sing la, liro, liro la, lilo.[6]

9. Shakespeare, *Twelfth Night*, I, i.   1. Shakespeare, *The Merchant of Venice*, v, i.
2. E.g., the King in J. Shirley, *The Politician*, II, i; Merione in Fletcher, Massinger, and Field, *The Queen of Corinth*, III, ii.
3. Holyday, *Technogamia*, III, iv.
4. Fletcher and Massinger, *The Lover's Progress*, III, iv.
5. Middleton, *A Chaste Maid in Cheapside*, v, ii. Other references to song as an antidote to sadness occur in "T. B.," *The Country Girl*, v, ii; Beaumont and Fletcher, *Cupid's Revenge*, v, iv; Fletcher, *The Chances*, IV, iii; Fletcher and Massinger, *The Double Marriage*, II, i; Heywood, *A Maidenhead Well Lost*, II, ii; Knevet, *Rhodon and Iris*, I, iii; J. Shirley, *The Changes*, IV, i, and *The Maid's Revenge*, v, iii. Were one to include curative or soothing lullabies in this list, it might be extended almost indefinitely.
6. Marston, *Jack Drum's Entertainment*, III, i. Compare Linsey-Wolsey in Brome, *The City Wit*, III, iii; Miniona in Clavell or Marmion, *The Soddered Citizen*, IV, vii; and Valerio in Heming, *The Jews' Tragedy*, v, i.

In the seventeenth century it was accepted as a general truth, though in their context the words form part of a dancing-master's compliment to a singing-master, that "a merry heart makes a good singing-man."[7]

The sort of joy demanding expression in song is not necessarily a mood of the moment; frequently it is something deeper and more permanent. This idea is suggested indirectly in *Patient Grissill:*

> *Marq.* Stay you *Ianicola,* I haue heard you sing.
> *Ian* I could haue sung when I was free from care.

After making the old man sing a bridal song in honor of the girl who is to supplant Grissill, the Marquess asks him,

> Art thou as glad in soule as in thy song?
> *Jan.* Who can be glad when he indureth wrong?[8]

"Gladness of soul" is a good phrase for the state in question. The illustration just given suggests that the first requisite is peace and satisfaction with the external world; but the preceding scenes of the play have made it clear that Janicola enjoys something still more important: the inner peace of a clear conscience and a happy heart.

In *Tottenham Court* Nabbes has Bellamie state this same concept. Lost, lonely, and troubled, she hears singing off stage:

> . . . 'Tis a womans voyce.
> She sings; and in her musicks cheerefulnesse
> Seemes to expresse the freedome of a heart
> Not chain'd to any passions.

The song is a charming one about the happy life of the milkmaid, who "dabbles in the dewe, And sings to her Cowe." As it ends, Bellamie repeats her interpretation:

> What a blest state is this? the minds content
> Sweeten's all sufferings of th'afflicted sense.[9]

This understanding of song as a manifestation of abiding happiness, as well as of the more transient shades of joy such as triumph or elation, will be essential to a point of interpretation to be made subsequently.[1]

Axiomatically, if music can express joy, it can induce at least the more ephemeral kinds of joy. Its power to do so is recognized explicitly:

---

7. Middleton, *More Dissemblers besides Women,* v, i. For other references connecting mirth and music, see Beaumont (and Fletcher?), *The Knight of the Burning Pestle,* II, viii, and v, iii; Brome, *A Jovial Crew,* v, i; Cowley, *Love's Riddle,* I, i, and *passim;* Dekker (?), *The Weakest Goeth to the Wall,* ii (B2r); Heywood, *The Rape of Lucrece,* II, i, iii; III, v; Middleton, *A Chaste Maid in Cheapside,* I, ii.

8. Dekker, Haughton, and Chettle, *Patient Grissill,* xi (K3r, v).

9. Nabbes, *Tottenham Court,* I, iii. For much the same idea, see Brome, *A Jovial Crew,* I, i, and W. Rowley, *A Shoemaker a Gentleman,* I, ii.

1. See below, pp. 42 ff.

Weele haue a three-men song, to make our guests merry.[2]

God blesse my Lord *Mavortius,* & his merry men all,
To make his honour merry, we sing in the hall.[3]

Since joy and grief are opposites, all the examples of the employment of
song to combat sorrow are applicable here as well.

3. *"Enthusiasme"*

As third among the principal causes of music Ravenscroft names "Enthusiasme or ravishing of the Spirit." In the seventeenth-century sense
of the word, possession by a god, enthusiasm is negligible as a cause
of song in the Stuart drama. Perhaps the only case that is wholly relevant
occurs in Jonson's *The Devil Is an Ass,* where Fitzdottrel pretends to
be bewitched and possessed by a devil. Though he does not actually sing,
he talks in rhyme: a point considered noteworthy by Sir Paul Eitherside,
one of the observers.[4]

But there are other factors which, by depriving a man of the power
of control over his own speech and conduct, produce effects hardly to
be distinguished from those of enthusiasm. One is madness; another is
drunkenness.[5]

It may be significant that these two states are linked to each other and
to song in a passage in *The Loyal Subject.* The fanatically loyal old
general Archas, having been commanded to send his two innocent, coun-
try-bred daughters to the court, orders his son Theodore to escort them
thither. Theodore, a quick-tempered young colonel, is astounded that
his father should even consider sending the girls to what promises to be
their certain moral ruin. He expresses his incredulity in a line which
Colman[6] and most subsequent editors of the play have taken as a snatch
from a familiar song and have, accordingly, marked to be sung (the
second folio text has no such indication):

> *The.* Is this the business? I had thought your mind, Sir,
> Had been set forward on some noble action,
> Something had truly stir'd ye. To th' Court with these?

---

2. Heywood, I *King Edward IV,* Pearson reprint, I, 51.

3. Marston, *Histrio-Mastix,* II, iv. Additional references to song as an inducement
to or manifestation of mirth are found in Cartwright, *The Ordinary,* III, v, and IV, i;
D'Avenant, *The Wits,* v, ii; Dekker (?), *The Weakest Goeth to the Wall,* vii (D4v);
Marston, *What You Will,* II, i. There are many others.

4. Jonson, *The Devil Is an Ass,* v, viii.

5. One primitive explanation of madness was, indeed, possession by an evil spirit
(e.g., the madness of Saul, I *Samuel* 16:14 ff.).

6. *The Dramatick Works of Beaumont and Fletcher,* ed. George Colman (London,
1778. 10 vols.), III, 363. Seward (ed. 1750) had italicized the line; Weber (ed. 1812)
and Alexander Dyce, ed., *The Works of Beaumont and Fletcher* (London, Moxon,
1843–46. 11 vols.) followed Colman in marking it to be sung.

Why, they are your Daughters, Sir.
Arc. All this I know, Sir.
The. The good old Woman on a Bed he threw:
To th' Court?
Arc. Thou art mad.
The. Nor drunk as you are:
Drunk with your duty, Sir.[7]

If one accepts the editorial treatment of the irrelevant line, this passage implies that madness and drunkenness were the two alternative explanations which might occur to a Stuart Englishman for a snatch of song thus ejaculated in a serious conversation.

Actual references to drunken singing are rare in the Stuart drama.[8] In general, the almost innumerable passages which link singing with drinking make the connection social rather than physiological. That is, the intoxicated man's impulsion to sing (a phenomenon still to be observed) is taken for granted; but the practice of group singing as one of the customary pleasures of conviviality is mentioned very often. The social drinking song stems from joy rather than from drunken enthusiasm:

Musicke, and songs, good cheere, and wine; and wine,
And songs and Musicke, and good cheere.[9]

A mad man, like a drunken one, is literally ecstatic, not in command of his own speech. Burton, the best authority on the subject, names singing as a symptom of melancholy or madness, particularly if the melancholy proceed from blood adust.[1] The ordinary man and his chronicler, the dramatist, could hardly be expected to share Burton's technical understanding of madness; it was sufficient for them to observe that the mentally unbalanced person behaved in strange ways, one of the most striking of which was a tendency to break into disjointed fragments of song. One of Shirley's characters, for example, describes lunatics as people

. . . that look twenty ways
At once, that sigh and curse, and sing mad carols.[2]

The matter-of-fact linking of song and madness by several other dramatists is evinced by casual passages in their plays.[3]

7. Fletcher, *The Loyal Subject,* III, ii.
8. Note, however, a reference to singing as a proof of drunkenness in Massinger, *The Duke of Milan,* I, i.
9. Fisher, *Fuimus Troes,* III, vii.
1. Burton, *op. cit.,* part. I, sec. 3, mem. I, subsec. 3; (London, Chatto & Windus, 1891), p. 262.
2. J. Shirley, *The Changes,* IV, ii.
3. E.g., Ford, *Perkin Warbeck,* III, ii; Marmion or Clavell, *The Soddered Citizen,*

According to the axiom, if song can express madness, it should be able to cause madness. Burton says it can, and cites Plutarch in proof: *"Musica magis dementat quàm vinum;* music makes some men mad as a tiger . . ."[4] Like enthusiasme proper, this idea is negligible in its effect on the Stuart drama, although a character in *Lust's Dominion* demands the music of trumpets and drums to madden a couple of imprisoned and helpless enemies.[5]

Much more important dramatically, however, is the universal faith in the efficacy of music as a cure for virulent melancholy or madness. It would be interesting to trace this concept to its ultimate source. Burton devotes an entire subsection to it,[6] one of his earliest examples being the soothing effect which the boy David's harp-playing had upon King Saul. Certainly practical recognition of this quality in music preceded by many years any attempt at a philosophical interpretation of it; so that the Old Testament example does not invalidate Dover Wilson's case that the Renaissance attitude evolves from Plato and ultimately from the Pythagorean idea of the soul as essentially a harmony.[7] The enlightened citizen was well aware of this evolution;[8] the common man, however, was quite willing to accept the fact without questioning its background:

> There is a power in harmony, some say,
> To charm the unruly motions of the brain:
> Love is itself a melancholy madness;
> Why should not music cure the wound of love?[9]

It seems probable that the concept of enthusiasme as a basic cause of song may have yet a third manifestation, in addition to drunkenness and madness: the Stuart dramatists' long recognized practice of assigning songs to supernatural characters.[1] This device is in effect more a dramatic convention than the direct reflection of universal psychological principles

---

i, i; Middleton and Rowley, *The Changeling*, iii, iii; Webster, *The Duchess of Malfi*, iv, i.

4. Burton, *op. cit.*, part. 2, sec. 2, mem. 6, subsec. 3; (1891), p. 369.

5. Day, Dekker, and Haughton, *Lust's Dominion*, v, v. This case may, however, have little more significance than another where music is employed to prevent prisoners from sleeping. Heming, *The Fatal Contract*, v, ii.

6. Burton, *op. cit.*, part. 2, sec. 2, mem. 6, subsec. 3; (1891), pp. 367–9.

7. J. Dover Wilson, "Shakespeare's Universe," *The University of Edinburgh Journal*, 11 (Summer, 1942), 216–33, at 223–5. Cf. John Burnet, "Shakespeare and Greek Philosophy," *A Book of Homage to Shakespeare* (Oxford, Oxford University Press, 1916), pp. 58–61. See also below, pp. 45–7.

8. E.g., Chapman (?), *Sir Giles Goosecap*, iii, ii; Marston, *Jack Drum's Entertainment*, v, i.

9. J. Shirley, *The Changes*, iv, i; see also Dekker, *The Wonder of a Kingdom*, i, ii.

1. Over 75 years ago, for example, A. S. Richardson found it advisable to devote to "Songs of Fairies and Spirits" a separate section in his anthology, *Songs from the Old Dramatists* (New York, Hurd & Houghton, 1873).

like the ones already discussed, so that one would not expect to find it treated by contemporary musicians or philosophers; neither does any of the major dramatists take his public behind the scenes to show them just why song seemed appropriate to supernatural beings. Probably it was merely a matter of convenience: spectral effects through lighting were not available, and complicated stage machinery was not always either practical or desirable. But if the human beings in a play habitually conversed in blank verse or prose and the supernatural beings employed song or octosyllabic couplets, a continuing distinction was achieved with complete economy.

One can only guess as to just how this convention evolved. But a form of enthusiasme which would have been familiar to the Stuart Englishman was the "furor poeticus," in which a god, spirit, or devil, having taken possession of a man's mind and body, speaks through that man's lips in song or, at any rate, in some medium different from that of ordinary human conversation. Presumably, then, this supernatural being would use much the same form of communication when speaking in its own person and not through a human mouthpiece. Whether or not this is the actual background of the practice, however, the point at issue is simply the fact that supernatural singing is compatible with the psychology of song as understood in the first half of the seventeenth century.

If this compatibility is allowed, several other groups of songs fall into the over-all psychological pattern. Most obviously, song becomes useful to any character who has reason to impersonate a supernatural being. At the same time, it is appropriate for those who deal with gods or devils through witchcraft or the more legitimate channel of priestcraft, and for their coney-catching imitators who rely on impressive hocus-pocus to prepare their victims for being gulled.

Here as elsewhere it must be remembered that the Stuart psychology of song is not an academic structure so much as a digest of past observation of the effects of music. Since the most primitive times, music has been connected with both magic and religion.[2] It is not necessary, then, to seek a definite source in the liturgical tropes for songs imitating Christian ritual or in "the taste of the masque-loving age" for those of pagan ritual.[3] Such songs are primarily a matter of simple fidelity to real life. But even when, in scenes of magic or enchantment, song is employed to suggest unreality, its use is still, in the final analysis, only a paradoxical

2. See, for instance, Rudolf Felber, "Music and Superstition," tr. Theodore Baker, *Musical Quarterly, 17* (April, 1931), 235, and Edward Evans, "The Analogies and Associations of Music and Literature," *Transactions of the Royal Society of Literature,* Ser. II, *32* (1913–14), 219.

3. J. R. Moore, "The Song in the English Drama to 1642" (Ph.D. dissertation, Harvard University, 1917), pp. 1, 9 (of Christian ritual and angelic singing); Moore, "The Function of the Songs in Shakespeare's Plays," *Shakespeare Studies by Members of the Department of English of the University of Wisconsin* (Madison, University of Wisconsin Press, 1916), p. 87 (of pagan ritual).

phase of the purpose of almost all dramatic song, which is to achieve psychological realism.[4]

4. Love

Ravenscroft's statement that "Love teaches a man Musick, who ne're before knew what pertayned thereto" is accepted and documented by Burton: "Plutarch . . . telleth us moreover in what sense, *Musicam docet amor, licet priùs fuerit rudis,* how love makes them that had no skill before learn to sing and dance."[5] Burton considers that "A sweet voice and music are powerful enticers" to love.[6] He also endorses Ravenscroft's ascription of therapeutic qualities to music; for love-melancholy he prescribes "music, feasting, good wine."[7] But he is somewhat apologetic about discussing love-melancholy; he cites Erasmus to the effect that people will feel "that it is too light for a divine, too comical a subject to speak of love symptoms, too fantastical, and fit alone for a wanton poet . . ."[8] or some such person.

Since the data compiled by Burton were part of the heritage of all contemporary thought, his opinions, albeit they are those of a philosopher and scientist, are also indicative of those held by the dramatists and the enlightened public. In general, then, music or song was considered to be the natural language of a lover; it was at the same time, under a considerate arrangement by Providence, a stimulus to love. In case the courtship did not come to a happy conclusion, music might serve to alleviate the sufferings of the unsuccessful suitor. But the passion of love was not a very dignified one.

In the drama, therefore, the lover's tendency to burst into song is conventional:

> I think he is in love; he's often heard
> To sigh a Ladies name, and sing sad Sonnets

4. One stock explanation for supernatural song and instrumental music has been that something was needed to drown out the creaking of the machinery by which supernatural beings were lowered from the heavens or otherwise made to appear. This observation probably is justified in respect to masques but applies in very few of the cases where supernatural beings are introduced as characters on the professional stage.

On the other hand, Percy Scholes has argued, on the basis of its effectiveness, that the music in Shakespeare's plays is intended almost exclusively to produce a feeling of mystery and unreality. "The Purpose behind Shakespeare's Use of Music," *Proceedings of the Musical Association* (43d sess., 1916–17), pp. 1–15. Scholes's opinion has not met universal acceptance; it imposes, in effect, a limitation on Shakespeare's originality and scope.

5. Burton, *op. cit.,* part. 3, sec. 2, mem. 3; (1891), p. 578. Burton also gives a very similar quotation as from Erasmus (*ibid.,* [1891], pp. 576–7).

6. *Ibid.,* part. 3, sec. 2, mem. 2, subsec. 4; (1891), p. 534.

7. *Ibid.,* part. 3, sec. 2, mem. 5, subsec. 1; (1891), pp. 586–7; see also his subsection on music as a cure for melancholy in general, *ibid.,* part. 2, sec. 2, mem. 6, subsec. 3; (1891), pp. 367–9.

8. *Ibid.,* part. 3, sec. 1, mem. 1, subsec. 1; (1891), p. 466.

In [a] dissolving passion . . .[9]

But it is treated with mild ridicule; so that *Musicam docet amor* becomes in *The Queen of Corinth,*

Oh, love would make a dog howle in ryme.[1]

This ambivalence in the popular attitude toward lovers' singing is attested by numerous glancing references in the plays under examination;[2] in all likelihood it is responsible for the odd treatment accorded the serenade in the Stuart drama.[3]

More than merely a reliable symptom, music is "the food of love,"[4] "the quiver of young *Cupids* dart."[5] Consequently, it is the accepted way of winning a fair lady:

> *Bra.* Gods pretious, I forgot to bring my Page
> To breathe some Dittie in my Mistris eare.
> *Pla.* Wouldst have a Ballet to salute her with?
> *Bra.* No, but a Song. How wouldst thou court thy Mistresse?[6]

It is a rare mistress indeed to whom a serenade would not be appropriate —perhaps the only one in the Stuart drama is the ancient but wealthy widow courted by Vasco in D'Avenant's *Love and Honor:*

> *Fri.* Thou dost not meane
> To court her at her window with rare musick?
> *Vas.* No, she's very deafe, so that cost is sav'd.[7]

A recognition of the fundamental kinship between love and physical desire is evident in the interest Stuart audiences took in the bedding of newly married lovers and in the prominence of the deferred consummation as a dramatic motif. A harsher name for physical desire is lust. One would not expect a musician and apologist for music like Ravenscroft to draw attention to the connection between music and lust; but the reformer Gosson complains with Plutarch that ignorant men "abuse the majestie of auncient musike" by bringing it into theaters, where, instead of acting as a spur to virtue, it serves as a prick to vice: "Ovid,

---

9. Jordan, *The Walks of Islington and Hogsdon,* iv, iv. Cf. similar statements in Heywood, *Love's Mistress,* ii, iii; Lower, *The Phoenix in Her Flames,* ii, i (C3v); Lyly, *Midas,* iii, iii.
1. Fletcher, Massinger, and Field, *The Queen of Corinth,* iv, i.
2. See, in the Beaumont and Fletcher canon alone, *Cupid's Revenge,* ii, iv; *The Elder Brother,* ii, ii; *The Fair Maid of the Inn,* i, i; *The False One,* iii, ii; *The Humourous Lieutenant,* iv, i; v, ii; *The Lover's Progress,* i, i; *Monsieur Thomas,* iii, iii; *The Wild-Goose Chase,* i, ii; ii, i.
3. See below, pp. 18–23.   4. Shakespeare, *Twelfth Night,* i, i.
5. Marston, *Jack Drum's Entertainment,* iv, v.
6. *Ibid.,* ii, iii. Though it occurs in a satirical passage, Proteus' advice to Thurio to serenade his lady Sylvia (Shakespeare, *The Two Gentlemen of Verona,* iii, ii) is orthodox; cf. similar advice by Melancholy in Nabbes, *Microcosmos,* iii.
7. D'Avenant, *Love and Honor,* ii, iii.

the high Martial of Venus feeld, planteth his mayn battell in publike as-
semblies, sendeth out his scoutes to Theaters to descrye the enimie, and
in steede of vaunte curriers, with instruments of musick, playing, singing and dauncing gives the first charge."[8] Burton cites Plato as forbid-
ding "music and wine to all young men, because they are most part
amorous, *ne ignis addatur igni,* lest one fire increase another."[9] In fact,
it would be hard to determine by how many centuries Darwin was anticipated in his recognition of music as a means of sexual attraction. In the
reading or experience of Gosson and Burton, moreover, music figures
as an attribute of certain infamous women,[1] as a stimulative when used
as an accompaniment to sexual pleasure,[2] and as the subject of a particular abuse by brothel-keepers.[3]

The Stuart dramatists—even those to whom we attribute a genuine
love of music—and, presumably, their audiences accepted this aspect
of music as a matter of course. In other words, its effect on the passions
was a scientific fact, not a moral one. Dramatic references are likely to
include music or song among other provocatives; thus the Genoan court
is described as presenting perils to "a Lady gardianlesse":

> . . . heating delicates,
> Soft rest, sweete Musick, amorous Masquerers,
> lascivious banquets, sinne it selfe gilt ore . . .[4]

The efficacy of song in this respect was recognized and exploited by
the would-be seducer of either sex:

> And you must use all art for his content,
> With Musicke, Songs, and dancing, such as are
> The stirrers of hot appetites.[5]

> . . . let sweet musicke plead
> with ravishing notes to winne her maidenhead.[6]

The result in the drama (and conceivably also in real life) was the development of a familiar and highly stylized song type which will be
discussed more fully in the following chapter.[7]

8. Stephen Gosson, *The School of Abuse* (Shakespeare Society reprint, London,
1841), pp. 18–19. Boyd, *op. cit.,* quotes Prynne and others to similar effect.

9. Burton, *op. cit.,* part. 2, sec. 2, mem. 6, subsec. 3; (1891), p. 369.

1. *Ibid.,* part. 3, sec. 2, mem. 2, subsec. 4; (1891), pp. 534, 542; Gosson, *op. cit.,* p. 13.

2. Burton, *op. cit.,* part. 2, sec..2, mem. 6, subsec. 3; (1891), p. 369.

3. Gosson, *op. cit.,* p. 26; see below, p. 31.

4. Marston, *The Malcontent,* III, i. See also Davenport, *A New Trick to Cheat the
Devil,* I, ii, and Tourneur (?), *The Revenger's Tragedy,* III, v.

5. Marmion, *Holland's Leaguer,* II, ii; cf. Brome, *The City Wit,* IV, i.

6. Anonymous, *The Two Noble Ladies,* V, ii. See also Heywood (?), *A Cure for a
Cuckold,* IV, ii; Massinger, *The Renegado,* II, iv; J. Shirley, *The Traitor,* II, i.

7. See below, pp. 26–30.

Moreover, this stimulative effect of music could be useful not only in a seduction but in heightening the pleasure of an encounter already agreed upon, licit or illicit. A waggish maid, for example, says that if she were being married, she would ply her groom with wine until he saw double,

> While waggish Boyes should with their wanton Songs
> Prepare our thoughts to our ensuing pleasures.[8]

The material just presented, in combination with the axiom that song can manifest any state of mind it can help to create, indicates a further conclusion to be logical: that singing should be a distinguishing characteristic of people who deal in the passions—courtesans, bawds, and panders—of wanton people, and of people who for some reason desire to be thought wanton. This idea seldom finds explicit statement in Stuart plays,[9] but there is proof of its validity in the dramatists' very frequent use of song for the purpose of characterizing such people. This evidence will be presented in Chapter II.[1]

5. The Divinity of Music

Although the ability of song to arouse sexual desire is accepted objectively as a scientific phenomenon by the Stuart dramatists, it would be unfortunate to let this concept stand as the last word in an analysis of their philosophical views on music. Shakespeare's love and respect for the art are familiar; less familiar but no less sincere are tributes to it by several of his contemporaries.[2] Goffe expresses the consensus when he makes an unhappy lover dismiss his singing boy with the words,

> Why should I tax thy power gentle Boy,
> That holds so much Divinity, it awes
> Not mortalls only, but makes other powers
> *Sub-Deities* to thine?[3]

It is such exalted opinions as this that are responsible for the ascription to music of beneficent powers far outranging those already mentioned in connection with the cure of madness and the relief of love-

---

8. Freeman, *Imperiale,* III, i. Cf. D'Avenant, *The Just Italian,* III, iii.

9. Notice, however, Chough in Middleton, *A Fair Quarrel,* IV, iv: "Stay, Trim; I have heard your tweaks are like your mermaids, they have sweet voices to entice the passengers." Cf. Fletcher, *The Humourous Lieutenant,* II, iii, where the business-like bawd Leucippe alludes to the pecuniary value of the good singing voice of a prospective courtesan.

1. See below, pp. 30–3.

2. Some of these are quoted below, pp. 45 ff. The anonymous author of *Two Wise Men and All the Rest Fools,* alone among the dramatists, shares Gosson's concern over the contemporary abuses of music (VI, i).

3. Goffe, *The Careless Shepherdess,* I, i. See Boyd, *op. cit., passim,* for corresponding material from nondramatic literature.

melancholy. These powers include efficacy (deriving in part from the sleep-inducing qualities of music) in cases of anxiety, trouble, and even physical sickness. Holyday is only half in jest in this passage from *Technogamia:*

> *Geog.* Nay, I do beleeue there is a great vertue in Musicke.
> *Mus.* O Sir, 'tis your onely medicine of the minde.
> *Geog.* Indeed I thinke so, and that's the reason, 'tis likely, why *Apollo* is the god both of Musicke and Physicke.[4]

In the very exceptional cases where any doubt is expressed of the ability of music to help cure even a physical ailment, the skeptic is likely to be either a comic character or an unsympathetic one.[5] There is, of course, classical authority for the belief that music has therapeutic powers: even Gosson refers to Homer's curing pestilence-stricken soldiers in the Greek camp with his music, though he interprets the story symbolically rather than literally.[6]

Bishop Hooker's idea of music as a moral force is also reflected to some extent in the drama. Wendoll contemplates a song to drive away his passion for Anne Frankford in *A Woman Killed with Kindness,* but immediately discards the idea.[7] If his faith is infirm, however, that of the bereaved Earl of St. Anne is not:

> . . . to lift all his thoughts
> Vp to another world, where she expects him,
> He feedes his eares with soule-exciting musicke.
> Solemn and Tragicall, and so Resolues
> In those sadde accents to exhale his soule.[8]

While Chapman's concept here is an exceptionally lofty one, it should be obvious by now that in the early seventeenth century everyone— philosopher, dramatist, and ordinary private citizen alike—regarded music not as desirable only for the intrinsic pleasure it gives but as meaningful and closely related to life. It should be equally obvious that to neglect this fact in a study of the incidental lyrics of the Stuart drama would be to neglect a principle which not only governs the use of these lyrics but is probably the ultimate reason for their very existence.

If, according to the seventeenth-century view of life, music was a spontaneous expression of certain primary emotional states and could induce certain emotional states in its hearers, one might expect to find the Stuart drama reporting this aspect of life as any other—to find the characters in the plays singing in the grip of strong emotion and, perhaps,

4. Holyday, *Technogamia,* III, iv.
5. E.g., Dekker, *The Wonder of a Kingdom,* III, ii.
6. Gosson, *op. cit.,* pp. 15–16.   7. Heywood, *A Woman Killed with Kindness,* II, iii.
8. Chapman, *Monsieur D'Olive,* I, i.

using song to influence the emotions of other characters. One of the aims of the following chapters necessarily will be to show that they do both these things. But this concept of song was a dogma of popular psychology; everyone accepted it, and everyone understood it. What would be more natural, then, than for the intelligent dramatist to put psychology to work—not to stop with making his characters sing as they would in real life but to use the expressive qualities of song on a semantic level to tell the audience something about those characters? Or, better yet, to apply the emotional force of song directly to the audience, on whose responses his livelihood depended? The Stuart playwright appreciated both these possibilities so keenly and exploited them so ably that the song became an essential part of his dramatic technique. It is primarily this point that the succeeding chapters are intended to demonstrate.

II

Psychology in Action: Songs of Love and Lust

THE VALIDITY of our proposed analysis of the techniques of the dramatic lyric rests on the premise that Stuart dramatic practice was a faithful mirror of Stuart philosophical thought—specifically, that the songs in the plays actually are used in accordance with the psychological principles already explained. This premise can be proved.

If it is true that music stems from a limited number of specific emotional causes, one might expect to find the dramatic lyrics conforming to a few rigid types: the song to express joy, the song to induce joy, the song to express sorrow, the song to induce sorrow, and so on. Such a pattern exists, but it is an intricate one. Because a given lyric may arise from one of the principal causes or from any combination of them, and because each of the principal causes has a variety of shades, the dramatic use of song has a breadth and flexibility which preclude any rigid classification. That is to say, there are common song types which arise from particular causes and which are handled consistently, even conventionally, by the playwrights to achieve definite effects; but it is impossible to draw precise boundaries between these types.

It will not be necessary to treat in detail all the song types deriving from all the emotional causes in order to show that the songs in the plays really do embody the concepts of contemporary psychology. The nature of the pattern underlying their use will be made sufficiently clear by a careful exposition of the kinds of song originating from a single cause. It is the purpose of this chapter to present such an exposition and so to lay the foundation for the analysis of the lyric's contribution to dramatic technique. For this purpose let us consider that emotional state which, because it includes and embraces all the principal causes of song, is the most important, most interesting, and most varied in its manifestations: love, with its obverse, lust.

1. The Song to Induce Love: the Serenade

To most people a love song is a serenade. In the following discussion it will be convenient to use this term but to extend its meaning to include any song offered by a suitor to his beloved as an act of courtship. Such a song type as the *aubade,* for instance, differs from the true serenade only in external circumstances.

The definition of the serenade as an act of courtship makes obvious its psychological correctness. While it is, in a sense, the expression of the suitor's love, its real function is to induce love in the one serenaded. This point is essential to the understanding of why the Stuart dramatists handle the serenade as they do.

The word "serenade" evokes in the average person a highly romantic mental picture of a handsome youth singing in the moonlight beneath his lady's window; one expects the music to dissolve into an idyllic love scene. But the person who approaches a Stuart play thus conditioned by modern musical comedy will be sorely disappointed,[1] for there the conventional treatment of the serenade calls for a suitor who is ridiculous, repulsive, evil, or otherwise unacceptable to sponsor a love song which, though sometimes it may be comic, is more often acceptable or even quite charming. For examples one need look no further than Shakespeare's "Who is Sylvia," sung by professional musicians for the lumpish Thurio, and "Hark, hark, the lark," also performed by musicians for the despicable Cloten.[2] Similar cases dot the drama from *Roister Doister* to Glapthorne's *Wit in a Constable;*[3] the very names of the serenaders— Sir Gregory Fop, Puffe, Mammon, Knowlittle[4]—are enough to characterize them. In two cases out of three the suitor is someone who clearly has no chance of winning the girl, and in two-thirds of the remaining cases, his chances at the moment are definitely slim.[5]

When comedy is the dramatist's primary end in this unromantic treatment of the serenade, the fact is generally made clear by the text of the song.[6] More interesting dramatically, however, is another common effect. Marmion's Aurelio, for instance, is a perfectly presentable young man, and his instructions to his hired singer are appropriate for a romantic lover:

> This is the window! Now, my noble Orpheus,
> As thou affect'st the name of rarity,
> Strike with the soul of music, that the sound
> May bear my love on his bedewed wing,
> To charm her ear: as when a sacrifice,

1. Perhaps only Freevill's serenade to Beatrice in Marston, *The Dutch Courtezan,* II, i, would satisfy him completely. Honorio's serenade to Dulcimenta in Sharpe, *The Noble Stranger,* II, i, comes close to meeting the requirements of the sentimentalist but is sung vicariously.

2. Shakespeare, *The Two Gentlemen of Verona,* IV, ii, and *Cymbeline,* II, iii.

3. Udall, *Roister Doister,* II, iii; Glapthorne, *Wit in a Constable,* III, iii.

4. Beaumont and Fletcher, *Wit at Several Weapons,* III, i (Fop); Marston, *Jack Drum's Entertainment,* II, i (Puffe and Mammon); Randolph, *The Drinking Academy,* V, iii (Knowlittle).

5. The reader may verify these figures for himself by reference to the Appendix, which lists, classifies, and suggests the circumstances of all the songs under consideration.

6. E.g., the lisping serenade provided by Fulgoso as appropriate to his lisping lady Amoretta in Ford, *The Lady's Trial,* IV, ii,

> With his perfumed steam flies up to Heaven,
> Into Jove's nostrils, and there throws a mist
> On his enraged brow. Oh how my fancy
> Labours with the success![7]

Though the words of the ensuing song are lost, their nature is easily conjectured. But Lucretia's response shatters the mood:

> Cease your fool's note there! I am not in tune
> To dance after your fiddle. Who are you?
> What saucy groom, that dares so near intrude,
> And with offensive noise, grate on my ears?

Nor can she be softened by sweet speeches. Though it later transpires that this display was a form of coquetry and though Aurelio eventually wins Lucretia, the fact remains that as far as this serenade scene goes, he could take his place with the comic lovers.[8]

The dramatic effect achieved here is, of course, surprise. The perfervid poetry leading up to the song and the professionally performed song itself have a lulling effect on the audience and prepare their subconscious for a tenderly romantic dialogue. Consequently, the unexpected reversal of mood in Lucretia's tirade at once affords the spectators a dash of pleasing excitement and startles them into closer attention.

Sometimes the reversal takes a different form. In *The Laws of Candy*, for example, a serenade has results not merely disappointing but catastrophic to its sponsor.[9] Philander hires musicians in the hope of pleasing the proud Erota. Their song does please her, but it also suggests to her that Philander, who woos her so movingly, is just the person to plead her love to his rival Antinous, whom she herself has been unable to soften. Thus the audience have their emotions excited almost simultaneously by the two well-tried devices of the reversal and the love dilemma.

On the few occasions when an apparently favored lover sings to his mistress, he generally does so under unromantic circumstances—for example, he may use his song as a means of summoning his lady to an interview, perhaps in broad daylight.[1] As a rule the dramatists carefully avoid the traditionally sentimental treatment of the courtship song, preferring even such bizarre variations as making the lady sing the serenade

---

7. Marmion, *The Antiquary*, II, i.

8. Though the reversal becomes more effective as the acceptability of the suitor makes it less expected, it is not therefore limited to serenades provided by the juvenile lead. Witness, for example, Barry, *Ram-Alley*, v, ii, where a comic senile amorist provides an *aubade* for a charming widow only to be greeted from her bedroom window by his own son, who has already taken the lady by storm.

9. Massinger and Fletcher (?), *The Laws of Candy*, III, iii.

1. E.g., Piorato in Massinger (?—revising Beaumont and Fletcher?), *Love's Cure*, III, ii.

to the man[2] or making a husband sing or provide a serenade to his own wife.[3]

The actual ownership of the singing voice is not an aspect of the dramatic technique of the serenade. The reason why it is not becomes obvious when one remembers what the serenade is: an act of courtship intended to induce love in the hearer. The identity of the singer is of no more consequence than the identity of the boy who delivers the flowers a modern wooer sends to his sweetheart. Whether a suitor in a play does his own singing or hires musicians to do it for him is determined by such considerations as social decorum and perhaps the exigencies of casting.[4] It does not, however, have anything to do with the ends sought by the dramatist in using the serenade.

These ends may be considered on two planes of practicality, the lower of which is the immediate dramatic effect or function. We have seen that the serenade may be handled for comic appeal. It may be employed for direct characterization, serious or comic, as when a miser sponsors an *aubade* urging his suit on the basis of his wealth:

> Those that are farre more yong and wittie,
> Are wide from singing such a Dittie
> As Chunck, chunck, chunck . . .[5]

It may develop suspense or dramatic irony or both, as does the air demanded by Antonio of his friends to waken his bride-elect Mellida: the audience know that a cruel plot is already working against her but still are not quite prepared for the opening of her curtains a little later to reveal the butchered body of Feliche:[6]

Sometimes the serenade even has a plot function, as it does in D'Avenant's *The Spanish Lovers*.[7] This is perhaps the most complex use of the love song for dramatic ends in the Stuart or any other period; it utilizes two serenades, each followed by a surprising reversal, and makes each the starting point for one half of the double plot. First Orgemon serenades Claramante and calls her to appear; instead, her brother, mistaking Orgemon for his enemy Dorando, steps forward, challenges him, and eventually wounds him. To find how his wound is healing, Claramante leaves home in disguise, and her ensuing adventures constitute half the play. In the very next scene Orco, disguised as a fiddler, sings to the co-heroine Amiana a comic serenade which has the unlooked-for effect of suggesting to her that she commit herself to him for protection

---

2. E.g., Oriana to Gondibert in Beaumont, *The Woman-Hater*, iii, i; Camelia to Planet in Marston, *Jack Drum's Entertainment*, iv, v.

3. E.g., Lopez in Fletcher, *Women Pleased*, iii, iv; Sforza in Massinger, *The Duke of Milan*, i, iii (the latter song is conjectural; see below, pp. 95 ff., and cf. E. B. Reed, *Songs from the British Drama* [New Haven, Yale University Press, 1925], p. 346).

4. See below, pp. 44–5, 122 ff.

5. Mammon, in Marston, *Jack Drum's Entertainment*, ii, i.

6. Marston, *Antonio's Revenge*, i, ii.   7. D'Avenant, *The Spanish Lovers*, ii, ii, iii.

and guidance to the house of his favored rival Androlio. Thus each serenade is directly responsible for a maiden's leaving home, and for the rest of the play the two maidens are moved about like two peas under three walnut shells.

Beyond these immediate dramatic effects, however, the serenade has a higher functionalism which explains the antisentimental treatment conventionally accorded it by the Stuart dramatists: it is a kind of idiomatic communication between the playwright and the audience for establishing a triangular situation. The most highly stylized examples occur in the second or third act of the play or, if later, at least in the early stages of the courtship of which they form a part.[8] This fact is evidence of their expository nature.

The communicative value of the serenade lies in the fact that to the seventeenth-century playgoer it was not the idle courtesy of a summer's evening; it was a calculated move in a carefully planned campaign. Whatever the qualities of the suitor, his use of song (especially if it is, like Cloten's, in itself acceptable) immediately marks him as determined and resourceful—a corner of the triangle to be reckoned with. His recourse to song emphasizes the desirability of the lady who seems to him to justify such pains and expense. Simultaneously, her rejection of both song and suitor underlines her haughtiness, devotion to another lover, or whatever other motivation the dramatist chooses to give her.

The seriously conceived romantic lover, the third corner of the triangle, ordinarily does not need to serenade. On the realistic plane, if the lady's heart already belongs to him, there is no point to his using a device whose purpose is to induce love. On the communicative plane the dramatist is able to forego the characterizing values of the serenade because he is prepared to devote acting time to a romantic love affair and to exert his full poetic power in the creation of effective love scenes. In other words, his sense of proportion requires him to develop a major romance by strictly dramatic means, whereas a secondary one can be sketched in with a serenade and little more. A Romeo does not sing, but a Paris relies on musicians to help his courtship to a successful conclusion.

Structurally, too, the stylized serenade is significant as one aspect of a technique which will be considered in greater detail in a subsequent chapter.[9] It will be demonstrated there that the audiences whom the practical Stuart playwright sought to please demanded, along with characters and situations to which they had become as accustomed as to their own everyday doublets, the emotional excitement of novelty, surprise, and even shock. In the stylized serenade we have a good illustration of how the dramatist could reconcile those elements. The serenade itself was a familiar situation. Equally familiar was the concept of the lover as a slightly ridiculous figure; Burton might put it in Seneca's pungent words,

8. See Appendix.   9. See below, pp. 56 ff.

"Amare simul et sapere ipsi Jovi non datur,"[1] but everyone else had the same idea. This concept is uniformly embodied in the lovers of the serenade scenes. But at the same time the serenade in real life should logically dissolve into a love duet; and when he makes it do something very different, the dramatist has achieved one of the surprises, the little independent climaxes, in which his public delighted.

When Cowling[2] and Wright[3] tell us, then, that the Stuart songs were introduced "merely in deference to popular liking," we should remember that their musical attractiveness was seldom more important than their dramatic effect as a cause of their popularity with a public whose taste, after all, helped to give us Shakespeare. As we have seen and as we shall see, a careful examination of the functions of the songs in the Stuart drama reveals the deceptive nature of this half-truth of popular liking.

2. The Song as an Expression of Love: the Complaint

Song as the spontaneous expression of love occupies in the Stuart drama a place equal in importance to that of the serenade, the song to induce love. But the modern theater-goer, accustomed to light-opera practice, will be disappointed again if he looks to find the love duet used in these plays as the lyrical expression of a strong mutual affection. The reason has already been suggested: that the dramatist preferred to build a genuine romance by dramatic and poetical means rather than by the shorthand of song. This explanation finds support in the circumstances of the two or three lovers' duets which are to be found in all these hundreds of plays. In *Jack Drum's Entertainment,* for instance, Marston makes a duet between Camelia and Ellis serve as the musical condensation of an entire courtship.[4] Camelia forsakes Brabant Junior for Ellis and Ellis for Ned Planet; but since her affairs constitute only one subplot of the play, Marston cannot afford more than a few lines to establish her love for Ellis as a temporarily serious attachment. The use of the song enables him to do so economically by giving him the benefit of a set of conditioned responses in his audience.

On a very few occasions love expresses itself musically in the person of a favored wooer who pauses in the midst of a conversation *à deux* to

1. Burton, *The Anatomy of Melancholy,* part. 3, sec. 2, mem. 3; (1891), p. 562.
2. Cowling, *Music on the Shakespearian Stage;* the words quoted are from p. 97.
3. Wright, "Extraneous Song in Elizabethan Drama after the Advent of Shakespeare," *passim;* especially p. 274: "practical playwrights, then as now, supplied the public with what it wanted, even at the expense of their artistic ideals."
4. Marston, *Jack Drum's Entertainment,* III, ii. Ellis may sing alone, but the context implies that this song is a duet; both Ellis and Camelia sing elsewhere in the play, so no question of either actor's vocal ability arises. Cf. the duet of Jasper and Luce in Beaumont (and Fletcher?), *The Knight of the Burning Pestle,* III, i, where there is too much else going on for Beaumont to develop the romance at length, and the duet of Lysander and Gloriana in Tatham, *Love Crowns the End,* ix, a miniature pastoral the one-act dimensions of which require the economy of the song.

sing directly to his lady.[5] But the most important song type deriving from the concept of song as the expression of love is one which owes much to another of the principal causes, doulour. Like the serenade, it is a highly stylized form: the lyric expression of the emotions of an unhappy lover. Let us call it the "complaint."

The ancestry of the complaint is ancient and not wholly dramatic, although Helen Hull Law points out the existence in the Plautine comedy of an important group of "reflective-emotional songs . . . sung by the *adulescentes* on the general topic of love" and ordinarily lamenting the pains and other disadvantages of love.[6] The Stuart dramatists were aware of these *cantici* but also knew the more purely lyrical laments of some of the Greek and Latin poets. Chaucer's complaints suggest the popularity of the form in the Middle Ages—and, in the fact that he could parody it, the extent to which it had become stylized. It was a familiar type in Tudor literature, not only in the drama[7] but in the pastoral romances; in fact, the complaint seems closely related to the pastoral tradition. Some of the complaints in Sidney's *Arcadia,* for example, are carried over directly into dramatizations from that work. One in the version attributed to Shirley is sung off stage by Pyrocles in his disguise as Zelmane; though the words of the song are lost, its effect is described in terms which might apply to almost any example of the genre:

> *Pyr.* It was no light air, I'm sure.
> *Gyn.* Indeed it carried some thing, methought,
> Of sorrow's descant; I heard love in't too.[8]

The dramatic complaints cover a fairly wide range of circumstances. The difference is essentially slight between the emotion expressed by a temporarily frustrated lover and a forsaken one or one who is actually bereaved. The gradualness of the progression from a complaint like Zelmane's to a dirge over a coffin, like Luce's in *The Knight of the Burning Pestle,*[9] shows that there can be no clear-cut boundary between the songs of love and those of doulour.[1] It must always be remembered, therefore, that such general classifications as are used in this study are intended to facilitate discussion, not to pigeonhole the lyrics according to an artificial system.

5. E.g., Manuel to Clara in J. Shirley, *The Court Secret,* i, i; Irus to Samathis in Chapman, *The Blind Beggar of Alexandria,* iii.

6. Helen Hull Law, *Studies in the Songs of Plautine Comedy* (Menasha, Wis., George Banta, 1922), p. 38.

7. One of the best-loved examples is "Cupid and my Campaspe," attributed to Lyly (*Campaspe,* iii, v). On the authorship of the songs in Lyly's plays, see below, pp. 105 ff.

8. J. Shirley (?), *The Arcadia,* ii, i. Cf. Parthenia's complaint in Glapthorne, *Argalus and Parthenia,* ii, ii. The pastoral complaint is burlesqued in J. Shirley, *Love Tricks,* v, i.

9. Beaumont (and Fletcher?), *The Knight of the Burning Pestle,* iv, iv.

1. In fact, both these causes are combined with a third, madness, in the singing of Constance in Brome, *The Northern Lass,* iii, ii.

In the broad category of complaints, however, two elements are usually present in varying proportions. One is the simple welling-over of love and grief; the other derives from the universal faith in what Ravenscroft calls the "Cure and Remedy" which music affords to the "Infortunate Sonnes of Love." Thus the complaints range from the soliloquy of grief (usually, of course, sung by the sufferer himself) to the consolatory song performed or provided by the friends or servants of the unhappy lover. Aspatia's poignant little song is simply the cry of heartbreak:

> Lay a Garland on my Hearse
> of the dismal yew.[2]

Consolatory or soothing music is exemplified by the boy's song to Mariana at the moated grange, "Take, O take those lips away," of which Mariana says apologetically,

> My mirth it much displeas'd, but pleas'd my woe.[3]

These are two of the songs of which Symonds wrote, "These songs cannot be regarded as occasional ditties, interpolated for the delectation of the audience. On the contrary, they strike the key-note of the playwright's style. They condense the particular emotion of the tragedy or comedy in a quintessential drop of melody."[4] Now, such criticism is creative rather than constructive. It offers a subjective interpretation conceived and expressed with beauty and some broad truth; but it misleads the reader who takes it too seriously. We shall see later that the aim of the Stuart dramatist was to produce a play full of variety, surprises, reversals, moral dilemmas;[5] both *Measure for Measure* and *The Maid's Tragedy* are such plays, and neither of them can well be said to have a "particular emotion" which could be summed up in a single lyric. One dramatic effect sought in these two songs is immediate: the creation of a mood which is to continue only so long as it can be sustained without relaxing in intensity, and which is then to be succeeded by a contrasting mood. The song in *Measure for Measure* has another function equally practical: it literally introduces Mariana to the audience, who, although they have heard about her, do not see her until she enters with the boy who sings. The nature of his song establishes her at once as a typical forsaken lady and an object for sympathy.

The functions of the complaint, then, like those of the serenade, arrange themselves on two planes. Immediately, the song may have a foreshadowing effect;[6] sung by an attendant, it may lull a character to sleep

2. Beaumont and Fletcher, *The Maid's Tragedy,* II, i.
3. Shakespeare, *Measure for Measure,* IV, i.
4. John Addington Symonds, "The Lyrism of the English Romantic Drama," *In the Key of Blue and Other Prose Essays* (New York, Macmillan, 1893), pp. 252–3.
5. See below, pp. 56 ff.
6. E.g., Aspatia's song, Beaumont and Fletcher, *The Maid's Tragedy,* II, i.

and so make possible a prophetic vision;[7] its being overheard may result in a meeting of characters.[8] Quite often the playwright uses it structurally, like the serenade, lulling the audience into a state of emotional relaxation in order to exaggerate the surprise of a subsequent twist of the plot, whether that twist be a happy reversal or an unexpected deepening of the lover's misery.[9]

Its higher function, again like the serenade's, is in what might be called expository characterization; that is, it identifies a character as belonging to a type familiar to contemporary audiences, particularly when it occurs in one of the earliest appearances of that character on the stage. Because of the mild amusement already described as customarily associated with the idea of a man in love, the character thus introduced or typed is, in most cases, a woman.[1] Her complaint, whether she is bereaved or merely unhappy, evokes from the audience the formula reaction associated with a formula character; simultaneously, as we shall see later, the emotional effect of the music is exerted on the audience themselves to induce the mood of pathos which the dramatist desires at the moment.[2]

3. The Song to Induce Lust: the Seduction Song

The line between love and lust is hard to draw, and doubtless one of the reasons for the seventeenth-century Englishman's faith in the serenade as a means of courting a reluctant lady was the universally held concept of music as a stimulant to passion. Sykes recognized Dekker's appreciation of music and his "great idea of its power to excite amorous desire."[3] In fact, he cited the use of music for this purpose at the opening of *Lust's Dominion* as evidence of Dekker's authorship of that play. The fact that he could do so demonstrates the need for just such a study as this; for all the major dramatists of the time except Chapman recognize this quality in music, and most of them use it dramatically. Cowling, again, accused Beaumont and Fletcher of regularly associating music with wantonness and went so far as to say that this was the only respect in which they delighted in reproducing the musical life of their times.[4] To single out these authors for such an attack is a little like damning Sophocles, alone among the Greek tragedians, for not being a Christian.

7. E.g., Brome, *The Love-Sick Court,* III, iii.

8. E.g., Glapthorne, *Argalus and Parthenia,* II, ii; J. Shirley, *The Opportunity,* II, iii.

9. Both these effects, in the order named, follow the sad song for Onaelia in Dekker and Day (?), *The Noble Soldier,* I, ii.

1. When Antonio's boy, for example, sings to express his master's grief over the supposed loss of Mellida, Antonio's passions are a shade overdone, and Marston achieves comic irony by having Mellida herself, in disguise, stand by and watch the performance before revealing herself. *Antonio and Mellida,* IV, i.

2. See below, pp. 49 ff.

3. H. Dugdale Sykes, *Sidelights on Elizabethan Drama* (Oxford, Oxford University Press, 1924), p. 101.

4. Cowling, *op. cit.,* pp. 102–03.

In fairness to the Stuart dramatists and audiences, it should be said that they were no more interested in matters of sex than their present-day counterparts. If anything, their approach to the subject was franker, more objective, and healthier in general. When their treatment of sex was comic, the end sought was usually the belly laugh rather than the nervous snigger; when it was serious, it reported human behavior as that behavior was then understood. Accordingly, if a plot called for an attempted seduction, song was almost invariably employed, because people in general believed song to be helpful in such an attempt. The result was another highly stylized song situation and song type.

It may be conceded, in justice to Cowling, that among the best and most frequently anthologized songs of this type are those of Beaumont and Fletcher, notably the two in *Valentinian*. Here the emperor has long sought to corrupt Lucina, the chaste wife of Maximus. When he at last finds a way to lure her to the court by trickery, his first thoughts about practical preparations for her seduction involve the providing of music;[5] the additional stimulus of perfumes and the temptation of a display of jewels are afterthoughts. The placement of the musicians is a matter of concern.[6] Finally, as Lucina enters the court, two songs are sung in immediate succession. The first begins,

> Now the lusty Spring is seen,
> Golden yellow, gaudy Blew,
> Daintily invite the view.
> Every where, on every Green,
> Roses blushing as they blow,
> And inticing men to pull,
> Lillies whiter than the snow,
> Woodbines of sweet hony full.
> All Loves Emblems and all cry,
> Ladys, if not pluckt we dye.[7]

Most of the surviving seduction songs resemble this one fairly closely. The imagery is sensuous and focused on such ephemeral beauties of nature as flowers and fruits, and the argument is invariably that one should gather one's rosebuds while they still are worth the gathering. Most of the songs of this group, incidentally, have high poetic merit, and few are salacious. It is rather interesting that their percentage of success is extremely low. Perhaps the only one to achieve its purpose occurs in Massinger's *The Renegado;* there Donusa welcomes Vitelli with a song which is presumably instrumental in winning her his attentions.[8]

The ultimate end sought by means of a song of seduction is not always the obvious and immediate one. Thus, in Massinger's *Believe as You*

5. Fletcher, *Valentinian*, II, i.
6. *Ibid.*, II, iv.
7. *Ibid.*, II, v (II, iv, in F2).
8. Massinger, *The Renegado*, II, iv.

List and Cartwright's *The Royal Slave,* ostensible seduction attempts are actually stratagems aimed at diverting the one seduced from activities which threaten to disturb the obtaining political balance.[9] In other plays yet higher stakes—human souls—are on the table. Both Dekker and Middleton show a man tempted to physical lust by song provided by an evil spirit, the audience understanding clearly that if he yields, he cannot escape damnation.[1] The same device is employed by a human agent in *The Bloody Brother* when Edith sets out to avenge her father's death.[2] According to Renaissance ethics a revenge was incomplete unless it accomplished the destruction of the victim's soul as well as the killing of his body. This concept is most familiar from *Hamlet* but is a factor in many contemporary plays. Edith's plan for ensuring Rollo's eternal damnation is to dispatch him when he is inflamed with lust. Accordingly, an important detail in her arrangements for assuring that his passions will be roused fully is the providing of a song to greet him when he enters. The one she chooses is that sung to Mariana in *Measure for Measure,* with an added second stanza. The resultant debate over the authorship of the lyric has obscured the significant fact that this second stanza, purposely one of the most frankly sensual of the seduction songs, is employed in what amounts to a coldly scientific spirit.

An interesting variation of the use of music to inflame the passions is its employment by lovers whose desire is mutual and who are concerned with refining their pleasure to the most excruciating degree possible. The Spenserian scholar may be reminded of Acrasia's bower;[3] in the drama, one of the most interesting illustrations occurs in Marston's *The Insatiate Countess.*[4] Here Isabella, having had two husbands and a lover, is beginning an affair with a fourth man, Gniaca, who is to steal home from a hunting party for an assignation. When he is seen approaching, Isabella orders music to be sounded. Soon after he enters she says,

> Cease admiration, sit to *Cupids* feast,
> The preparation to *Papheon* daliance,
> Hermonius *Musicke* breathe thy silver Ayres,
> To stirre up appetite to *Venus* banquet,
> That breath of pleasure that entrances soules,
> Making that instant happinesse a heaven,
> In the true taste of loves deliciousnesse.

Gniaca replies gallantly that he does not need music to stimulate him in Isabella's presence; but when she goes into her bedchamber he apparently changes his mind:

9. Massinger, *Believe as You List,* iv, ii; Cartwright, *The Royal Slave,* ii, iii.
1. Dekker, *If This Be Not a Good Play,* xiii (Pearson reprint, iii, 332); Middleton, *A Mad World, My Masters,* iv, i.   2. Fletcher, *The Bloody Brother,* v, ii.
3. Spenser, *The Faerie Queene,* Bk. II, canto 12, stanzas 74-5.
4. Marston, *The Insatiate Countess,* iii, iv.

Gnia. Sing notes of pleasure to elate our bloud :
Why should heaven frowne on joyes that doe us good?
I come *Isabella* keeper of loves treasure,
To force thy bloud to lust, and ravish pleasure. [*Exit.*

After some short Song enter Isabella *and* Gniaca *againe, she hanging about his necke laciviously.*

This particular song is one of Louis B. Wright's examples of extraneous musical entertainment; he says of it, "The purpose of the song, aside from mere entertainment, could be only to gain time for a change of costume, but there is no evidence of any necessary change."[5] As the context makes perfectly obvious, however, the fact that the selection of this song seems to be left to the discretion of the stage manager is not evidence of its extraneous quality. Others in addition to Wright have argued that a "blank" song cannot be functional.[6] But what is actually proved by an example like this is merely that the psychological implication of the music is the factor determining the use of song; one may assume that the manager had no difficulty in choosing a lyric appropriate to these circumstances, but the text was of secondary importance.

Clearly, the song just described is functional in two respects. To the characters on the stage it is a means of titillating the passions; to the dramatist, on the other hand, it is a means of indicating a lapse of time, and probably also a symbol of off-stage adultery. There is always a danger of reading more into an old play than the author could possibly have intended, and one may hesitate to accept a symbolic interpretation of a song which has other functions that are quite clear and direct. But there are other songs in the Stuart drama which seem to demand this interpretation,[7] and recognition of the symbolism would illuminate still other passages and enrich their significance for modern readers.[8] The drama has always required symbols for sexual intercourse, off stage or on. Not long ago the one favored by the motion picture industry was a

5. Wright, *op. cit.,* p. 270.
6. E.g., John Robert Moore, "The Songs of the Public Theaters in the Time of Shakespeare," *JEGP, 28* (April, 1929), pp. 172 ff.
7. Reed, *op. cit.,* p. 314, believed that the song in Mayne, *The Amorous War,* iv, v, was inserted to allow a change of costume, but the characters involved do not reappear until after an intervening scene; then they re-enter, apparently in the same clothing but, according to the stage direction, "buttoning themselves" (v, i). Mayne's intention seems unmistakable. Songs in Marston, *The Malcontent,* ii, iii, and Massinger, *The Fatal Dowry,* iv, ii, almost certainly combine this symbolism for intercourse with their other functions.
8. This interpretation of Suckling's familiar "Why so pale and wan, fond lover?" (*Aglaura,* court version, iv, ii) would explain the severity of the punishment meted to Odella at the end of the play. Similarly, if Imperia's song in Middleton, *Blurt, Master-Constable,* v, ii, is a device to symbolize love-making more passionate than could be shown on the stage, Bullen's attempt to whitewash the character of Fontinelle is defeated. A. H. Bullen, ed., *The Works of Thomas Middleton* (London, 1886), i, xxii–xxiii.

panoramic view of cumulus clouds framed by peach blossoms, with a burst of choral music on the sound track. On the stage Eugene O'Neill once achieved the same end more prosaically by blacking out the lights for a moment.[9] Anyone who reads the Stuart dramatists carefully will agree that in resourcefulness they rivaled O'Neill and the employees of Metro-Goldwyn-Mayer.

Music without song serves as an accompaniment to adultery in *The Bloody Banquet* and *The Revenger's Tragedy,* and it is part of Mullisheg's plans for a night with Bess in *The Fair Maid of the West,* Part II.[1] But the stimulative uses of music are not confined entirely to illicit applications. On at least two occasions it is demanded by a wife whose husband has just returned after a long absence;[2] on at least two more it is prescribed by a parent or guardian for a frigid or uninterested girl whom he hopes to render more receptive to the idea of marriage.[3]

4. The Song as an Expression of Wantonness

After seeing the powers attributed to song as a sexual provocative, one would naturally expect to find it used by the people who earn their living by satisfying sexual desires: bawds, panders, and courtesans. Such is indeed the case. A. J. Walker, in an unpublished dissertation, has already demonstrated that courtesans are regularly singing characters on the Stuart stage. His only comment in explanation of this phenomenon, however, is that it is a projection of life applying to all sorts of people low in the social scale—to thieves, gypsies, artisans, as well as to courtesans.[4] This is a half-truth; these other groups sing, but not for the same reason that courtesans do.

Song by courtesans is not a mere Stuart dramatic convention. In Heywood's *The Captives* Palestra and Scribonia, though not courtesans, have been trained for that profession, and part of their training has consisted in their "beinge brought vpp to musick and to sing."[5] But in this detail Heywood is following one of his sources, Plautus' *Rudens,* where also the girls are given musical training in preparation for a career of prostitution. Here, then, is an idea shared by peoples so widely separated in time and place as to suggest that it is founded not on national *mores* but on the popular psychology of song.

This supposition is supported by the uses which courtesans make of song in the plays. One is for advertising. Thus, two virtuous girls who

9. O'Neill, *The Great God Brown,* Prologue.
1. Dekker (?), *The Bloody Banquet,* III, iii; Tourneur (?), *The Revenger's Tragedy,* III, v; Heywood, 2 *The Fair Maid of the West,* I, i.
2. Heywood, *The Silver Age,* II, i; H. Shirley, *The Martyred Soldier,* I, ii.
3. J. Shirley, *St. Patrick for Ireland,* songs by the Bard in IV, i; *The Sisters,* proposed song in III, ii.
4. A. J. Walker, "Popular Songs and Broadside Ballads in the English Drama, 1559-1642," pp. 161 ff.   5. Heywood, *The Captives,* II, i.

impersonate courtesans, Brome's Victoria in *The Novella* and Dorcas in *The Weeding of Covent Garden,* both stand on their balconies and sing to the lute.[6] Victoria makes her purpose explicit:

> Give me my Lute; and set me for the signe
> Of what I meane to be, the fam'd *Novella.*

Though only Brome seems to have used this particular concept dramatically, the courtesan Lamilia in Greene's *Groatsworth of Wit* employs exactly the same device, "Hiena-like alluring to destruction."

A more common use of song represents it as part of the entertainment offered by a courtesan. Franceschina, Marston's Dutch Courtezan, is perhaps the most familiar example of a woman who entertains her guests by singing and dancing for them, but there are a score of others.[7] In fact, in *Your Five Gallants* Primero is able to pass off his brothel as a music school, with song as part of the entertainment offered to visitors.[8] Not long before, Gosson had charged real-life brothel-keepers with this very abuse: "If their houses bee searched, some instrumente of musicke is laide in sighte to dazell the eyes of every officer, and all that are lodged in the house by night, or frequent it by day, come thither as pupilles to be well schoolde."[9]

Whether used as advertising or as entertainment, song obviously is employed in these cases for its quality of arousing or increasing physical desire. In this fact lies the Stuart dramatists' consistent assignment of song to their courtesans. The concept was so firmly established and so universally accepted that the playwrights were able to utilize it to ends of comedy or grim irony by making characters mistake other kinds of music for this preparative type.[1] Moreover, as these examples suggest, song occurs almost as frequently in cases where someone is pretending to be a courtesan or is mistaken for one as it does with genuine courtesans. When one finds throughout the drama instances of women impersonating courtesans largely by the simple expedient of singing, one is justified in assuming that such an idea would not contradict the experience of the members of the audience or at least would not confuse them. In their acceptance of the device is solid evidence of its psychological soundness and therefore of its value to the dramatist as a shorthand method of characterization.

Although, as has been shown, the use of song might be simply a business matter to the courtesan, it might also be a reflection of her own tastes—an expression, that is, of her wantonness. Walker has recog-

6. Brome, *The Novella,* II, ii; *The Weeding of Covent Garden,* I, i.
7. Marston, *The Dutch Courtezan,* I, ii; II, ii; v, i; see Appendix for other examples.
8. Middleton, *Your Five Gallants, passim;* song in II, i.
9. Gosson, *The School of Abuse,* p. 26.
1. E.g., Brome, *The Northern Lass,* II, iii (comedy); D'Avenant, *The Unfortunate Lovers,* v, v (grim irony).

nized and has demonstrated at length that song is indeed widely used in the Stuart drama as an external manifestation of wantonness.[2] Our recognition of the psychological basis of song enables us to consolidate his findings, however, and to see that the explanation of song by wanton women is the same as that for song by courtesans—that the distinction between the two groups is simply the distinction between the amateur and the professional in any field.[3]

The uses of song to characterize a wanton range from the forthrightness of what Walker calls the "sung soliloquy"[4] to the more subtle (and more common) device of having her sing snatches of some familiar song or ballad, preferably a bawdy one.[5] Occasionally, even, it behooves some chaste lady to feign wantonness—Fletcher's Florimel in an attempt to cool the ardor of a would-be seducer by shocking him,[6] Brome's Millicent in the hope of so scandalizing her repulsive old bridegroom that she will not be forced to go to bed with him.[7] Florimel sings art songs, Millicent ballad snatches, but both girls are successful in their stratagems.

Walker's conclusion from this and similar material is that, in regard to women who are or pretend to be wanton, "It is not the fact that they sing that marks them as wanton, but their choice of words."[8] There is considerable evidence in support of this interpretation but perhaps not enough to invalidate the theory that singing itself is a natural expression of wantonness. In the first place, courtesans and wantons who call for song stipulate liveliness often, bawdiness seldom.[9] (Incidentally, another manifestation of moral laxity is dancing, sometimes to the accompaniment of a song by musicians,[1] although a chaste woman feigning lewdness may provide her own accompaniment by singing meaningless syllables.[2a]) In the second place, a girl who feigned wantonness out of desperation would naturally exaggerate the symptoms. Third, even a chaste heroine feigning wantonness does not invariably choose bawdy words. Thus, in Wilson's The Swisser the King has committed a rape; his sister Panopia, to show him how ugly his conduct would appear in another, pretends a violent passion for Arioldus, announces that she wishes she could rape him, and finally sings,

2. Walker, op. cit., pp. 192-7.

3. That Walker does not himself make this connection appears from the fact that he separates his observations on the two groups by some 25 pages on such miscellaneous singing types as poetasters, gallants, roarers, and mad people.

4. E.g., Fletcher, The Faithful Shepherdess, I, iii.

5. E.g., J. Shirley, Love's Cruelty, IV, i.

6. Fletcher and Rowley, The Maid in the Mill, V, ii.

7. Brome, The English Moor, I, iii.   8. Walker, op. cit., p. 192.

9. E.g., Margarita in Fletcher, Rule a Wife and Have a Wife, III, i; Lillia-Bianca in Fletcher, The Wild-Goose Chase, II, ii; Imperia in Middleton, Blurt, Master-Constable, II, ii.

1. Dancing is directed or implicit in the three cases cited in n. 9.

2a. E.g., Penelope in J. Shirley, The Gamester, III, i, and perhaps also Donna Zoya in Marston, The Fawn, II, i, and the Wife in Anonymous, The Honest Lawyer, I, i.

> Hee's a Cabinett of treasure
> The very Soule and life of Pleasure,
> Spirit and Genius of the Age,
> Natures primest Equipage:
> All that's good and Louely, wee
> Find in him: And this is hee.[3]

These words could hardly be called bawdy.

It seems fairly certain, then, that the psychological explanation of wanton singing is the valid one. In an appropriate context lively singing and dancing are unmistakable manifestations of genuine or pretended wantonness; the selection of immodest words is an underlining of the idea, but not the essential element.

Under a double standard of morality, wantonness is not a quality one thinks of in connection with men, since it is their normal instinct to pursue; but theoretically the accident of sex should make no difference in the manifestation of wantonness by song. It does not seem to have been noticed that a considerable number of dramatists make certain clownish characters sing in contemplation, either anticipatory or retrospective, of sexual gratification.[4] Although other causes for song (such as triumphant elation or drunkenness) are present in some of these cases, all are so similar as to indicate that their real basis is the element which all have in common.

In summing up the dramatic aspects of song as related to sex, one finds the same levels of functionalism as were apparent in the relationship between the song and love. The immediate dramatic ends are varied. A Stuart audience would have found comic values in most instances of wanton singing. In every seduction song and in most cases of the purposive feigning of wantonness, there is a strong element of suspense. Wanton singing, moreover, is a form of direct characterization. There is stylized characterization in the circumstances of the seduction song: its use demonstrates that the would-be seducer is dangerous and determined, and this fact emphasizes the victim's constancy—to virtue or to another love—in that he can withstand such an assault.

But it must not be forgotten that the Stuart Englishman understood the effect of music to be two edged, and that its second, or inductive, effect was not necessarily limited to the characters on the stage. How the dramatist exploited this fact for his own ends, particularly in the case of the seduction song, will be demonstrated later.[5]

By now it should be quite clear that the seventeenth-century psychology of song was not mere academic lore relegated to the library shelf, but a

---

3. Wilson, *The Swisser*, v, iii.
4. E.g., Philarchus in Anonymous, *The Ghost*, IV, iv; M. John fo de King in Marston, *Jack Drum's Entertainment*, III, i; IV, iv. See Appendix for other examples.
5. See below, chap. iv, esp. pp. 54 f.

part of everyday life. The psychology was based on the observation of life; the dramatists, in creating their illusion of life, either followed consciously the guidance of the psychological principles or unconsciously corroborated the principles by their own observation.

In more concrete terms, love is a principal cause of song; it can be emotional or sensual. The love songs in the Stuart drama either express or attempt to induce love in one or the other of these aspects. Precisely the same demonstration could be made with one of the other principal causes of song as the subject. An equal number of illustrations could be presented to show that the plays contain songs which spontaneously express joy or which are intended to induce joy—or doulour or enthusiasme.

The value of what we have done thus far lies in the fact that we now know that we have attuned our thinking to the thinking of the Stuart dramatists. We know that our method of reconstruction is realistic rather than imaginative, and we can proceed with assurance to a systematic analysis of the technical functions of the dramatic lyric.

III

Functions of Song Deriving from the Psychology of Music: Song for Characterization

WE HAVE SEEN, now, that the Stuart dramatic lyric is not a haphazard thing to be used as the caprice of the playwright suggests; rather, it is subject to a psychological principle understood by dramatist and audience alike. Chapter I showed, without direct reference to the lyrics themselves, what that principle is: that song is normally either the spontaneous expression of one of several emotional states or an attempt to induce one of those states. Chapter II demonstrated that theory and practice are identical—that the songs in the drama actually bear out the abstract principle. This establishes the foundation for the constructive part of this study, an analysis of the effects of the principle on actual dramatic technique. In Chapters III and IV we shall attempt to discover just what it meant to the practical dramatist to have reliable machinery for expressing or inducing certain emotions and just how he used that machinery. Parts of this analysis have been anticipated in Chapter II, where it seemed best to explain immediately the technique of the serenade, for example, rather than to describe the serenade there and come back later to account for its being handled as it is. But this and the following chapter will assume the psychology of song as proved and will concentrate directly on the analysis of the practical techniques deriving from the psychological principle already established.

We have seen that both the Stuart playwrights and their audiences thought of song in general as either expressing or inducing certain basic emotions and that, on the whole, the songs in the drama conform to this interpretation. Their dramatic function, then, should be either to express or to induce emotion. Obviously, the use of song to express the emotions of the persons in a play is a form of characterization. The use of song to induce emotion is a more complex matter. On the one hand, a character may employ music in an attempt to control the emotions of another character; in such cases he ordinarily states explicitly what he is doing and why. At the same time, however, the dramatist may use song to control the emotions of his audience in order to bring about their fuller participation in the emotional experiences of the characters.

For purposes of discussion it will be convenient to make an academic distinction between the use of song for characterization and its employment for emotional effect. The two are not mutually exclusive; in fact, they cannot exist independently of each other. When one of Dekker's carefree apprentices enters singing blithely, his cheerfulness spreads contagiously to the audience. In contrast, the audience are saddened by the song, "Take, O take those lips away," which is a vicariously sung soliloquy of Mariana's grief and an attempt to relieve it by giving it expression. While both these songs illustrate the dual nature of music, they are differentiated dramatically by the primary intention of the playwright: Dekker is interested first of all in establishing that his apprentice is joyful, perhaps in order to show his spirits dashed a moment later. Shakespeare, on the other hand, is more interested in arousing the audience's pity for Mariana than in merely showing her to be sad. If we remember that the active and passive qualities of music are in fact inseparable, if we realize that we are simply agreeing to divide our material into easily comprehensible units by observing which quality is more important in any given song and that we are not attempting to impose an arbitrary system of classification on the lyrics, then we can profit from the distinction between songs of characterization and songs used primarily for their emotional effect on the audience.

1. Direct Characterization

Shakespeare, his contemporaries, and his successors were practical playwrights who knew the importance of characterization and did their best to achieve clarity in it. That they valued it (and rightly) above a Belascan realism is clear from their use of the soliloquy, in which a character deliberately explains his motives to the audience to insure against possible misunderstanding. Certainly these dramatists appreciated the usefulness of any device which would help them to achieve, with speed and economy, lucid, clear-cut, forceful characterization. Such a device they found in the song.

The techniques of song for characterization are widely diversified. The most direct is to make someone analyze his own motives in a "sung soliloquy"; a very charming example is the wistful song of the little schoolboy in Neale's *The Ward*.[1] On about the same level is the song in which one person candidly describes another, as do the monks with Constantius in Middleton's *The Mayor of Queenborough*.[2] Under these circumstances, obviously, much of the characterizing value of the song lies in the text rather than in the fact of singing, although the little ward's childish innocence is suggested by his singing, and the monks' song covers a religious procession.

---

1. Neale, *The Ward*, ii, iv.
2. Middleton, *The Mayor of Queenborough*, i, i. This and one other song are not found in printed editions of the play earlier than that by R. C. Bald, which was published under the alternate title, *Hengist, King of Kent*, in 1938. For the history of these songs, see below, p. 99.

But from such unabashed statements to the audience the techniques of song for characterization range upward in subtlety and sophistication. One may learn much of a given character from the fact that he sings, from what he sings, from the circumstances under which he sings, from his response to what someone else sings, from the sort of song he writes for someone else to sing. For instance, a wounded duelist who insists on hearing the warlike ballad of "John Dory" during his treatment by the surgeon is evidently pugnacious but shows a saving whimsical humor.[3] Again, if a duke writes a passionate love song to his own wife and commands a eunuch to sing it at a public banquet, one assumes that duke to be uxorious, and one may see in his exalting of passion over strict decorum the forewarning of his eventual downfall.[4] While this may or may not be oversubtle analysis (it is, of course, impossible today to judge accurately what the impact of any such single song would have been upon a first-day audience in 1620), it is important to realize that in characterization song can do whatever the dramatist has the desire or the skill to make it do and that a definitive work on the use of song in characterization would require the dissection of perhaps hundreds of individual cases.

As a general principle, however, it can be said that the use of song for direct characterization is dictated by the psychology of music; that is to say, people who sing are joyous (or happy), dolorous (or melancholy), amorous (or wanton), or "enthusiastic" (for practical purposes, that is, drunken, mad, superhuman, or dealing with superhuman powers, celestial or infernal). This generalization must be qualified by the exclusion of two groups. Professional musicians, obviously, sing because they are paid to do so; their songs, nevertheless, are likely to tell us something about the people who have ordered them to sing. Moreover, since to people believing in the Aristotelian concept of the Golden Mean anything in excess is a vice, too much singing at inappropriate times occasionally identifies a frivolous, empty-headed person—an Asotus, Philautus, or Insatiato.[5]

Within this framework the utility of song for characterization combines considerations of realism and economy. People who sing on the stage are people who would sing in real life. But they sing on the stage chiefly because the playwright considers that he has something to gain by making them sing. Take the inebriate, for example: he sings today, as presumably he sang more than three centuries ago. But in the Stuart drama drunken singing is rare in proportion to the number of cases of drunkenness that are represented. The obvious reason is that even the

3. Fletcher, *The Chances*, III, ii.
4. Massinger, *The Duke of Milan*, I, iii. This song is conjectural; see below, p. 95.
5. Characters, respectively, in Jonson, *Cynthia's Revels;* Anonymous, *Every Woman in Her Humour;* and Anonymous, *Two Wise Men and All the Rest Fools.*

most inept actor can simulate drunkenness in pantomime, so that the further characterization of song is superfluous. Surely this is evidence that song is a device used intelligently by the dramatists for purposes of economy in communicating ideas to the audience.

Mad singing is likewise realistic; usually consisting of disjointed fragments of familiar songs or ballads, it suggests the incoherence of the conversation of mad people in real life.[6] It may, in addition, suggest the cause of the madness or the course which the malady is taking.[7] It may even intimate to the audience the attitude which the dramatist hopes they will adopt toward the mad person—an attitude of amusement, of pity, or of both.[8]

We have already observed how and why amorous people and wanton people sing. Our examination of happy song may be deferred for a moment.[9] Perhaps there is no such thing as a chronically sad person, but the melancholy man is a familiar character in the Stuart drama. Although he is not often a singing character, he is usually distinguished by a love of music and a yearning to hear it: a youth in *The Two Merry Milkmaids* says, when his coy sweetheart addresses him with unwonted kindness,

> O you speake musicke to the melancholly,
> Health to the sicke.[1]

One thinks of the Duke of Illyria,[2] Clarence in *Sir Giles Goosecap*,[3] Malevole in *The Malcontent*,[4] possibly even Hamlet. When a dramatic

---

6. When mad people do sing complete songs (e.g., Lyly, *The Woman in the Moon*, v, i; Webster, *The Duchess of Malfi*, iv, ii), the words are either incoherent or otherwise appropriate to the singer. Perhaps the only noteworthy exception is Fletcher's Passionate Lord (*The Nice Valor*, ii, i; iii, iii [two songs]; and v, i), who sings four art songs expressive of four different phases of his madness; he seems to be intended as a broad caricature of the conventional singing madman.

7. E.g., Ophelia in Shakespeare, *Hamlet*, iv, v; Constance in Brome, *The Northern Lass*, iii, ii; the Gaoler's Daughter in Shakespeare and Fletcher, *The Two Noble Kinsmen*, iii, iv, v; iv, i, iii.

8. Stuart audiences seem as a general rule to have found madness funny (F. L. Lucas, ed., *The Complete Works of John Webster* [New York, Oxford University Press, 1937], ii, 181; see also Edgar Allison Peers, *Elizabethan Drama and Its Mad Folk* [Cambridge, W. Heffer & Sons, 1914], chap. iii, *passim*) except in certain memorable cases most of which involve young girls like Ophelia. Perhaps the susceptibility of a masculine audience to the appeal of feminine beauty and fragility helped to set these cases apart; perhaps the clear voices of the boy actors were a factor. Male characters whose madness is meant to be pitied do not sing; this holds true particularly of men like Pasquil (Marston, *Jack Drum's Entertainment*, iii, iii and ff.), Witworth (Marmion or Clavell, *The Soddered Citizen*, iv, i and ff.), and Aeglamour (Jonson, *The Sad Shepherd*, i, i and ff.), whose madness, being due to love, comes perilously near to the comic anyway. The singing of bedlams, half-wits, and sham lunatics carries no pathetic overtones.

9. See below, pp. 42 ff.   1. Anonymous, *The Two Merry Milkmaids*, iii, ii.

2. Shakespeare, *Twelfth Night*, i, i; ii, iv.

3. Chapman (?), *Sir Giles Goosecap*, i, iv; iii, ii.

4. Marston, *The Malcontent*, i, i.

character is subjected to a prolonged spell of genuine unhappiness, music generally is involved sooner or later; but, as we shall see,[5] this technique ordinarily aims at ends more complex than the simple identification of the character as an unhappy person.

Priests, pagan or Christian, who sing in the drama normally do so under the circumstances in which they would sing in real life—as a part of some religious ceremony. The same thing is true of magicians and enchanters, whose rites are a sort of counterfeit of religious ritual. Finally, although one can hardly say with assurance that supernatural beings sing in real life, there is, as has been suggested, logical reason for supposing that they might; moreover, music can express directly and clearly the essential qualities of fairies, witches, and angels, the three classes of supernatural being for whom song is almost mandatory in the drama.[6]

The conclusion to be drawn here is that in the use of song for direct characterization, the lyric is a device for realism and not merely a dramatic convention. It is not enough to say, "In the Stuart drama madmen sing; supernatural beings sing," and let it go at that. The use of song follows a logical pattern which is adumbrated in the text from Ravenscroft; dramatic singing is done by people in the grip of emotions with which song is associated in popular psychology, and, in consequence, it works both practical and psychological realism.

Moreover, in addition to what we ordinarily think of as characterization, song is useful toward another end. There are innumerable occasions in the Stuart plays when it is dramatically desirable to portray a character's temporary mood, not as an end in itself but as a subsidiary factor contributing to an end. Let us say that this end is to be a comic reversal: a character is to enter in high spirits and to be dashed by unexpected news. This person's permanent characteristics are immaterial to the effectiveness of the reversal itself; only his temporary mood is of moment. But his joy is important only in that it makes possible the reversal. The dramatist who has any sense of proportion cannot take time to lay a foundation under the foundation by devoting precious minutes of acting time to establishing that his character is joyful. But he does not need to when he has a ready-made device for doing just that—a device, too, which the audience are bound to interpret correctly because they themselves would show happiness in exactly the same way.

In *The Little French Lawyer* La-Writ, an inoffensive little man going busily about his affairs, encounters three strangers who literally force him to be a fighting second in a duel under French rules. *Mirabile dictu,* the little lawyer, who has never before used a sword, disarms not only

5. See below, pp. 49 ff.
6. Ghosts (which, however, may dance in a dignified manner), devils, genuine genii, and pagan gods (with the exception of Cupid) seldom sing in the drama. The smaller fry—succubi, goblins, elves, and so on—adapt themselves to their authors' needs. See Appendix.

his own antagonist but his associate's opponent as well. Naturally, the effect on him is tremendous; he is a Walter Mitty whose dream-self has suddenly become real. His next appearance is heralded when the audience hear him singing offstage, and he enters still singing,

> He strook so hard, the Bason broke,
> And *Tarquin* heard the sound.[7]

At intervals during the ensuing dialogue, which happens to be with a swordsman who could easily carve La-Writ to pieces and who is in a mood for doing so, the lawyer continues to sing lines, half-impudent, half-triumphant, from the ballad of "The Noble Acts of King Arthur." When he leaves, he is still singing.

This scene is reminiscent of the old movie favorite in which the timid hero pokes a ferocious lion with his umbrella, supposing it to be a tame one whose teeth have been removed. That La-Writ emerges unscathed is due to his mood of triumphant self-confidence, which baffles and denies the initiative to his antagonist. Thus this mood is essential to the success of the scene. It is established, instantaneously and unmistakably, even before La-Writ himself appears on the stage, through the medium of his song. It is the fact of his singing which is significant, moreover; mere solmization would be enough to convey the impression of a heart bubbling over with self-satisfaction. That La-Writ's song happens to be a ballad of tremendous deeds of chivalry, and so is, to him, an appropriate expression of his own deeds, only adds to the fun.

That this and many similar cases of singing are intended purposively by the dramatists seems clear from their location. Most of them occur, like this one, either at the beginning of the scene or at the entrance of the singing character; others occur toward the end of the scene. The inference is obvious: when a character enters singing cheerfully, the audience know instantly that he is joyful, and the action can proceed with no time lost on preliminaries. If, on the other hand, the circumstances justify some dramatic development of the character's mood, then his subsequent breaking into song amounts to an exclamation point for emphasis. Such singing is, in a word, a short cut to the establishment of a character's mood when it is demanded for the full realization of the dramatist's purposes but is inhibited by the inexorable limitation of playing time.

In regard to the use of song for direct characterization, either of permanent traits or of temporary moods, two further observations are pertinent. First, the characterizing values of song are recognized by the persons in the plays, as well as by the playwrights; consequently people who have occasion to feign the qualities manifested by song employ song as part of their pretense. In *The Maid's Tragedy* Amintor, accused of being in low spirits the morning after his marriage to Evadne, wildly suggests

7. Fletcher and Massinger, *The Little French Lawyer*, ii, iii.

that a friend join him in singing a catch.[8] He is so distraught that his suggestion only increases the suspicion he means to allay; but Isabella actually sings a little song under very similar circumstances in *The Witch* with fair success.[9] If such characters as these are aware of the power of song to convey the impression of a particular emotion, it would be ridiculous to suppose that their creators, the playwrights, were ignorant of that power or unappreciative of its value to them in conveying to their audiences the emotions of their dramatic creatures.

Second, dramatic singing is not inevitably done by the person who is being characterized. A person of high degree may demand a song by a servant to express or accord with his emotional state, as does Helena in the bliss of a new love,[1] or Piero when he carouses to the ghosts of the enemies he has murdered.[2] This practice of vicarious singing will be discussed subsequently,[3] but it may be stated as a general rule that the aristocrat who demands a song by a servant does so under exactly the emotional stresses that would cause a poor man to sing for himself.

2. *Stylized Characterization*

Most dramatic characterization involves two processes—recognition and understanding. As we have just seen, song is of great value to the dramatist in achieving the first of these responses by his audience, in that it is an identifying trait of certain groups of people—the joyful, the sad, the amorous, the mad, and so on. The particular quality which is to be identified is emphasized by the act of singing, although the identification itself is aided by the words of the song, the nature of the music, the context in the play, and the physical appearance of the character.

Beyond this benefit, however, the dramatist may gain from his use of song a further response by the audience in the form of a connotative relating of the particular character on the stage with a background of elementary psychological theory and practical experience. For example, it has been shown how in a serenade or a seduction song are implicit the determination of the lover, the desirability of the beloved, and other less salient traits of both. In a complaint may be suggested all the pathetic steadfastness of a bereaved or forsaken lover. A supernatural song may convey the dainty gaiety of fairies, the grisliness of witches, or the spiritual purity of angels.

In each of these instances much of the characterizing value of the song applies directly to the individual on the stage. But some of it lies in the fact that he behaves as other individuals in somewhat the same situation have behaved. Thus when a complaint is sung for Mariana, the audience subconsciously transfer to her the fund of sympathy they have acquired

---

8. Beaumont and Fletcher, *The Maid's Tragedy*, III, i.
9. Middleton, *The Witch*, II, i. 1. Heywood, *A Challenge for Beauty*, III, ii.
2. Marston, *Antonio's Revenge*, V, ii. 3. See below, pp. 44–5, 122 ff.

through their literary associations with other forsaken maidens. The result is the equivalent in effectiveness of an exhaustive characterization, but it is achieved with little effort on the part of the dramatist and, still better, with little expense of playing time. Moreover, the effect of the device is cumulative; that is, the more times song is associated with a Mariana—or a Thurio, or an Appius, or a witch—the more firmly that association becomes fixed in the minds of the audience and the fuller and more certain is the audience response.

This is a different concept of type characterization from that which has previously been applied to the singing in the early drama. The usual practice has been simply to catalogue particular trades and miscellaneous social groups—shoemakers, tinkers, courtesans, rogues, rustics, merry old men—as singers and to leave the matter there. But it seems implausible that a drama as good as that of the Stuart period could have been created by quite such mechanical methods of characterization. Moreover, the compartments tend to break down on close examination. Should separate pigeonholes be allotted to "merry old men" like Merrythought and merry young men like Randall?[4] If one category is to include merry old men, should it take in Janicola in *Patient Grissill*? He is old, and he sings; but he is hardly effervescent enough to be called merry. Moreover, he and his family sing as they work at their trade of basket-making;[5] perhaps he should be called a singing artisan, and not a merry man at all. Finally, when we find it said of singing tradesmen in general that their singing identifies their particular trade but does not characterize them further,[6] the argument becomes very hard to follow. In the Stuart drama there are singing apprentices, botchers, cobblers, and so on down through the alphabet. A tinker can be distinguished from a tiler by his costume, by his tools, and by what he works on; but when both tinkers and tilers sing,[7] it is rather difficult to see precisely how their singing identifies their particular trades and why such additional identification is necessary.

Most of these difficulties can be resolved, however, if one remembers Ravenscroft and postulates as a common trait in all these miscellaneous groups the most important of the principal causes of song—joy. Merrythought sings perennially because he is too happy to be concerned about maintaining the dignity consistent with his white hairs. Janicola is perfectly adjusted to and content with his humble way of life. And as for the singing artisans, Thomas Deloney cited as an "old proverb" even in his day that

---

4. Characters, respectively, in Beaumont (and Fletcher?), *The Knight of the Burning Pestle,* and W. Rowley, *A Match at Midnight.*
5. Dekker, Chettle, and Haughton, *Patient Grissill,* ii (A4v, B1r).
6. Walker, "Popular Songs and Broadside Ballads," p. 141.
7. E.g., a tinker sings in Wild, *The Benefice,* IV, i; Dr. Sands sings as part of his disguise as a tiler in Drue, *The Duchess of Suffolk,* II, ii.

They proue seruants kind and good,
That sing at their businesse like birds in the wood.[8]

If Simon Eyre's men sing not merely because they are shoemakers but because they "followed their business with great delight, which quite excluded all weariness," as Deloney tells us, then they are singing for the very same reason as Merrythought and Janicola. These "singing artisans" and these "merry old men" share an important trait of character: that inward peace with the world and with self that was stressed in Chapter I.

Although Merrythought's normal medium of expression is song, it is noteworthy that he continues to sing in adversity, even when he faces actual hunger; Janicola and his family sing in spite of poverty. Worldly position has a semantic value in literature as it does in life, and the virtues of the lowly and the lofty go by different names. What is a humble acceptance of fate in Merrythought and Janicola becomes, in titled characters singing in the face of less prosaic hardships, heroic fortitude and a noble superiority to external circumstances. In the drama this applies particularly to prisoners, like the King of Tidore in Fletcher[9] and Pyrocles and Musidorus in Shirley's *Arcadia*.[1] Lear suggests the pastime to Cordelia.[2] But whether a singer happens to be at the top or the bottom of Fortune's wheel, as long as the reason for his singing is related to the basic concept of joy, we are being given a clue to his character far more significant than the mere identification of his trade or social class. Let us consider that clue in all its implications.

3. Song and the Nature of Man

It is a surprising fact, but a fact nonetheless, that in the hundreds of plays upon which this study is based, the reader can count on the fingers of one hand all the human beings who sing and yet are utter, fearsome, irredeemable villains. These lonely villains are Franceschina, who sings because that is part of her business as a courtesan;[3] Nero, who sings during the burning of Rome presumably because some unidentifiable leading man was unable to fiddle;[4] and, most notably, Iago, who sings not because he loves song but because he is pretending to be a good fellow.[5] Such unanimity of practice can hardly be accidental. The conclusion seems inescapable that people who sing *are* good fellows, or at least are,

8. Thomas Deloney, *The Pleasant History of the Gentle Craft*, Pt. I, chap. x, in *The Works of Thomas Deloney*, ed. Francis Oscar Mann (Oxford, Clarendon Press, 1912), p. 110.
9. Fletcher, *The Island Princess*, II, i.   1. J. Shirley (?), *The Arcadia*, v, i.
2. Shakespeare, *King Lear*, v, iii. This idea is very common in the Stuart drama; its familiarity is attested by burlesques in Marston, *Antonio's Revenge*, v, i; Middleton, *The Spanish Gypsy*, v, iii; and J. Shirley, *The Court Secret*, v, i.
3. Marston, *The Dutch Courtezan*, I, ii and ff.   4. Anonymous, *Nero*, III, iv.
5. Shakespeare, *Othello*, II, iii.

despite appearances, up to no great mischief. When a gang of thieves or gypsies or beggars first break into song, one knows immediately that they are Gilbert and Sullivan rogues, not scoundrels. The dramatist is not taking any chances on letting his audience adopt the wrong attitude toward his characters; he is, literally, saying, "These people are sympathetic. See how jolly they are? You will like them."

Naïve as this interpretation may seem, it is sound, practical theater. It should be acceptable to any thoughtful playgoer today whose interest in the drama takes him to plays both good and bad, whether experimental works or professional productions in the tryout stage. The realization is forced on such a playgoer that it is not enough for the dramatist to understand his own characters; he must make sure that the members of his audience understand them, too, and that their sympathies cannot be misplaced. The stake is satisfaction on the one hand, confusion, disappointment, and resentment on the other. Consider Shakespeare: no attempt to "explain" *Measure for Measure* and, perhaps, *Troilus and Cressida* can quite conceal the fact that they are failures and that they fail primarily because the audience do not know what position to take toward certain central characters. Talent is less likely to make mistakes than genius, however, and in the minor plays of the English Renaissance there are very few perplexing characters. Song is, of course, only one means of distinguishing sympathetic characters, but it is a reliable and a popular one.

As has been suggested, this is not to say that all singing characters are wholly sympathetic; they may be unsympathetic but harmless. Nevertheless, the generalization is valid, and re-examination quickly discloses the irrelevance of most objections to it. George Bernard Shaw, for example, is reported to have said that he would not like to sit down to dinner with the singers in Shakespeare—for songs are sung in Shakespeare's plays by fools and servants, by Autolycus, Pandarus, Falstaff, Petruchio, Mercutio, the grave-digger in Hamlet—in fact, by only one respectable gentleman (Amiens) and one noble lady in full possession of her intellect.[6] One may choose between considering Shaw a colossal stuffed shirt and believing merely that he preferred to be the only wit at the dinner table. But the answer to his class-conscious objection is, of course, that it is invalidated by the code of decorum governing the actions of all the characters on the Renaissance stage. If kings, dukes, and ladies do not ordinarily sing in Shakespeare, it is simply because for them to do so would be a breach of propriety; they can and do have pages and fools to sing for them, however, and so Shakespeare's songs may, with some misrepresentation, be said to be limited to people unacceptable as dinner

6. H. B. Lathrop, "Shakespeare's Dramatic Use of Songs," *MLN, 23* (January, 1908), 1–5, at 1.

companions. But most of Shakespeare's singers would be very stimulating company.

Again, it is not altogether relevant that the singing characters occasionally fail to pattern their conduct on conventional standards of morality. Walker, for example, deprecates the fact that a number of them, by their sheer attractiveness, escape absolute justice.[7] Under the Stuarts there was, indeed, no Legion of Decency to deplore the effect of Autolycus on the young. But, as Harbage warns us, "We must not be too narrow in our view of what constitutes morality."[8] If a character in the drama is attractive enough, we should be prepared to overlook his minor sins. We can be assured that he is not guilty of very heinous ones so long as his conscience allows him to sing.

This generalization that a singing man is a sympathetic character (or at least not an unsympathetic one) does not depend entirely on negative evidence. Everyone is familiar with Lorenzo's lines to Jessica:

> The man that hath no music in himself,
> Nor is not mov'd with concord of sweet sounds,
> Is fit for treasons, stratagems, and spoils;
> The motions of his spirit are dull as night,
> And his affections dark as Erebus:
> Let no such man be trusted.[9]

Caesar, were he liable to fear, would fear Cassius, who "hears no music."[1] Both these speeches deserve more thoughtful attention than they get from people who see in them merely further proof of Shakespeare's "surpassing love for music" or who accept as just a charming romantic idea the concept that a man's attitude toward music is a touchstone to his character.

The important fact about this idea of Shakespeare's is that it is not peculiar to him; it is shared by every dramatist of the time. Not all of them cared to, or could, document it as well as the author (probably Chapman) of *Sir Giles Goosecap:*

> According to my master *Platos* minde
> The Soule is musick, and doth therefore ioy
> In accents musicall, which he that hates
> VVith points of discorde is togeather tyed
> And barkes at *Reason,* Consonant in sence.[2]

Day, for instance, is less specific but has the same general attitude toward "heavenly music":

7. Walker, *op. cit.*, p. 115, n. 5.
8. Alfred Harbage, *As They Liked It* (New York, Macmillan, 1947), p. 141. Harbage's whole discussion of "Justice in Comic Fable" (pp. 117–41) is relevant here.
9. Shakespeare, *The Merchant of Venice,* v, i.   1. Shakespeare, *Julius Caesar,* I, ii.
2. Chapman (?), *Sir Giles Goosecap,* III, ii.

> . . . since all conclude
> It is an art divine, we were too rude
> Should we reject it.[3]

Samuel Rowley stresses the training in music given to Edward, Prince of Wales, and makes the prince say of music,

> Truly I love it, yet there are a sort,
> Seeming more pure than wise, that will upbraid at it,
> Calling it idle, vain, and frivolous.
> > *Tye.* Your grace hath said, indeed they do upbraid
> That term is [it] so, and those that do are such
> As in themselves no happy concords hold:[4]

Other writers who do not discuss the matter so directly make their position clear by the sort of characters to whom they assign a dislike of music: Beaumont's Gondibert, an eccentric and ridiculous woman-hater;[5] Shirley's Bubulcus, a rich gull;[6] Glapthorne's Covet, a comic alderman, who objects to it on the ground that it

> Does but cloy
> The eares, but never fills the purse sonne.[7]

The agreement of still other dramatists is evident in the symbolic use they make of music. The recapitulatory masque at the end of Brome's *The Antipodes* introduces Discord, attended by "Folly, Iealousie, Melancholy and madnesse," to sing a "Song in untunable notes," which is contrasted with the pleasant song performed immediately afterward by Harmony and her attendants, Mercury, Bacchus, Cupid, and Apollo.[8] Thomas Randolph does almost exactly the same thing in *The Muses' Looking-Glass;* with a masque by the seven deadly sins he contrasts a song and dance by the virtues.[9] The stage direction does not state that the music of the sins is "untunable," but the text of their song makes the idea clear:

> Disorder is the Masque we bring,
> And Discords are the Tunes we sing.

Even in a play as apparently ingenuous as *Histrio-Mastix,* the eight songs prescribed all occur, at the cost of some crowding, during the reigns of Peace and Plenty; singing is conspicuously and significantly absent under Pride, Envy, War, and Poverty.[1] Definitely this concept of a re-

---

3. Day, *Humour Out of Breath,* I, i.
4. S. Rowley, *When You See Me, You Know Me,* viii (ed. Elze, p. 52).
5. Beaumont (and Fletcher?), *The Woman-Hater,* III, i.
6. J. Shirley, *Love Tricks,* II, i.   7. Glapthorne, *Wit in a Constable,* III, iii.
8. Brome, *The Antipodes,* v, x, xi.
9. Randolph, *The Muses' Looking-Glass,* I, iv, and v, i, ii, respectively.
1. Marston, *Histrio-Mastix;* all the songs occur in I, II, and VI.

lationship between music and all good qualities—virtue, harmony, order —is not just a quaint idea. It is an integral part of Renaissance philosophy, a practical development of the Pythagorean-Platonic theory that a celestial music is produced by the spheres as they revolve in harmony with a divinely ordered plan.[2]

The concept of a sympathy between music and the good is used both positively and negatively for sound but economical dramatic characterization. Demagoras is shown to be not simply a military man but a brute when he rejects a song which is part of "rurall pastimes" in his honor with the comment,

> 'Tis too effeminate this; I had rather heare
> The cryes of dying men than these nice straines,
> Or Souldiers with loud clamours rend the aire
> With shouts of victory.[3]

He is demonstrated to be capable of doing what he later really does: avenge Parthenia's indifference by smearing her face with a poison which destroys her beauty.

In *The Malcontent* Pietro is a usurper and a villain. But about the middle of the play, when he seems committed to a career of bloodshed, he suddenly appears in a very charming scene; he gives over a hunt to engage in a gentle wit-combat with a page and demands a song from two other pages.[4] To a hasty reader the scene would appear completely extraneous; but to a Jacobean audience Pietro's kindness to a child and even more emphatically his interest in music would have been a warning not to misjudge him, quite sufficient preparation for the complete repentance and conversion which he in fact undergoes only a little later.[5]

It is not too much to say, then, that song, in the hands of the Stuart dramatists, is an invaluable tool for characterization. It may identify an individual with a type to which a particular audience response attaches.

---

2. Burnet, in "Shakespeare and Greek Philosophy," pp. 58–61, and Wilson, in "Shakespeare's Universe," 223–5, discuss this philosophic theory but do not relate it to dramatic characterization. The theory is summed up in Armin (?), *The Valiant Welshman*, III, ii, when Gald attempts to reconcile Caradoc to some bad news:

> What, Royall Prince, can chaunce predominate
> Ouer a mind, that, like the soule, retaynes
> A harmony of such concordant tunes?
> No sudden accident should make to iarre.
> This tenement of clay, in which our soule
> Dwels in, vntill the Lease of life indures,
> Of learned men was well called, *Microcosme*,
> Or, little world . . .

3. Glapthorne, *Argalus and Parthenia*, I, ii.
4. Marston, *The Malcontent*, III, ii.
5. Other characters whose singing may be intended as preparation for their conversion to more sympathetic behavior are Lopez in Fletcher, *Women Pleased*, III, iv, and Pallatine Senior in D'Avenant, *The Wits*, IV, i.

It may reflect or underline any of the "Principall Causes" as elements of character. By the use of the "sung soliloquy" or by developing a character's response to song, the playwright may achieve subtler nuances of characterization. But broadest and most valuable to him, song is a convention for separating the sheep from the goats—for adjusting his audience's perspective and clarifying to them the alignment of the characters. All these things song does quickly, economically, and effectively; it seems a pity to attack it (as so many scholars have done) because it also does them pleasantly.

IV

Functions of Song Deriving from the Psychology of Music: Song for Emotional Effect

U NDER OUR ACADEMIC DIVISION of the functions of the dramatic lyric according to the primary intention of the playwright, the second principal purpose served by song is the influencing of the emotions of the audience, rather than the expression of the emotions of the characters. It must be remembered that this division is made solely for convenience in discussion. We have just seen that the value of song in the characterization of a good man depends in part on the sympathetic response of the audience; in a moment we shall see that much can be learned of the character of a woman from her use of song for its emotional effect upon others. The benefit of our subdivision of the material into more easily comprehensible units will become a disadvantage if the interdependence of the active and passive qualities of song is forgotten.

1. Song and the Audience

The subplot of Fletcher's play *The Captain* affords a good introduction to the use of song for evoking a desired emotional response from the hearers. Lelia, an artful prostitute, wants a husband and has made up her mind to have Julio. Inadvertently she has frightened him badly by a premature mention of marriage, and so she is faced with the difficult task of winning him back, either to marry him or to be revenged on him. The difficulty is increased by Julio's wariness: when he next comes to call, intending to rail at Lelia, he brings along his friend Angelo to see that he does not fall under her spell again. But Lelia is both resolute and resourceful. Determining to work on the emotions of Julio, she assumes the role of an innocent girl heartbroken at her abandonment by a beloved but callous suitor. These are her instructions to her waiting woman:

> Give me my Vail, and bid the Boy go sing
> That song above, I gave him; the sad song;
> Now if I miss him, I am curst, go, wench,
> And tell 'em I have utterly forsworn
> All company of men, yet make a venture

At last to let 'em in; thou knowst these things,
Do 'em to th' life.[1]

Accordingly, as Julio and Angelo enter, they hear the pathetic song, "Away delights, go seek some other dwelling, For I must dye." By the time it ends, both young men's sympathies are so affected that Julio is wax in Lelia's hands and Angelo is in love with her too.

This is not Lelia's only use of music. Though she has one eye on future security, she is unwilling to sacrifice present pleasure. To this end she sends her maid to invite a likely looking stranger to her house; when he enters he finds himself alone in a rich chamber with a sumptuous banquet set out and hears a song of a different sort—one in the provocative seduction pattern already described—which is intended to prepare him for Lelia's entrance and her dishonorable proposals.[2]

Obviously Fletcher, who created Lelia, understood as well as she the potentialities of song for influencing human emotions. Fletcher's livelihood depended largely on his ability to control the emotions of his audiences. In these two scenes he is, like a master magician, letting the audience in on the secret of one of his tricks, confident in the knowledge that he has a whole bag full of others. Few of Fletcher's contemporaries could match him in the sheer dexterity of his use of song, and consequently few of them follow him in exposing the arcana of the craft; but all of them use the technique employed by Lelia.

In essence, this technique is much the same as that of modern background music: sad music for a pathetic scene, martial music for a war-like scene, horrid music for an infernal scene. This comparison may seem inappropriate in that today we understand that the score of a motion picture is aimed directly at our emotions and that the music is not heard by the characters on the screen. Our acceptance of such music, however, should be recognized for what it is: a convention, in exactly the same sense as the soliloquy and the aside were conventions. It is a convention which has no direct counterpart in the Stuart drama; the Stuart audience never hear music which is inaudible to the characters. Therefore the Stuart playwrights, recognizing and seeking the same emotional values which we attribute to background music today, had to devise techniques by which their emotive music might plausibly be performed in the presence of the characters on the stage.

Modern background music, however, is almost invariably an auxiliary, aimed at intensifying a mood induced by the dramatic action.[3] The Stuart dramatists go further, attributing to song the ability to induce a desired mood virtually by itself. This sounds like an extreme statement.

1. Fletcher (and another?), *The Captain,* iii, iv.   2. *Ibid.,* iv, v (iv, iv in F2).
3. Although the emotional tone of a moving picture is sometimes set by the music accompanying the "credits," little is made of the possibilities of overture music in the cinema. Sir Laurence Olivier's *Hamlet* is a happy exception.

But, as we have seen, Lelia's effects are achieved through music almost alone; and, as we shall see, the dramatists sometimes achieve equally definite effects with a song and little else.[4]

That the Stuart position is fundamentally sound could probably be proved by documentation, but a little introspection on the reader's part will serve equally well. Certain melodies recall particular memories and, with them, moods; different types of music, too—a lullaby and a Sousa march, let us say—evoke different emotional responses. If one approaches music in a passive or, still better, a receptive mood, one can be moved by it toward gaiety, melancholy, sentimentality, or spirituality —that is, to Ravenscroft's principal causes.

If, then, music can influence the emotions of a theater audience, it assumes value to the dramatist as a means of making that audience not merely passively receptive to a particular scene but in effect emotionally participant in it. The intimate nature of the platform stage was probably more conducive to such an empathic relationship of audience to actors than the picture-frame stage, which enforces objectivity by keeping the audience on the outside, looking in. Consequently, the Stuart audiences were prepared to be stirred. But their dramatists were too adept (and too practical) to neglect any device that might make this empathy more complete. If a sad song, for example, could transform an audience from observers of a tragic scene to participants in it, then they employed a sad song.

Simultaneously, such a song could perform another function. It is generally recognized that such realism as could be achieved on the platform stage was a realism of total illusion rather than of physical detail. If one thinks of the minuteness of the directions for stage settings supplied by, say, O'Neill, one will realize forcibly how the picture-frame stage has changed the nature of the drama. When certain types of songs became associated with certain situations both on the stage and in real life, however, those songs inevitably recalled to the audience similar situations from other plays or from their own experience, thus suggesting a richness of detail perhaps not actually developed by the particular scene being unfolded. This is exactly the same sort of connotative value as was attributed in Chapter III to certain characterizing songs; a complex of associations can build up about a situation just as it can about a type character.

To sum up, the song sung purposively by one character to another character may be copied directly from a corresponding situation in real life. But the Stuart dramatists did not forget—nor must we—that its effect was felt by its hearers in the pit as well as by those on the stage. This effect was all the more insidious precisely because it did not seem to be directed at the audience. One may recognize the "art" in modern

4. See below, pp. 58 ff.

background music; one is less likely to recognize it in a song that seems to be part of the dramatic action, open and aboveboard. Thus the audience, hearing a song, were convinced of the authenticity of the accompanying action because they saw people behaving as people would behave under similar circumstances in real life. At the same time, though they did not realize it, they themselves were influenced by the emotive power of the music to a more complete participation in the scene. This empathic participation was reinforced by the fact that the songs had connotative values which rounded out the total illusion of the scene, making the surrender of the auditors to that illusion more rapid and more satisfying. The proof of the argument lies in the existence, in the corpus of the Stuart drama, of a clearly defined code of song types applicable to particular situations and conventionalized in exactly the same way as the player piano rendition of "Hearts and Flowers" and the "Light Cavalry Overture" became conventionalized for the love scene and the chase in the silent moving pictures of twenty-five years ago.

2. *The Conventional Songs of Situation*

There is nothing new about recognizing stylized song types in the Stuart drama; everyone who has ever written on the dramatic lyrics has had his own classification. In fact, the orthodox position in regard to these songs is like the orthodox position in regard to song for characterization: a tendency to catalogue rather than to analyze and interpret. Nothing would be gained by repeating any of these catalogues here or by attempting a new one; the fact that certain types of song are conventional is beyond dispute.[5] But some important things remain to be said about the songs which are conventional in particular situations.

First, the conventional songs are, in the emotions which they express or induce, consonant with the general psychology of song—which is, be it remembered, not a rigid system but a comprehensive principle. Obviously the serenade is associated with love, the dirge with doulour. Equally common, however, are song types which combine two or more of the basic emotions, or which range from one basic emotion to another, like the shades between two primary colors. Thus the wedding song is a conventional form; its dramatic manifestations range the gamut from songs symbolizing the actual wedding ceremony (i.e., songs of religious enthusiasme)[6] to songs which are simply a part of a general happy cele-

5. A sampling of a few pages of the Appendix will demonstrate both the nature and the extent of the conventionality of these types. The serenade, seduction song, and complaint already have been discussed. Other familiar groups include the songs of religious ritual, secular ceremony, and social festivity, the drinking song, the curative-consolatory song, and so on.

6. E.g., Marston, *Sophonisba*, I, ii; Mayne, *The Amorous War*, v, ix; Goffe, *The Courageous Turk*, IV, ii.

bration (i.e., songs of pure joy).[7] Within the general classification of songs performed as part of the entertainment at social gatherings, typical lyrics range from the catch sung by a group of drinkers whose gaiety has begun to pall (i.e., a song conventional in the particular situation but sung in this case in an attempt to induce joy homeopathically)[8] to the lyric performed under circumstances reminiscent of the drawing-room ballad of a generation ago (a purely social song but one that recalls Burton's observations on young women who forget their expensive musical training as soon as they find husbands).[9] It is clear, then, that most of these songs are realistic socially and that all of them are realistic psychologically.

A second point to be emphasized is that these songs are used purposively, for their effect on the audience as well as on the characters in the play. The nature of the effect desired has been described. Perhaps no one would be disposed to question the ability of music to induce sensations of sadness, cheerfulness, or sentimentality, or to convey a mood suitable to the introduction of certain types of supernatural beings. The hard-headed twentieth-century reader may, however, find some difficulty in accepting the theory that song was expected to be equally effective in inducing in the audience the other emotions included among the principal causes of music. Let us, therefore, examine a couple of representative cases.

That music can influence a man toward that special form of enthusiasme which we might call religious awe is indicated by the fact that it forms part of the ritual of most creeds and sects today. An occasion where some such mood assumes importance to the dramatist occurs in *Cupid's Revenge*. The plot of this play narrates the vengeance exacted by the god on the royal house of Lycia when the Duke rashly, at the request of his daughter, destroys the images and abolishes the worship of Cupid. The request is made and the orders for its fulfillment are given in the opening scene; the dramatic interest of all the rest of the play lies in the retribution which overtakes the Duke and his children. But to a seventeenth-century audience of good Christians, the destruction of heathen idols might seem to be a good idea; the dramatist therefore needed in some economical way to suggest that to the Lycians the worship of Cupid was an authentic religion. Accordingly he provided a short scene set in the temple of Cupid; in it a priest speaks briefly, and a boy sings in praise of the god.[1] By seeing this service and, through the music, sharing in it, the audience

---

7. Such songs are especially appropriate as a cap to a comedy; e.g., Chapman (?), *Sir Giles Goosecap;* Field, *A Woman Is a Weathercock;* Fletcher, *Wit without Money;* Jonson, *The New Inn.* It is possible that more plays were intended to end in this way than we suspect; Rutter's *The Shepherds' Holiday* and Brome's *The Court Beggar,* for example, both provide opportunity for an afterpiece of hymeneal song and dance.

8. J. Shirley, *The Politician,* iii, ii.   9. Middleton, *Women Beware Women,* iii, ii.

1. Beaumont and Fletcher (and another?), *Cupid's Revenge,* i, ii.

are satisfied that Cupid worship actually is a genuine religion, any dese-
cration of which will be a sacrilege fully deserving punishment. This
particular song has other functions in addition to its basic one, moreover.
Being in the seduction pattern already described, its text suggests the
erotic element to which the Duke's daughter objects; and when Fletcher
has soldiers interrupt the service to destroy Cupid's image, he achieves
a shock effect which emphasizes the sacrilege.

Perhaps, then, the only aspect of the theory at which the modern
reader will still be inclined to boggle is the apparent absurdity of the
implication that a song might be intended to induce lust in the audience.
But even this absurdity is more apparent than real. Any man who saw
Sir Laurence Olivier's motion picture version of *Henry V* must remember
the momentary shock he felt when the charming actress who played
Katharine faded into a heavily rouged boy actor as the scene contracted
in a royal palace and expanded again into the Globe theater. The whole
essence of the drama is contained in that sense of shock. The boy represents what the Elizabethan playgoer saw with his physical eye; the girl
represents what he saw with his mind's eye.

A modern audience, its imagination atrophied by exposure to scenery,
lighting, and sound effects, could hardly have realized the full emotional
power of *Henry V* had the entire play been filmed as it was acted on the
stage of the Globe; the Elizabethan audience, accustomed to the bare
stage and the boy actor, presumably saw in imagination something reasonably like what we saw in the picture. But their being accustomed to
the physical conditions of their theater was only part of the reason for
their ability to appreciate; the rest lay in their willingness to surrender
themselves emotionally to the control of the dramatist. The dramatist,
on the other hand, recognized fully the limitations of his stage; sometimes (as Shakespeare did in *Henry V*) he chafed at them; but always
he made the best of them by whatever means were at his disposal.

To see how all this applies to the apparent absurdity of using song to
excite lust in the audience, let us think of any of the scenes in which
a woman attempts to seduce a man. If the audience see nothing but a
mascaraed boy, there is no sense of temptation, no dramatic tension, no
thrill. If, however, they see a beautiful and alluring woman, then they
can share in the temptation and in the triumph of resisting it. How can
they be made to see the woman instead of the boy? Partly by costume,
make-up, clever acting; more by the power of the total illusion; but no
little by the subtle stimulus of the song which actually helps to create in
the audience the emotion which the protagonist is supposed to be feeling.
And whether or not we today believe that it *can* create that emotion,
we know that the Stuart dramatists believed that it could, because most
of them tell us so explicitly.

Since the advent of actresses, the dramatist no longer has to bother about exciting physical passion by artificial means. But a general empathic participation by the audience is as indispensable today as it ever was. One need not read books on the drama to be told that "what we want above all in the theater is to be moved"[2]—one need merely remember how one's wife enjoys sobbing through a pathetic scene in the movies. Such participation is the whole object of going to the theater. A play in which the audience cannot take sides may be good dialectic, but it is seldom good drama. That the Stuart dramatists needed no one to tell them so is attested by the skill with which they used song to help their audiences choose the right side and, having chosen it, share all the emotions of the hero and heroine.

That certain song types should have become conventionalized is what one would normally expect of a drama so conventionalized in general as the Stuart drama. Even the reader whose acquaintance with the literature of the period extends little beyond the covers of a standard anthology of plays knows the extent to which these plays repeat certain stock devices (such as the "bed trick" or the Friar Lawrence potion which induces a deathlike sleep); certain stock characters (such as the heroine disguised as a page or the comic senile amorist); and certain stock dilemmas (such as the conflicting claims of love and friendship or the heroine's choice between saving her own honor or the life of a loved one).

The third essential fact to be remembered about the conventional songs of situation, then, is the extent of their conventionality. Although, as has been shown, the effects of the "Principall Causes" overlap to an extent that makes it uncritical to attempt a strict classification of the resulting types, recognition of a general pattern not only is possible but is actually forced on the reader. No one but the scholar is likely to have the rewarding experience of reading a particular play for the first time and saying to himself on reaching a certain kind of scene, "Here should be a song," turning the page, and finding it—or the even more exciting experience of discovering later that a manuscript of the play in question contains a song at that very point, the directions for it somehow having failed to find their way into the early printed editions.[3] Nevertheless, the non-specializing student can find convincing evidence of the conventionality of these song types in the frequency with which they recur, as demonstrated in the appendix to this study.

Further proof of their conventionality is the fact that every one of these song types is, at one time or another, parodied or burlesqued. It is manifestly impossible to burlesque a convention that does not exist; the effectiveness of any travesty, moreover, is in direct proportion to the familiarity of the subject. For instance, the soldiers' drinking song is a

2. Alan Reynolds Thompson, *The Anatomy of Drama* (Berkeley and Los Angeles, University of California Press, 1946), p. 132.
3. See below, pp. 97 f., 99.

common subclassification of the convivial type. Representative examples are sung by the watch in *The Knight of Malta,* by Bellario and the artisan-soldiers in *The Faithful Friends,* by the loyal and treacherous officers in *Wallenstein.*[4] Fletcher's comedy *The Woman's Prize* concerns itself with a pair of Jacobean champions of women's rights who support their cause by barricading themselves away from their menfolk. In the ensuing siege they are relieved and victualed by an army of sympathetic city and country women. The general mock-heroic treatment is funny, but the climax to this part of the comedy comes when the embattled dames proceed to get drunk and to sing in true military fashion a drinking song in honor of "the woman that wears the breeches."[5]

The conventional hymeneal song is travestied in the satiric one sung by Crack in Brome's *The City Wit;*[6] Shirley makes the clever servant Gorgon disguise himself as Mopsa and burlesque the pastoral tradition by singing a doleful mock complaint;[7] the songs forming part of the secular ceremony of the coronations of Valentinian[8] and of Anne Boleyn[9] have their mischievous counterpart in the coronation of Claus as King of the Beggars,[1] that at the induction of a Knight of Malta[2] in one at the comic induction of a Knight of the Twibill.[3] Nothing is sacred in this business of burlesque, not even the sentiment of the serenade[4a] or the awe of religious ritual.[5a]

But the clearest evidence that certain song types not only were used conventionally by the dramatists but were accepted accordingly by the audience is the fact that occasionally there is little or nothing but a song to establish a specific situation and induce the appropriate mood. Full understanding of this technique, however, requires a brief examination of exactly what the Stuart dramatist wanted to achieve and how he went about achieving it.

3. The Conventional Song as an Element of Dramatic Structure

The completely unprejudiced attempt to discover the conscious aims of the early dramatist is a critical approach of fairly recent inception. One of the clues it has followed is found in the uneven dramatic intensity of the Tudor and Stuart plays—an unevenness which partly justifies the practice of excerpting selections like Lamb's. Some of the romantic critics recognized this clue without being quite able or willing to interpret it.

---

4. Fletcher, Field, and Massinger, *The Knight of Malta,* III, i; Anonymous, *The Faithful Friends,* I, ii; II, iii; Glapthorne, *Wallenstein,* V, ii.
  5. Fletcher, *The Woman's Prize,* II, vi.   6. Brome, *The City Wit,* V, i.
  7. J. Shirley, *Love Tricks,* V, i.   8. Fletcher, *Valentinian,* V, viii.
  9. Shakespeare and Fletcher, *Henry VIII,* IV, i.
  1. Fletcher and Massinger, *Beggar's Bush,* II, i.
  2. Fletcher, Field, and Massinger, *The Knight of Malta,* V, ii.
  3. Glapthorne, *The Hollander,* IV, i.   4a. E.g., Fletcher, *Monsieur Thomas,* III, iii.
  5a. E.g., Anonymous, *The Faithful Friends,* IV, v.

Thus Gifford, long ago, in pointing out the "heart-rending pathos" achieved by the dirge sung at Calantha's death in the last scene of Ford's *The Broken Heart,* commented that the audiences of Ford's day had firm nerves

—and they needed them: the caterers for their amusements were mighty in their profession, and cared little how highly the passions of the spectators were wound up by the tremendous exhibitions to which they accustomed them, as they had ever some powerful stroke of nature or of art at command to compose or justify them.[6]

But they *did* care, if only as a matter of business. Modern criticism has shown that the "great scene," like this one of Ford's, was a conscious part of seventeenth-century dramatic technique:

the men who crowded The Phoenix or The Red Bull lived, both in the theatre and outside it, far more in the moment for the moment's sake than the cultured classes of today; and accordingly it was a succession of great moments that they wanted on the stage, not a well-made play. . . . If a dramatist gave them great situations, ablaze with passion and poetry, it would have seemed to them a chilly sort of pedantry that peered too closely into the machinery by which these were produced. They did not want their fireworks analysed. They were, in fact, very like a modern cinema-audience, with the vast difference that they had also an appetite for poetry. And so all their playwrights, Shakespeare included, worked predominantly in scenes. Scenes were the essential units. That is the first thing to realize about their plays.[7]

Now, the preceding pages of this study have attempted to demonstrate that the conventionally handled song is a device aimed at intensifying the scene in which it occurs by evoking in the audience the mood most conducive to emotional participation in the scene and therefore most productive of full appreciation. But it is possible to analyze this dramatic technique more minutely.

From Dekker's prologue to *If It Be Not Good* (Q 1612) George F. Reynolds draws four concepts which, he says, were the conscious aims of a popular Elizabethan dramatist (as distinguished from a "pseudo-classic" dramatist like Jonson).[8] As first in importance he names poetry (or at least rhetoric)—the magic of words; second is "the quick creation of vivid audience responses"; third is the necessity of giving the actor

6. *The Works of John Ford,* ed. Alexander Dyce with notes by William Gifford (London, 1869), I, 319, n. 18.

7. Lucas, ed., *The Complete Works of John Webster,* I, 17.

8. George F. Reynolds, "Aims of a Popular Elizabethan Dramatist," *Renaissance Studies in Honor of Hardin Craig* (Stanford University, Stanford University Press, 1941), 148–52.

"a good opportunity to display strong emotions, 'Sorrow, Rage, Joy, Passion' "; and last is the stipulation that "these emotions must be arranged to provide striking contrasts—'sometimes drawing out Teares, then smiles.' " Reynolds' second point is, of course, an aspect of his fourth one: the effect of any contrast depends on the intensity and the close juxtaposition of the elements contrasted, so that the slow, laborious creation of an audience response would destroy the vividness of the contrast.

Obviously, song can be instrumental in the attainment of all four of these ends. In proof of its poetic quality there is the long series of anthologies from the playbooks, not to mention the sort of criticism (or, rather, appreciation) represented by Symonds' thesis that "the bias of poetical literature in England during the Elizabethan age was lyrical" and that, from Marlowe to Ford, the blank verse abounds in passages of lyrism which climb higher and higher until they reach their culmination in the actual songs.[9]

It is evident, too, that the use of song helps to give the actor a chance to display strong emotions. Song is a natural expression of all the emotions named by Dekker except rage. Even when the song is sung by someone else, the principal actor gains by it an opportunity for pantomimic action before an audience prepared by the emotional effect of the music to respond to his performance.

But song is particularly valuable for implementing Reynolds' second and fourth aims, which might be elided into a single one: the achieving of striking emotional contrasts by the quick creation of vivid audience responses. That this was basic to Stuart dramatic technique is supported by Lawrence B. Wallis' demonstration that the main aim of Fletcher was "variety of emotional impact on his audience."[1] Wallis shows how intricately the better plays of the Beaumont and Fletcher canon are constructed on an emotional pattern of contrasts, antitheses, and reverses; he adds, perhaps without adequate emphasis, that the aims of Fletcher's contemporaries were substantially the same.

There is nothing about this technique, however, that is peculiar to the seventeenth-century stage. Students of the modern drama call it "surprise" and value it as one of the chief sources of dramatic effect. Thompson says that surprises arising from plot are particularly important; when such a surprise is "especially well devised and startling," it is called a *coup de théâtre*. He explains that melodrama and farce are the dramatic types most dependent on coups.[2]

Much Stuart tragicomedy is essentially melodramatic, and much Stuart comedy is farcical; so that, far from being an esoteric technique,

---

9. Symonds, "The Lyrism of the English Romantic Drama," pp. 244 ff.
1. Lawrence B. Wallis, *Fletcher, Beaumont & Company* (New York, King's Crown Press, 1947), p. 217.   2. Thompson, *op. cit.*, pp. 135 ff.

the construction of a play to create a series of effective surprises—"emotional patterning" or "striking contrasts," if one prefers—is exactly what one should expect to find in the work of the Stuart dramatists, who were, above all, practical men of the theater. It remains now to show how song is helpful in this connection.

Consider a brilliant coup de théâtre: the opening scene of *The Two Noble Kinsmen*. The play begins with the movement of the wedding procession of Theseus and Hippolyta toward the temple. All the resources of the platform stage are called upon to enhance the spectacle: stately movement, colorful costumes—and song. No words are spoken, but the hymeneal song at once explains the situation and intensifies the mood. By the final stanza the audience have surrendered wholly to the frame of mind that even today attaches to any big church wedding. Then, without warning, three queens in somber black step forward silently, ominously, and the stately procession halts.

The stunning effect of this reversal happens to be irrelevant to the total plan of the play. The three queens have, of course, come to ask Theseus to postpone his wedding and recover for burial the bodies of their husbands, slain at Thebes; in complying with their request, Theseus takes Palamon and Arcite prisoner, and the plot proper gets under way considerably later. But it would be a cold-blooded critic who could raise this fact in objection to one of the most sensational openings in the drama of the Jacobean or any other period.

The significant aspect of the scene in relation to this study is the fact that the reversal is accomplished without the use of spoken words. The wedding mood is created wholly by visual and musical means. Here, then, is one ultimate dramatic value of song: the creation, with absolute economy, of a mood the sole end of which is to furnish theatrical sensation by being shattered with a contrasting mood. When such a coup is an end in itself, as it is in *The Two Noble Kinsmen* and in most other cases, there is no time to spend on a lengthy development by dramatic means of the mood to be shattered; but song can induce it almost instantaneously, as the playwrights knew from popular psychology as well as from practical experience. The result is a dramatic device which might justly be called the "Fletcher effect," since no other dramatist of the period uses it so consistently as Fletcher does, or achieves his powerful compression with it.

It is demonstrable that Fletcher's employment of this device is no mere happy accident. Nearly every wedding song in the entire Beaumont and Fletcher canon shows its influence. The action of *The Little French Lawyer* really begins when a wedding procession with song is interrupted by Dinant's rude denunciation of the bride, her father, and the groom.[3] In *The Fair Maid of the Inn* the effect of a lost but presumably

3. Fletcher and Massinger, *The Little French Lawyer*, I, i.

hymeneal song as wedding guests gather is reversed by the arrival of the bride-elect's father and brother to forbid the ceremony.[4] In *The Maid's Tragedy* the effect is protracted and made less sensational in keeping with the prevailing spirit of the play, which is tragic rather than melodramatic, but the result is the same: the magnificence of the wedding masque, with its three songs,[5] makes more horrible by contrast the actual circumstances of the marriage of Amintor and Evadne—circumstances which have been foreshadowed but which are not fully revealed until the following act.

Application of the Fletcher effect is by no means confined to wedding songs, however. It underlies the conventional treatment of the serenade which has already been explained, not only in the plays of Fletcher but in those of all his contemporaries.[6] It is developed from a pagan ritual song in *Cupid's Revenge;*[7] from a consolatory song in *The Honest Man's Fortune*, where the sad peace of a page's song to the heroine is shattered by the abrupt entrance of the hero, sword in hand and fainting with exhaustion;[8] from a dirge in *The Knight of the Burning Pestle*, where Luce sings over Jasper's coffin, then removes the cloth and is amazed to see her supposedly dead lover sit up;[9] from a soporific song in *Valentinian* when at the end of the soothing "Care-charming sleep" the emperor, dying of poison, bursts out into explosive groans and demands for drink.[1] The effect is inverted in *The Mad Lover* when a pagan ritual processional song recaptures a solemn mood after a farcical scene in which a comic soldier and the priestess of Venus are nearly caught swiving in the temple.[2]

Fletcher is neither the first nor the only Stuart dramatist to understand the efficacy of song in building up to a surprise. Marston, for one, pioneered in many of the dramatic effects commonly used later, including this one. In *Sophonisba,* for example, he has an exact parallel to Fletcher's treatment of the wedding song: the entrance of Massanissa to the bedchamber of his bride is made the occasion for a remarkable oratorio-like performance, with Sophonisba singing or declaiming an irregular Shakespearian sonnet while a chorus accompanied by cornets and organ responds at intervals, "Io to Hymen." This is a build-up to the coup at the end of the song:

> *Chorus.* Io to Hymen.
> *Enter* Carthalon *his sword drawne, his body wounded* . . .[3]

4. Fletcher (or others?), *The Fair Maid of the Inn*, v, iii.
5. Beaumont and Fletcher, *The Maid's Tragedy*, i, ii.   6. Above, pp. 19 ff.
7. Beaumont and Fletcher (and another?), *Cupid's Revenge*, i, ii; described above, pp. 53 f.
8. Fletcher, *et al.*, *The Honest Man's Fortune*, iii, i.
9. Beaumont (and Fletcher?), *The Knight of the Burning Pestle*, iv, iv.
1. Fletcher, *Valentinian*, v, ii.   2. Fletcher, *The Mad Lover*, v, i.
3. Marston, *Sophonisba*, i, ii; cf. Armin (?), *The Valiant Welshman*, ii, i.

And the wedding mood is dashed as Massanissa is called away to defend Carthage against the Roman invaders.

The Fletcher effect remained a popular device to the closing of the theaters. It is used by many of the Caroline playwrights, among whom perhaps Glapthorne most nearly approximated Fletcher's skill with it. The massacre of Wallenstein's loyal officers is made more shocking by the fact that their murderers have just joined them in a carefree drinking catch,[4] and in *Argalus and Parthenia* a song and dance by shepherds and shepherdesses in honor of Pan sets up a cheery pastoral mood which is demolished a moment later by the appearance of Parthenia, veiled in black, and her announcement of Demagoras' brutal destruction of her beauty.[5]

Surprise, then, is a dramatic technique depending on contrast: the sudden supplanting of one clearly defined mood or emotion by a very different one. The dramatist may, of course, harness his contrasting emotions abreast rather than in tandem and drive them through as many scenes or acts as he sees fit. The effect so achieved, though not the same as surprise, still depends on an emotional antithesis. This practice, too, can be illustrated from the wedding songs—the paradoxical "sad epithalamion" in *The Custom of the Country*[6] and the dirge which greets a bridal couple on their return from the church in *Sicily and Naples*.[7]

As the most striking form of surprise is the coup de théâtre, so the most striking form of the continued contrast is dramatic irony. The practical value of the term "irony" has suffered recently from a multiplicity of critical definitions of the word. Thompson distinguishes between the verbal irony of having the hero "unconsciously use ambiguities of language which have a harmless meaning to him but another and ominous meaning to us" and the Sophoclean irony of showing the protagonist "as joyful on the very brink of disaster."[8] Because he feels that "a consistent attitude of detachment would simply make tragedy impossible," he disagrees with Sedgewick, whom he quotes as finding irony a combination of "superior knowledge" and "detached sympathy."[9] But the two views are perhaps not irreconcilable: Sedgewick's concept of superior knowledge is essentially the same as Thompson's "verbal irony," the degree of audience sympathy determining whether the effect of the irony is tragic or comic. On the practical level irony is inherent in any situation where the audience have significant knowledge denied to one or more of the characters on the stage.

By these terms, when the gentleman usher Bassiolo imagines himself a lion watching over its cubs and (unaware of "the bug, the Duke" looking down balefully from the upper stage) bursts into vainglorious

---

4. Glapthorne, *Wallenstein*, v, ii.   5. Glapthorne, *Argalus and Parthenia*, ii, iii.
6. Fletcher and Massinger, *The Custom of the Country*, i, ii.
7. Harding, *Sicily and Naples*, iii, ii.   8. Thompson, *op. cit.*, pp. 142-3.
9. G. G. Sedgewick, *Of Irony, Especially in Drama*, quoted by Thompson, *op. cit.*, p. 87.

song while he guards two young lovers,[1] the audience have superior knowledge which results in comic irony because their sympathies are not deeply involved. On the other hand, one cannot well view a pair of doomed lovers with detachment, so the irony is tragic in *A Wife for a Month* when a gala hymeneal masque, with song, is performed for a groom who expects to be executed at the end of a month with his bride; the audience know, however, that a plot is working to deny him even his brief month of happiness.[2] Tragic irony occurs when Shirley's Bard, sent to cheer the unaccountably depressed Emeria, attempts to do so by singing bawdily of fallen maidens, thus unwittingly rubbing salt into the wounds he is trying to heal;[3] comic irony occurs when Antonio passionately laments the loss of Mellida and makes his page sing a doleful song to which Mellida herself listens interestedly from concealment.[4]

The relationship between irony and surprise appears clearly in a popular comic device used by Marston and others. In *Jack Drum's Entertainment* the usurer Mammon hires a man to murder his rival in love Pasquil. Pasquil, however, bribes the assassin not to kill him but to report the deed done; then, smearing his breast with cosmetics, he lies down and pretends to be a corpse. Mammon, coming to inspect the body, bubbles over with evil glee:

> *Mam.* Dead *Kate,* dead *Kate,* dead is the boy,
> That kept rich *Mamon* from his joy.
>
> Mamon *sings.* Lantara, &c. Pasquill *riseth, and striketh him.*[5]

The fun, naturally, lies in the abruptness of Mammon's discomfiture at the height of his triumph. Mammon himself is surprised. The audience are not, but, knowing what is coming, they get the full benefit of the two excellent dramatic devices, comic irony and comic suspense.

All the examples just cited show precisely how song is of value in the attainment of dramatic irony. Irony is based on contrast, and song emphasizes or actually creates one of the antithetical emotional elements— happiness in the presence of unsuspected disaster or sorrow in the presence of an unsuspected joy. Thus the use of song to achieve irony, like its use to achieve surprise, rests ultimately on a psychological foundation.

But every function of song yet described depends largely on the same property—its power to express or induce one or a combination of the basic emotions. It is this power which enables the dramatist to establish certain stage-setting situations instantly; to separate for the audience some of his sympathetic characters from his unsympathetic ones; to communicate more specific information about the characters, about either their permanent traits of personality or the fine shadings of their transient

---

1. Chapman, *The Gentleman Usher,* v, i.   2. Fletcher, *A Wife for a Month,* ii, vi.
3. J. Shirley, *St. Patrick for Ireland,* iv, i.   4. Marston, *Antonio and Mellida,* iv, i.
5. Marston, *Jack Drum's Entertainment,* ii, ii. Cf. Dekker, *Old Fortunatus,* iii, ii, and Dekker (?), *The Weakest Goeth to the Wall,* ii (B2r–B3r).

moods; to induce in the audience an empathic concern over what takes place on the stage; to intensify the emotional and dramatic power of the great scene which was his unit of composition; to achieve the special effects of surprise and dramatic irony; and to do all these things pleasantly, quickly, unobtrusively, and economically. It becomes clear that the dramatic song in the hands of an intelligent playwright is a tool which, for versatility, mechanical simplicity, and all-around usefulness, is comparable to the soliloquy, to the aside, indeed to all the other familiar technical devices put together.

V

Nonpsychological Functions of Song

BY NOW the value of the song to the Stuart dramatists should be clear, as should the psychology upon which its main functions are dependent. But together with its psychological connotations, song possesses certain intrinsic, accidental qualities such as the fact that it takes some time in the singing and that its text receives emphasis from the rigidity and compression of its metrical form as well as from the melody which sets it off from spoken dialogue. The skillful dramatist was able to use these properties to achieve, in addition to the major effects already described, various other ends which may be classified for discussion as dramatic, realistic, mechanical, communicative, and comic.

When these effects were the immediate objective of the dramatist, the psychological implications of the music were, except in a few cases, of secondary importance. But it must be understood that those implications were never wholly unfelt. By analogy, tonal quality in a musical instrument or voice depends not on its scientific purity of pitch but on the overtones which make the sound of a violin distinguishable from that of a trumpet or an oboe. In much the same way, whatever the immediate purpose of a Stuart dramatic lyric happened to be, the audience's understanding of the meaning of music created emotional overtones which gave that lyric a richness and beauty of effect over and above its direct function.

Because some of the most ingenious uses of dramatic song are peculiar to a single author or to a single play, it is impossible in a study as broad in scope as the present one to give them the attention their interest demands. Among such techniques are Ford's of beginning a scene with a song that suggests intermission entertainment, covers the entrance of the characters, and, by preparing the audience emotionally for what is to follow, partially foreshadows the action;[1] and Marston's of plotting in song the curve of a protagonist's career.[2] Similarly, it would be impractical to attempt to describe all the Pied Piper tricks[3] and other individual purposive uses to which song is put by characters in the plays, and yet the ingenuity of such purposes is an accurate index to the ingenuity of

1. Ford, *The Broken Heart,* III, ii; IV, iii; *The Lady's Trial,* II, iv.
2. Marson (?), *Eastward Ho* (Gertrude, Quicksilver); *Histrio-Mastix* (humanity as protagonist).
3. Fletcher and Rowley, *The Maid in the Mill,* II, i; Fletcher and Massinger, *The Little French Lawyer,* IV, vi.

the dramatists responsible for them. Thus a couple of Fletcher's characters give ballads to the servants of the prospective victim of a robbery to the end that the servants' singing will drown out the master's cries for help.[4] All these techniques are part of the total picture of the use of song by the Stuart dramatists; the few to be mentioned here can only suggest the range and variety of effects which they can achieve by it.

1. Dramatic Effects

Reed, in his valuable essay on "Some Aspects of Song in the Drama," confines himself to two examples of the dramatic use of song: one from *The Malcontent* and one from *Valentinian*.[5] In each case the song, as he says, both prolongs and intensifies a crisis; that is, it creates suspense. Reed's selection of examples is unfortunate in that it might lead one to think suspense to be the principal dramatic function of song, or perhaps the only one. That it is neither has been demonstrated in the preceding chapters. Song is, indeed, peculiarly adapted to the development of dramatic suspense because it is a definite interruption of the action for a definite period of time. Perhaps in this light almost all the dramatic lyrics are suspensive. But to the extent that suspense is simply the heightening of anticipation of what is to follow, the drama is all suspense, and the term becomes too broad to be of any use in discussion. Only when a song delays an event on which interest is highly focalized, then, is its suspensive effect specific enough to be considered a deliberate dramatic end.

In view of Reed's choice of an illustration from *The Malcontent,* it is rather surprising that he failed to stress the systematic pattern of suspense followed by Marston in his three plays of revenge. In each play the fifth act opens with the villain apparently triumphant and celebrating by some form of revel the imminent culmination of his plots. The audience may or may not know what events are shaping up, but they do sense that a climax of some sort is near. In each case a song postpones that climax, which follows almost immediately afterward.[6] Suspense, then, must be included among the other dramatic effects attributable to these particular songs: Sophoclean irony and the Fletcher effect of surprise.

Reed's mention of the seduction songs in *Valentinian* is a reminder that suspense is inherent in all seduction songs, despite their low percentage of success. Suspense is not, however, one of the more common uses of the song in the Stuart drama; only a few playwrights beside

4. Fletcher, *The Night-Walker,* iii, iv.
5. Reed, *Songs from the British Drama,* pp. 351–2. His examples are Marston, *The Malcontent,* ii, iii, and Fletcher, *Valentinian,* ii, v (ii, iv, in F2; described above, p. 27).
6. Marston, *Antonio and Mellida,* v, i (a singing contest); *Antonio's Revenge,* v, ii; *The Malcontent,* v, iii.

Marston exploit it to any extent.[7] Heywood employs it, for example, but without much subtlety. Thus, when in *A Challenge for Beauty* Bonavida is unjustly condemned to death, Helena (the only person who can save him) arrives in Seville on the very day set for the execution. With her escort Manhurst she happens to meet Bonavida's servant the Clown, and their conversation leads to Manhurst's singing a lengthy song, "The Spaniard loves his ancient slop." Afterward the Clown tells Helena of his master's danger; when she learns the situation, of course, she hurries off to save Bonavida.[8] Wright condemns this song as completely extraneous.[9] In relation to the particular scene of which it forms a part, the song seems indeed to be an excrescence; but when the scene is considered in relation to the whole action of the play, the functionalism of the song at once becomes clear. By causing the audience to wonder whether Helena will learn of Bonavida's danger in time, it postpones the denouement, which itself is swift.

"Suspense does not, like surprise, depend on the spectator's ignorance of what is to follow."[1] Effective suspense may arise from delaying the discovery by a character of something already known to the audience. Thus in *The Guardian* a wedding song develops comic suspense as to when Adorio will discover that he has eloped with the wrong girl and what he will do when he does realize his mistake.[2] Most of the ironic reversals involving comic characters also are suspensive in this way.[3]

A second dramatic effect, foreshadowing, is achieved by the songs of Desdemona and Aspatia.[4] These are so familiar and so effective that one is surprised to discover no others in the Stuart drama comparable to them and but few which aim at such an effect at all. The proportion is negligible even allowing for the fact that foreshadowing is basically a function of content and seldom can be postulated of "blank" songs. There is a small group of supernatural songs which warn villains of impending doom,[5] and other miscellaneous examples occur now and then.[6] But the

---

7. Brome uses a focalized suspense in *The Queen and Concubine*, v, ix; *The Love-Sick Court*, v, iii; and possibly *The City Wit*, v, i, and *The Court Beggar*, iv, ii. Cartwright consistently uses song for suspense; *The Royal Slave*, v, vii, offers a particularly good example, but there is suspense also in several of the songs in *The Siege* and occasionally elsewhere in his work.

8. Heywood, *A Challenge for Beauty*, v, ii. Note also *The Golden Age*, iv, v; *A Maidenhead Well Lost*, v, ii; *Thomas Lord Cromwell*, iii, ii.

9. Wright, "Extraneous Song in Elizabethan Drama," p. 272.

1. Thompson, *The Anatomy of Drama*, p. 146.

2. Massinger, *The Guardian*, iv, ii; cf. Fletcher, *Women Pleased*, iii, iv. For other suspensive songs in Massinger, see Aymer's two songs in *The Fatal Dowry*, iv, ii, and the conjectural birthday song in *The Duke of Milan*, i, iii.

3. See above, p. 62, and n. 5.

4. Respectively, in Shakespeare, *Othello*, iv, iii, and Beaumont and Fletcher, *The Maid's Tragedy*, ii, i.

5. E.g., D'Avenant, *The Unfortunate Lovers*, v, v; Goffe, *The Courageous Turk*, ii, ii; v, iii; Heming, *The Jews' Tragedy*, iv, x; Richards, *The Tragedy of Messallina*, v, iv; Tatham, *Love Crowns the End*, ix (two songs).

6. E.g., H. Killigrew, *The Conspiracy*, ii, v; Massinger, *The Picture*, ii, ii, and pos-

pitfall of hindsight is gaping for the reader who seeks instances of fore-shadowing; what looks like a good example in the study might have no practical value as foreshadowing on the stage. Moreover, as we have seen, the Stuart playwrights preferred the unexpected turn to the long-awaited one; this particular device was not an important implement in their kit of techniques.

To be completely dramatic, perhaps a song should exert a direct in-fluence on the course of the plot. Tucker Brooke held that to an Eliza-bethan the word "reply" might mean "rhyme"; accordingly, when Portia provides the song,

> Tell me where is fancy bred,
> Or in the heart or in the head?
> How begot, how nourished?
> Reply, reply,[7]

she is telling Bassanio to choose the rhyme-word "lead."[8] Whether one accepts this explanation or not, the latter part of the song does afford Bassanio a definite hint (though not so broad as those in other plays where a character *sings* a secret he is forbidden to *tell*):[9]

> It is engender'd in the eyes,
> With gazing fed; and fancy dies
> In the cradle where it lies.

Bassanio immediately picks up the clue:

> So may the outward shows be least themselves:
> The world is still deceiv'd with ornament.

And so this song has an important effect on the course of events.[1]

In *The Lover's Progress* Lydian's "farewell to love and women" so affects Clarangé that he decides to become a friar and to cede Olinda to Lydian, his rival; this decision resolves one of the plots of the play.[2] D'Avenant's use of serenades to activate a series of complications has already been described.[3]

As a rule, however, those songs which do have plot function are less

---

sibly *The Duke of Milan*, I, iii (conjectural song; see above, p. 37). A foreboding note may be heard in the sensual nature of the love song to Beaumelle in Massinger, *The Fatal Dowry*, II, ii. Cf. also Ford's semiforeshadowing songs mentioned above, p. 64, n. I.

7. Shakespeare, *The Merchant of Venice*, III, ii.
8. This information was given me by Robert J. Menner.
9. Heywood, *The Rape of Lucrece*, IV, vi; Middleton and Rowley, *A Fair Quarrel*, V, i. Cf. W. Rowley, *All's Lost by Lust*, III, iii.
I. The informative nature of the content of this song has long been recognized (e.g., Moore, "The Function of the Songs in Shakespeare's Plays," pp. 93–4); but Brooke's explanation makes the clue much more meaningful than a mere caution to Bassanio not to be guided by outward show.
2. Fletcher and Massinger, *The Lover's Progress*, III, iv.
3. D'Avenant, *The Spanish Lovers*, II, ii, iii (*described above*, pp. 21–2).

decisive than the ones just mentioned and adhere to certain conventional lines. Thus a song may result in one character's finding or meeting another.[4] It may be a part of one of the highly theatrical devices so often employed by one character to gull, impress, or reform another[5]—or merely to announce her choice among several suitors.[6] There is a well-established tradition that thieves and pickpockets shall sing to distract or to disarm their intended victims.[7] Finally, curative songs are very apt to have plot function: they may accomplish a cure necessary to the denouement,[8] or they may lull the patient to sleep to clear the way for a prophetic dream or vision, a theft, or even a murder.[9] This last convention, that a song is an acceptable means of putting a character to sleep while the audience wait, is a particularly handy one for plot manipulation.

2. Realistic Effects

The fact that the English were a singing people during the late Renaissance suggests that ordinary realism is sometimes a desideratum in the dramatic use of song. Song for realism occurs frequently in connection with court scenes, masques, and triumphs, where the music gives an impression of opulence probably unattainable on the platform stage by visual means alone.[1] In a few instances, also, characters announce that they are going to sing to while away the time; this may be intended as a humanizing touch.[2] But the most vivid of all realistic songs are those which even in the reading suggest the bustle of a fair or a market place,[3] or reproduce the atmosphere of a London street by imitating the cry of a seller of brooms or a buyer of coney skins,[4a] or round out the picture

4. E.g., J. Shirley, *The Opportunity*, ii, iii, and the argument for the unfinished portion of Jonson, *The Sad Shepherd*, iii.

5. E.g., respectively, J. Shirley, *The Constant Maid*, iii, ii; Fletcher, *The Wild-Goose Chase*, v, vi; J. Shirley, *The Witty Fair One*, iv, iii.

6. E.g., J. Shirley, *Honoria and Mammon*, ii, ii, and possibly also Middleton, *Your Five Gallants*, v, ii.

7. E.g., Autolycus in Shakespeare, *The Winter's Tale;* Nightingale in Jonson, *Bartholomew Fair;* Latrocinio in Middleton, *The Widow;* Higgen in Fletcher and Massinger, *Beggar's Bush.*

8. E.g., Wilson, *The Inconstant Lady*, ii, iv.

9. E.g., respectively, Brome, *The Love-Sick Court*, iii, iii; W. Rowley, *All's Lost by Lust*, iii, i; J. Shirley, *The Maid's Revenge*, v, iii. A song in Massinger, *The Roman Actor*, v, i, makes possible both a vision and a theft.

1. E.g., Beaumont and Fletcher, *Valentinian*, v, viii; Gomersall, *The Tragedy of Sforza*, ii, vi. See Appendix for other examples.

2. E.g., Beaumont (and Fletcher?), *The Knight of the Burning Pestle*, iii, i; Middleton, *The Widow*, iii, ii; J. Shirley, *The Bird in a Cage*, iii, iii. There are several other examples. The fact that such songs frequently occur in the third act may indicate the dramatists' intention of allowing a dramatic pause.

3. E.g., respectively, Jonson, *Bartholomew Fair*, ii, ii, iv; iii, v; Marston, *Histrio-Mastix*, ii, ii; and Massinger, *A Very Woman*, iii, i.

4a. E.g., respectively, Fletcher, *The Loyal Subject*, iii, v, and *Beggar's Bush*, iii, i. Note also the street-cry song which an unidentified player "adapted" for use in Heywood's *The Rape of Lucrece* merely by changing "London town" to "Rome's fair town."

of artisans or housewives busy at their work.[5] Such songs come directly (and purposively) from real life.

In the sense that nearly every song in the Stuart drama occurs under circumstances which in real life would probably give rise to singing, nearly every song might be considered an attempt at realism; but such a generalization is too sweeping to be informative. The dramatist must be discriminating in his selection of materials from life; all our own experiences have actually happened, yet how many of them would be good material for dramatization? When a Stuart playwright allots time to a song for purposes of realism he does so because that song can help him to achieve some particular effect more easily or more fully than would be possible by other means: an effect of pomp, bustle, gaiety, religiousness— the range is almost unlimited. But this is emotional rather than physical realism and, as such, is what one would expect to find on the platform stage.

Noble explains some of Shakespeare's songs as setting the stage in the literal sense; "Under the greenwood tree," for instance, and "Blow, blow, thou winter wind" are, he says, "definitely used as auxiliaries to describe scene."[6] Such a technique would, however, be a violation of the principle of dramatic economy, for the Stuart audiences were conditioned to pick up the essential data about time of day, weather, and physical surroundings from the first few lines of blank verse in a given scene. Moreover, the very location of these particular songs contradicts Noble. The first constitutes a scene by itself; the second comes at the very end of a long scene, and surely no sensible dramatist would set the stage just as his characters were leaving it. The setting of the Forest of Arden has been established some time before either song is sung.[7] Both these songs perform other functions, but their importance as "auxiliaries to describe scene" is negligible. There is little evidence that other dramatists used song for this purpose, either. Even such a beginning as the song and dance by a chorus of youths in Chapman's *May-Day* is intended not so much for physical stage setting as to establish the emotional atmosphere of the play.

3. Mechanical Smoothness

A third group of functions which the dramatic lyric is made to serve might be called mechanical ones, because, although they contain ele-

5. Artisans sing, for instance, in Dekker, *The Shoemakers' Holiday*, iv, ii; Jonson, *The Case Is Altered*, i, i; iv, v; Rawlins, *The Rebellion*, iv, vi; W. Rowley, *A Shoemaker a Gentleman*, i, ii. The housewife's song is almost peculiar to Chapman; note *All Fools*, ii, i, and *Sir Giles Goosecap*, ii, i. Parrott compares *Eastward Ho*, i, i.

6. Richmond Noble, "Shakespeare's Songs and Stage," in *Shakespeare and the Theatre*, a series of papers by members of the Shakespeare Association (London, Humphrey Milford, 1927), p. 128. The songs, of course, are in *As You Like It*, ii, v, vii.

7. Shakespeare, *As You Like It*, ii, i.

ments of realism and of dramatic effect, their primary purpose is simply to lubricate the wheels of the action—to keep the play moving along smoothly and to minimize the creakings of the machinery of presentation.

The importance of one such function has almost certainly been over-emphasized in the past : the employment of singing to cover entrances and exits.[8] The theory is that the nature of the platform stage made it desirable to relieve the awkwardness involved in a character's long walk to or from the door by assigning him a clever couplet or a snatch of song. It is illogical, however, to attribute to the Stuart dramatists a sense of embarrassment at the deficiencies of their stage when they knew no other stage and so hardly could have been conscious that their own was deficient.[9] Actual practice simply does not support the theory that singing was valued for this purpose. In the thirty-three plays of the Shirley canon, for instance, out of the hundreds of entrances and exits, only about fourteen are covered by song.

Nor has the lack of a front curtain any more to do with singing entrances than the floor plan of the platform. Many singing "entrances" are actually discoveries ; that is, the traverse is drawn to reveal characters on the inner stage, and these characters are singing.[1] Their singing has the realistic effect of suggesting that the action discovered has been continuing behind the curtain for some time—an effect which present-day dramatists sometimes attempt by this very means. But if the presence of an inner curtain encourages the use of song, then the absence of a front curtain should not have an identical effect.

Although there are many singing entrances and exits in the Stuart drama as a whole, in almost every case such song has at least one other function more important than the mere avoidance of possible awkwardness. Thus one considerable group of entrance songs sets the emotional tone for processions : triumphal, funereal, religious, hymeneal. Another group, also discussed earlier, indicates the mood of the character who enters. Still a third comprises the purposely theatrical effects sometimes staged by the characters themselves.[2] The few singing entrances and exits which do not fall into one of these categories mostly involve persons developed as singing characters who would sing anyway.[3]

8. See, for example, Richmond Noble, *Shakespeare's Use of Song* (London, Humphrey Milford, 1923), p. 84, and Walker, "Popular Songs and Broadside Ballads," pp. 61–81.

9. Most dramatists were, like Shakespeare, conscious of the limitations of their stage ; but these limitations are inherent in any stage. Any inconvenience felt to arise from the location of the doors would have been remediable.

1. E.g., the cobbler Juniper is discovered singing in his shop (Jonson, *The Case Is Altered*, I, i ; IV, v) ; Webster's Cornelia is discovered singing a dirge as she helps to wind the corpse of Marcello (*The White Devil*, v, iv).

2. E.g., Chapman, *The Gentleman Usher*, I, ii ; Middleton and Rowley (or Ford?), *The Spanish Gypsy*, III, ii.

3. E.g., Randall in W. Rowley, *A Match at Midnight, passim;* Alupis in Cowley, *Love's Riddle, passim.*

As Walker and others have pointed out, song may be employed to motivate or to cover the entrance of a non-singing character. Even here, however, other functions are likely to outweigh the possible one of getting him on stage gracefully: the situation may have values for characterization,[4] the song may be part of an effect planned by a character on stage,[5] or it may create a mood which the person who enters is to shatter in a coup de théâtre.[6]

On a few occasions a play opens with a song out of which the action develops more or less directly. *The Two Noble Kinsmen* is such a play; another is Chapman's *May-Day,* where Lorenzo enters during a song and dance by a chorus of youths, making their performance the occasion for an expository soliloquy. A variation on this technique starts the action of a medial scene with a dumb show during an inter-act song; this device is found chiefly in plays performed by children's companies, which specialized in music.[7] Less frequently there is some attempt in the closing lines of an act or scene to connect with the action song or instrumental music which clearly is meant primarily as intermission entertainment.[8] A third type of extra-dramatic song is sung at the very end of the play, as a sort of epilogue; it may be intended partly to get the actors off the stage, but more important functions are to sum up the content of the play,[9] to intensify the mood created by the closing scenes,[1] or simply to provide a rousing finale.[2]

It would be difficult to find a significant number of examples of entrance or exit singing not intended to achieve any of the effects just described. There is no dodging the conclusion that naturalness in an entrance or exit is not a primary consideration in the Stuart dramatists' use of song. The most one can say is that the natural entrance or exit is a welcome effect when it offers itself in connection with a more purely dramatic end.

There are, of course, many other mechanical uses to which song can be put; the number is limited only by the ingenuity of the dramatist. The

4. E.g., Fletcher and Massinger, *The False One,* I, ii. Many serenades, of course, motivate the entrance of the lady serenaded.

5. E.g., Fletcher, *et al., The Bloody Brother,* v, ii; Massinger, *The Renegado,* II, iv. Many other seduction songs have this effect, but it is, of course, not confined to seduction songs; note, for instance, J. Shirley, *The Constant Maid,* III, ii.

6. E.g., D'Avenant, *The Cruel Brother,* v, ii; *The Just Italian,* v, i.

7. E.g., Chapman, *The Gentleman Usher,* III, i; Marston, *What You Will,* v, i. More common, however, is a dumb show "whilest the Act is a playing," as in Marston, *The Fawn,* v, i; *The Malcontent,* II, i; *What You Will,* III, i; Massinger, *The Fatal Dowry,* II, ii (at end of act).

8. E.g., Middleton, *A Mad World, My Masters,* after II, i, and vii; Marston, *The Dutch Courtezan,* end of II, III, and IV, and in other plays; Field, *A Woman Is a Weathercock,* I, ii.

9. E.g., Jonson, *Cynthia's Revels* and *The Poetaster.*

1. E.g., Marston, *Antonio's Revenge* and *Histrio-Mastix;* Randolph, *Amyntas.*

2. E.g., Dekker, *Westward Ho;* Chapman (?), *Sir Giles Goosecap.* There are many plays (e.g., Barry, *Ram-Alley*) where the presence of such a concluding song is probable but not certain.

same time-consuming quality of song which fits it for suspense and for intermission entertainment makes it useful for covering a dumb-show interlude or stage business.[3] Some scholars have argued that this quality is also valuable to the dramatist who needs to indicate the passage of time; Richmond Noble, for instance, makes this claim for the singing of "What shall he have that killed the deer" in *As You Like It,* on the ground that it represents the interval between noon and two o'clock, when Orlando is to return to Rosalind.[4] Noble is undoubtedly right in respect to this particular case; but the general carelessness of the Stuart dramatists in regard to time suggests that one should be cautious about applying this explanation to any songs except those which cover specific action, like the off-stage adultery of Isabella and Gniaca or the nocturnal journey of Roman officers from the city to the camp at Ardea.[5]

4. Communication of a Message

The necessary suspension of action during the singing of a song has a tendency to focus the attention of the audience on the song text, a fact which makes the lyric a good vehicle for direct communication between the playwright and the audience. Although a dramatist may occasionally use a song or a song scene to save himself the time and trouble of providing a conventional dramatic statement of a particular idea (as May, for instance, makes a hedonistic banquet song serve as his sole statement to the audience of the kind of life led by Antony and Cleopatra[6]), emphasis on the philosophical message of a lyric is essentially not a dramatic device. In its most common form, it employs song to sum up or reiterate what didactic values a piece contains.[7] Thus it corresponds roughly to the somewhat forced "moral" so often found in the concluding lines of a Stuart play.

Jonson makes especial use of the song for the direct communication to the audience of his own ideas. In *Cynthia's Revels* the final palinode and the succeeding song constitute a summary of the types of evil the author has satirized in his play. *The Poetaster* concludes with a song very

---

3. E.g., Brome, *The Love-Sick Court,* III, iii; Dekker, *Westward Ho,* IV, ii; Heywood, *A Challenge for Beauty,* III, ii. Such dumb shows, of course, have their own functions, and the songs may have other functions in addition to that of covering the stage business.

4. Noble, "Shakespeare's Songs and Stage," p. 123.

5. Respectively, in Marston, *The Insatiate Countess,* III, iv, and Heywood, *The Rape of Lucrece,* III, v. On the other hand, in Heywood (?), *Thomas Lord Cromwell,* III, ii, it hardly seems probable that the song by Hodge is intended to indicate realistically the lapse of sufficient time to cover all the action which is supposed to take place off stage during one continuous scene.

6. May, *The Tragedy of Cleopatra,* I, ii. Cf. the somewhat similar functions of songs in Anonymous, *Narcissus,* vi, and Nabbes, *Hannibal and Scipio,* I, iii, and IV, v.

7. E.g., Cartwright, *The Lady Errant,* v, viii. The two songs prefixed to Brome, *The Queen and Concubine,* though Brome borrowed one and possibly both of them, express the philosophy presumably formed by the heroine Eulalia during her tribulations and passed on by her to the pupils who sing them.

similar in its intention. John D. Rea says that Nano's first song in *Volpone* is "the keynote of the whole drama," clarifying the theme of the play, which, he argues, is not greed but "folly in all its phases."[8]

The epilogue song of another famous fool, Feste, has been described by Morton Luce as containing, "in whatever humble guise, the philosophy of human life" and, moreover, as being a reminder "that we must return to realities, that life is a serious business, and that 'it is not good to stay too long in the theatre.' "[9] Other scholars, however, have attacked both Feste's and Nano's songs as meaningless clowning.[1] Contradictions such as these are likely to lead one into very subjective criticism; but the general practice of the Stuart dramatists supports Rea and Luce in their belief that these songs are functional. In any case, there is need for a thoughtful and impartial study of the extent to which the lyrics in the Stuart plays are the direct, nondramatic expression of the philosophical ideas of the playwrights.

5. *Comedy*

Next to the dual emotional effects discussed in Chapters III and IV, by far the most important single function of song in the Stuart drama is its use for comic purposes. This is not the place to attack or defend the popular taste which demanded comedy in the drama regardless of whether it was esthetically or emotionally appropriate; the demand existed, and the reasons for it do not concern us here. Neither is any systematic attempt made here to investigate the psychology of the comic; the point at issue is simply the ways in which song was used to make an audience laugh.

We can dismiss with a bare mention certain types of comic singing which are of little interest to this study because the part played in them by music is incidental, the comedy arising from content or singer. Thus one considerable body of singing passages depend for their effect not on the fact that they are sung but on their association with one or another of the stock jokes of the Stuart drama. Audiences of the early seventeenth century probably found amusement in all drunkenness and in most madness; song, as we have seen, was conventional in the representation of these states. In a sense, then, drunken or mad singing was comic.[2] Again,

8. John D. Rea, ed., *Volpone* (New Haven, Yale University Press, 1919), xxvii; the song occurs in I, ii.
9. Morton Luce, ed., *Twelfth Night* (English Arden ed. London, Methuen, 1918), p. 175 n.
1. Feste's by J. Dover Wilson, ed. (with Sir Arthur Quiller-Couch), *Twelfth Night* (The New Cambridge Shakespeare. Cambridge, Cambridge University Press, 1930), p. 170, and others. Willa M. Evans, *Ben Jonson and Elizabethan Music* (Lancaster, Pa., Lancaster Press, 1929), p. 62, actually suggests that Nano sang discordantly to implement his clowning. Wright, of course, condemns both songs (*op. cit.,* pp. 263, 267).
2. E.g., Cokayne, *The Obstinate Lady*, III, ii (drunkenness); Dekker, *Northward Ho*, IV, iii (madness). See Appendix for other examples.

like the New Yorkers who used to be convulsed by the mere mention of Hoboken, Stuart Englishmen felt themselves superior to the Welsh and the Dutch and were amused by songs actually or ostensibly in those languages.[3] Finally, one might see a rough equivalent to the "git gat gittle" of a Danny Kaye in the occasional but apparently popular songs in rogues' cant;[4] double talk itself was known,[5] but the preference seems to have been for a brand of unintelligibility that could be and sometimes was translated.

Equally independent of music for their effect were occasional indecent or obscene songs;[6] these we may deprecate, but the demand for them is perennial.

A third category of lyrics which had an appeal only remotely related to the fact of their being sung comprises those songs exciting laughter by the wit or humor of their texts. Paradox was popular;[7] satire found favor;[8] the nonsense rhyme appears, though infrequently;[9] and there are even examples of a genre we are apt to claim for our own generation, the "patter" song, like Randolph's of the schoolmen:

> Aristippus is better in every letter
>   Than Faber Parisiensis;
> Than Scotus, Socinus, and Thomas Aquinas,
>   Or Gregory Gandavensis:[1]

Also of value principally for their content are the many snatches from popular songs and ballads which delight by their unexpected patness to the circumstances under which they are sung. Such snatches are fundamental to the concept of singing characters like Merrythought or Randall,

3. Dutch songs occur in Heywood, *The Rape of Lucrece*, III, iii; Dekker, *The Shoemakers' Holiday*, II, iii; Dekker (?), *The Weakest Goeth to the Wall*, vii (D4v); there are others. In Marston, *Jack Drum's Entertainment*, v, i, Ellis sings an interminable cumulative drinking song which is described as "High Dutch" but is actually mostly in English. There is Welsh song in Armin (?), *The Valiant Welshman*, II, i, and Shakespeare, I *Henry IV*, III, i. See W. J. Lawrence, "Welsh Song in Elizabethan Drama," *TLS*, December 7, 1922, p. 810. Comic singing in supposedly Dutch, Welsh, or French accents is very common. Randolph alone seems to have used Latin in comic song (*Amyntas*, III, iv).

4. E.g., Brome, *A Jovial Crew*, II, ii (two songs); Middleton and Dekker, *The Roaring Girl*, v, i.

5. See the spoken conversation between Clove and Orange in Jonson, *Every Man Out of His Humour*, III, iv. The closest approach to a double-talk song seems to be Trincalo's "Moorish" serenade in Tomkis, *Albumazar*, III, viii.

6. E.g., Fletcher and Massinger, *Beggar's Bush*, III, i; Heywood, *The Late Lancashire Witches*, I, ii, and *The Rape of Lucrece*, II, iii, iv; III, v; and IV, vi (two songs, one a deplorable catch); J. Shirley, *St. Patrick for Ireland*, especially IV, i.

7. E.g., Jonson, *Epicoene*, I, i; Middleton, *Blurt, Master-Constable*, II, ii.

8. E.g., Jonson, *Cynthia's Revels*, IV, iii, and *The Staple of News*, IV, ii; Glapthorne, *Wit in a Constable*, v, ii; Cartwright, *The Ordinary*, IV, v; Wild, *The Benefice*, at end of IV.

9. E.g., Sharpham, *The Fleire*, II, i.

1. Randolph, *Aristippus* (no scene division). Cf. again Danny Kaye and the song of the Russian composers in *Lady in the Dark*.

but they are sung by ordinary characters as well. The popular "Go from my window," for instance, is sung or paraphrased in at least five plays under circumstances bearing some resemblance to those of its text.[2] In addition to the intellectual satisfaction in its aptness, the audience derive from such a fragment the pleasurable sensation of recognizing something familiar in the comparatively exotic environment created on the stage.

Wright believes that in some cases the effect of a comic song depended not on content, circumstances, or music but upon the man who sang it; he feels that such a song by a popular clown must be extraneous and undramatic.[3] It is true that a good number of comic figures are characterized, at least in part, by a tendency to sing at every opportunity; it is highly probable, too, that such a characterization was sometimes suggested by the talents of the actor who was expected to play that particular role.[4] But neither these considerations nor the personal appeal of the actor should obscure the fact that a love of song may be a legitimate character trait in just the same sense that, say, a love of money is dramatically legitimate in Shylock. The singing clown is a type; he is bumbling or impractical, but thoroughly likable, and his singing is a key to the significant aspects of his character.[5]

As has been said, the part played by music in the comic techniques already described is incidental, the comedy arising largely from content, associations, or singer. Much more interesting are the techniques which, while based on fundamental comic principles, implement these principles by what amounts to musical malapropism in the use of the psychology of song.

Misinterpretations and misunderstandings, for example, are standard comic situations. Such comedy usually takes an ironic turn (because the audience possess knowledge superior to that of the character making the mistake) and frequently involves comic suspense (the audience wonder when the gull will realize his error and what he will do then). The universal understanding of the psychology of music made possible to the Stuart dramatists a particularly piquant variation on the theme of mis-

2. Beaumont (and Fletcher?), *The Knight of the Burning Pestle,* III, v; Brewer, *The Love-sick King,* II, i; Fletcher, *Monsieur Thomas,* III, iii, and *The Woman's Prize,* I, iii; Middleton, *Blurt, Master-Constable,* IV, i; the song is appended in full to all five editions of Heywood, *The Rape of Lucrece.* Cf. the use of "For he did but kiss her" in Marston, *The Dutch Courtezan,* II, ii; J. Shirley, *Love's Cruelty,* IV, i; Anonymous, *The Two Merry Milkmaids,* I, ii.

3. Wright, *op. cit., passim.*   4. See below, pp. 119 ff.

5. Wright believes, too, that there was a custom of introducing extempore song on the stage (*op. cit.,* p. 266). He bases this opinion on a passage in *Histrio-Mastix,* II, v, wherein Posthaste the Poet volunteers to sing extempore—not, however, as part of the play which he and his fellows are presenting in the hall of Mavortius but in an attempt to salvage the evening after the guests have shouted the play off the stage. Since his song is not a part of the play-within-a-play, there is no reason for thinking extempore song to have been customary in the professional theater. It does appear, however, to have been a form of tavern entertainment. Brome, *The Weeding of Covent Garden,* III, i.

understandings—the mistake arising from or complicated by the application of the wrong psychological interpretation to a particular song. Fletcher manages this effect skillfully on two separate occasions in *The Chances*.[6] First, two clownish servants are terrified by the off-stage singing of Constantia No. 1, thinking the singer must be a devil—a dainty delicate one but a devil nonetheless. A little later this Constantia disappears. The Duke, who wants to marry her, thinks he has tracked her to a house in Bologna; when he hears a sweet singing voice inside the house, he is convinced that he is right. Actually, though, this voice belongs to Constantia No. 2, a prostitute, and the songs are appropriate to both her calling and her condition, which is slightly tipsy. Fletcher makes the most of the situation by playing up the Duke's bewildered attempts to find an explanation for such a song that is compatible with the innocence of his Constantia:

> *Fred.* This is the maddest song.
> *Duke.* Applyed for certain
> To some strange melancholy she is loaden with.

Of course, the simple mistaking of the identity of an unseen singer or of the person for whom a song is intended can stand alone without the psychological complication. Dekker, for example, enjoys making a lover provide a serenade or a seduction song for a supposed mistress who is actually a man in disguise,[7] and there are numerous other playwrights who take advantage of the comic possibilities inherent in such misunderstandings.

The comic principle of incongruity, too, could be worked out through song, thanks to the conventional association of certain types of song with certain types of people. For example, Brome, who is especially fond of the incongruous, has his Antipodean courtiers applaud a ballad appropriate to a carter and his senile schoolboys chant a truants' rhyme;[8] in *A Jovial Crew* he emphasizes of a drinking catch that the singers are all graybeards.[9] In a sense, incongruity is present in the whole concept of the merry old men who sing instead of behaving with the dignity that might be expected of them. On a few occasions the song is incongruous with the circumstances rather than with the singer, as when the Passionate Lord beats Lapet to music and the servants in *The Bloody Brother* sing their own ballad as they go to be hanged.[1] More rarely the incongruity may lie in the words of a song in a situation where music itself is appropriate, as when a courtesan finds enjoyment in a song praising chastity.[2] We already have discussed the travesty of the conventional song type;[3]

6. Fletcher, *The Chances*, II, ii, and IV, iii.
7. Dekker (?), *Look about You*, xiii (H2v; song conjectural); *Westward Ho*, IV, ii.
8. Brome, *The Antipodes*, IV, vi, and II, ix.   9. Brome, *A Jovial Crew*, IV, i.
1. Fletcher, *et al.*, *The Nice Valor*, III, iii, and *The Bloody Brother*, III, ii.
2. Middleton, *Blurt, Master-Constable*, II, ii.   3. Above, pp. 55–6.

there is no need to point out that this is another technique of comic song which would not have been possible without the conventionalization of the serious song, and that this conventionalization depended in its turn on the psychology of music. The mock serenade, the serenade by a ridiculous lover, the mischievous love song of a charming girl to a suffering misogynist are only a few of the comic possibilities suggested by a single type, and all the types are travestied.[4]

In addition to the comic song relying on content or singer for the production of laughter and the comic song that represents a ridiculous perversion of the psychology of music, there is another technique which is responsible for some of the most hilarious passages in the Stuart drama. It is the use of song as a principal structural element in a comic scene. Jonson is a past master of this technique for high comedy. There are no scenes elsewhere which can quite equal the professional jealousy between the singers Crispinus and Hermogenes in *The Poetaster*;[5] the long ballad of repentance sung by Quicksilver in *Eastward Ho,* with its absurd sequel by Security;[6] and, best of all, the comic irony of Nightingale's ballad warning against cutpurses which holds Cokes enthralled while his purse is stolen by Nightingale's accomplice.[7] From Jonson's classic scenes, examples of this technique range downward toward comedy which is more physical but no less effective—an exploitation of the combined elements of wit, a crowded stage, rapid movement in a sort of patterned confusion, and noise, with song occupying a focal position.[8] Almost all the comic scenes using song structurally are too good to summarize; the reader should go to the originals and do his best to visualize them as they must have been staged.

There is one other common comic technique in which the use of song might by courtesy be called structural: the employment of a lyric as either the climax or the *raison d'être* of a scene in itself essentially extraneous. This technique seems to owe its popularity to Lyly, who inserts into nearly all his plays at least one scene in which witty pages gather for some pattering conversation, sing a song, and scamper off.[9] It is most

4. For examples, see Appendix.   5. Jonson, *The Poetaster,* II, ii.
6. Jonson, *et al., Eastward Ho,* v, v. If additional evidence is needed that this part of *Eastward Ho* is from Jonson's pen, it exists in the fact that this very scene is foreshadowed in the sentence pronounced upon Bobadill and Matthew in the quarto version of *Every Man in His Humour,* v, iii. Quicksilver's ballad may have inspired that by Hob in Wild, *The Benefice,* v, i.
7. Jonson, *Bartholomew Fair,* III, v. Randolph copies this scene shamelessly in *The Drinking Academy,* III, ii, incidentally using a ballad which is sung also in Jonson's *Masque of Augurs.*
8. E.g., Brome, *The Court Beggar,* v, ii, and *The Northern Lass,* III, iii; Fletcher, *Monsieur Thomas,* III, iii (one of the gayest scenes in the Stuart drama), and *Women Pleased,* IV, iii. Other scenes built around song include Dekker, *Westward Ho,* v, ii; Middleton, *More Dissemblers besides Women,* v, i, and *The Widow,* III, i.
9. Lyly, *Campaspe,* I, ii; *Endymion,* IV, ii; *Gallathea,* I, iv; *Midas,* III, ii; *Mother Bombie,* II, i; *Sapho and Phao,* II, iii, and III, ii.

common around the turn of the century and in plays written for boys' companies, such as *What You Will* and *Blurt, Master-Constable* (both performed about 1601 by Paul's Boys).[1] Thereafter it becomes old-fashioned, appearing only rarely in plays for adult companies.[2] It is not really a dramatic technique at all; rather, it comes close to being a semidramatic introduction of intermission entertainment.

1. Marston, *What You Will,* III, iii; Middleton, *Blurt, Master-Constable,* I, ii.
2. E.g., Middleton, *The Widow,* IV, ii; Fletcher and Massinger, *The Tragedy of Sir John van Olden Barnavelt,* v, ii, and *The Spanish Curate,* III, ii.

VI

The Question of Song as Extraneous Entertainment

INASMUCH AS THE THESIS of this study is the essential functionalism of the Stuart dramatic lyrics, it is necessary to consider briefly the charges of extraneousness which have been leveled at these songs in the past. Three illustrations will afford an adequate sampling of their nature. Cowling, for example, wrote,

> But if we can imagine ourselves dramatic critics in the Elizabethan age forced to visit every new play . . . what could we say about their songs? We should be forced to admit that but few of them assist the unity of action, and that there is simply no excuse for the introduction of many of them.[1]

Cowling was particularly unappreciative of Beaumont and Fletcher, whose songs he called mere sops flung to public taste.[2]

An anonymous reviewer of Reed's *Songs from the British Drama* pontificated,

> The songs from the drama, of which so much has been made, were for the most part the result of a *confusion des genres* such as French criticism abominates. From Elizabethan days the popular audience demanded that a play should be a variety entertainment: there should be plenty of songs, and the clown must do his worst without check from the playwright.[3]

Probably the most vigorous attack on the dignity of the dramatic lyric is that by Louis B. Wright, who, after citing several dozen songs which he considers extraneous, concludes,

> Even in the last years before the Puritan prohibition in 1642, when playwrights were supposed to have learned more about dramatic structure and audiences were more sophisticated, there is scarcely a play which does not make a popular appeal through song, song that is frequently extraneous, and sometimes song that is of the grossest buffoonery. . . . practical playwrights, then as now, supplied the public with what it wanted, even at the expense of their artistic ideals.[4]

1. Cowling, *Music on the Shakespearian Stage*, p. 97.   2. *Ibid.*, p. 93.
3. Anonymous, "Song and Drama," *TLS* (March 25, 1926), p. 226.
4. Wright, "Extraneous Song in Elizabethan Drama," p. 274.

Wright deserves more consideration than the others because he alone makes an honest attempt to support his argument with a substantial body of evidence, some of which is discussed elsewhere in this study.[5]

In any controversial issue it is well to define the terms to be used. Wood says that no music is indispensable to the play in which it occurs.[6] This might be debated: what would *The Knight of the Burning Pestle* be without Merrythought's songs, *Eastward Ho* without Quicksilver's, or *Bartholomew Fair* without Nightingale's? But even in cases less obvious than these "indispensability" is not a fair criterion, nor is direct plot function. It would be more enlightening to consider how much patching a dramatist would have to do to eliminate any single lyric, what expenditures of oil, ink, and acting time would be required to make up for the characterizing and emotional values which would be lost with the song. If a song has these values and if it therefore helps the dramatist to achieve his primary ends with ease and economy, then it is functional. It would be extraneous if it were interpolated solely for its intrinsic appeal, at a sacrifice of artistic integrity. But the consideration that a song undoubtedly has an intrinsic ability to give pleasure is irrelevant unless no other reason can be found for its presence.

Then why should anyone criticize the songs? For one reason, changes in public taste and in dramatic practice make the songs in the early drama seem obtrusive to a modern reader when actually they are not. For another, there is still some tendency to pigeonhole the literary genres and to insist on a strict interpretation of the unities, although such purism is utterly foreign to the spirit of the Stuart drama; in Lucas' words, "as it happens, Aristotle was little thumbed on the Bankside; and those who lament this, might with poetic justice be condemned to read *Catiline* once a week for life."[7] Finally, the intrinsic merit of these songs has obscured their dramatic functions, so that it has been easy to assume that the Stuart audiences valued them for the same reasons that we do, and to let the matter drop at that.

The common charge against the songs is, as it has appeared, that they are a concession to the taste of an undiscriminating public; a secondary accusation is that songs are frequently included merely to give a musically talented actor a chance to show off his abilities. This latter charge involves a special problem which will be examined more minutely in a subsequent chapter. As for the first, it is worth while to set beside the songs actually called for the number of occasions on which song would be conventionally appropriate but is not employed. Song is a manifestation of madness, for example; but fewer than half the mad people in the Stuart drama ever sing. The proportion of songs to the total number

5. See above, pp. 28–9, 66, 75 and n. 5; below, pp. 109 ff.

6. Wood, "A Comparison between Shakespeare and His Contemporaries in Their Use of Music and Sound Effects," p. 69.

7. Lucas, ed., *The Complete Works of John Webster*, I, 19.

of scenes depicting conviviality or drunkenness is even smaller. And it must not be forgotten that about a third of the plays in question contain no singing at all.

A limitation of the discussion to a single canon will make possible a more specific argument. Beaumont and Fletcher are badly treated by Cowling and Wright. Yet of the fifty-five plays attributed to one or both of them, seven are without singing; these seven are spaced over the dramatists' creative span of a score of years.[8] In the way of songs conventional in particular situations, *Thierry and Theodoret* alone offers opportunities for a marriage song, a pagan ritual song, a banquet song, a masquing song, and a curative lullaby, but none are called for.[9] Bellario in *Philaster* is carefully described as a good singer—but does not sing.[1]

Even in the plays which have songs, there is room for more. Much is made of Piorato's "fine breast" in *Love's Cure,* for example, yet he sings only once.[2] Other people characterized as singers are not permitted to sing at all.[3] If Beaumont and Fletcher valued the popular appeal of vaudeville effects, as Wright insists, then it is hard to imagine what has become of the country sports contemplated in *The Prophetess* or the "Comicke Scene" which Ronvere suggests that the disguised Duke of Sesse and his crew of pirates prepare for the king in *The Double Marriage.*[4]

The significance of this evidence is not to be discounted because it is negative; it is, on the contrary, positive evidence that Beaumont and Fletcher recognized no obligation to give the public songs unless they felt they had something to gain dramatically by doing so.

Nor can those songs which are present be attributed solely to public demand. Wallis argues that Beaumont, in *The Knight of the Burning Pestle,* and Fletcher, in *The Faithful Shepherdess,* each began his dramatic career with a play written with a young man's idealism and de-

8. They are *Philaster* (1609); *A King and No King* (1611); *The Scornful Lady* (1613); *Love's Pilgrimage* (1616); *Thierry and Theodoret* (1617); *The Sea-Voyage* (1622); *The Noble Gentleman* (1626).

9. Fletcher, *et al., Thierry and Theodoret,* II, iv (wedding or banquet); III, ii (masquing); IV, i (pagan ritual); V, ii (therapeutic lullaby).

1. Beaumont and Fletcher, *Philaster;* reference is made to Bellario's singing in II, iii, iv, and III, ii, but in V, iii Bellario apologizes for not singing when the situation demands an epithalamium. Note that the supposed Alinda, a non-singing character in Fletcher's *The Loyal Subject,* I, ii, acknowledges to Olympia "her" ability to sing in phraseology almost identical with Bellario's in "his" similar acknowledgment to Arethusa.

2. Fletcher (later revised), *Love's Cure,* III, ii.

3. E.g., Septimius in Fletcher and Massinger, *The False One,* I, i; Malfort in Fletcher and Massinger, *The Lover's Progress,* I, i.

4. Fletcher and Massinger, *The Prophetess,* V, ii (V, iii, in F2), and *The Double Marriage,* IV, iv. When a Stuart playwright does go out for a vaudeville effect, there is no mistaking his intention. Thus the anonymous author of *The Two Merry Milkmaids* exhausts his source in two acts, pieces out his plot for two more, and gives Act V over to masquing, magic, song, dance, and comic turns under pretense of celebrating the happy outcome of Acts I–IV.

votion to his own artistic standards.[5] Neither play was successful. Yet Fletcher's contains four songs, Beaumont's upward of forty songs and snatches. These songs were not a concession to the public, nor did they please the public sufficiently to save the plays in which they occurred. That Beaumont and Fletcher continued to employ incidental lyrics in their later work is not, therefore, proof that they sacrificed their artistic integrity to Mammon.

The case of Ford throws similar light on dramatic conditions during the Caroline years. Critics as widely divergent in their views as Sherman (who says Ford is decadent) and Ellis-Fermor (who says he is not decadent) agree that his comic underplots are conscious, strained, and probably reluctant concessions to the taste of the groundlings.[6] Here, then, is a dramatist willing to adjust his own standards to popular tastes; one should expect to find his plays filled with songs like the plays of his contemporaries Brome and Glapthorne. Yet of the eight plays attributed to Ford alone, three are without formal songs and two more have only one song apiece.[7] Even Wright does not call any of Ford's lyrics extraneous. Now, if a playwright was demonstrably ready to make concessions to his audience but did not employ extraneous song, the logical inference is that his audience did not demand extraneous song but recognized (subconsciously, at least) the functional quality of the lyric as it was generally employed in the drama.

It should be realized that a song which is essentially dramatic sometimes gives the impression of being extraneous simply because it is introduced artlessly or clumsily. Manhurst's suspensive song in *A Challenge for Beauty*, already described, is a good example.[8] It jars on a modern reader, whereas a Stuart audience, accustomed to song as a normal part of everyday life, would presumably have accepted it without questioning its propriety and, accordingly, would have felt its suspensive effect.

Another practice somewhat offensive to modern readers is the piling up of songs where one or two might serve the dramatic purpose.[9] This is purely a question of changing tastes.

A third change in point of view involves the employment of song at what now seems an inappropriate and inopportune time. The modern reader is surprised and displeased when Volpone pauses in the midst of

5. Wallis, *Fletcher, Beaumont & Company*, pp. 177 ff.

6. Stuart P. Sherman, "Forde's Contribution to the Decadence of the Drama," *John Fordes Dramatische Werke* (Louvain, A. Uystpruyst; Leipzig, O. Harrassowitz; London, David Nutt; 1908), I, vii; Una Ellis-Fermor, *The Jacobean Drama* (London, Methuen, 1947), p. 227.

7. *'Tis Pity She's a Whore* (1627), *The Queen* (1628), and *Perkin Warbeck* (1633) are without songs; *Love's Sacrifice* (1627) and *The Fancies Chaste and Noble* (1635) contain one song apiece.

8. Heywood, *A Challenge for Beauty*, v, ii; see above, p. 66.

9. E.g., the series of songs sung by the Ancient's men in Fletcher, *The Loyal Subject*, III, v; by Higgen in Fletcher and Massinger, *Beggar's Bush*, III, i; and by Florimel in Fletcher and W. Rowley, *The Maid in the Mill*, v, ii.

what amounts to attempted rape and sings a love song to his Celia.[1] Subsequent generations turned Shakespeare into opera and developed Brome's *A Jovial Crew* into a musical comedy containing forty-three airs, but they eliminated Volpone's song.[2] They did so simply because they did not understand why he sings—because song is a powerful sexual provocative.

Even allowing for these changes in taste and in the philosophy of music, it must be conceded that there are some extraneous songs in the Stuart drama. There are, however, only two classes of considerable size which seem objectionable. One comprises those songs which characters sing or request merely to amuse themselves or to pass the time.[3] The fact that people in real life might sing under similar circumstances is not sufficient justification for their doing so in a play unless some additional end is served, like the shock effect of a reversal.[4] The other group consists of those songs which conclude or climax scenes which themselves contribute nothing essential to the play—where the singers say, literally or in effect, "Let's sing our song and go."[5]

But these two groups and such miscellaneous songs as might fairly be called extraneous amount to a very small percentage of the total number of dramatic lyrics—perhaps five per cent at the most. This figure could be verified statistically only by listing every song and demonstrating its functions, but the casual student can check the accuracy of the estimate by considering how few of the songs familiar to him do not fulfill one or more of the functions listed in the preceding chapters.

There are several other considerations upon which one should reflect before attacking the artistic integrity of the Stuart dramatists on the basis of even these questionable uses of the song. For one, the songs belonging to the Lylyan group already mentioned invariably occur in comic scenes, and the same thing is true of many other songs which have been condemned as extraneous. It is worth repeating that in such cases comedy is the end, song only the means, and that it is confusing the issue to attack such songs as extraneous. They are functional in producing a comic effect; the public demand for comedy is another question altogether.

Second, one should remember to distinguish between those songs which are part of the playwright's own design and those which are a matter of production. It is well known that the children's theaters specialized in elaborate concerts presented as preludes to their plays and that the

1. Jonson, *Volpone,* iii, vii.

2. Robert G. Noyes, *Ben Jonson on the English Stage 1660–1776* (Cambridge, Mass., Harvard University Press, 1935), pp. 55–6, 92–7.

3. E.g., the duet of Frank and Clora in Fletcher, *et al., The Captain,* ii, ii, and the song of the masquers in Middleton, *Blurt, Master-Constable,* ii, ii.

4. E.g., Veramour's song in Fletcher, *et al., The Honest Man's Fortune,* iii, i.

5. See above, pp. 77–8.

public theaters were popular for their jigs or afterpieces.[6] There is less agreement on the extent to which inter-act and inter-scene music was employed; but the plays afford ample evidence that there was such music and that it not infrequently took the form of song.[7] If dramatists like Chapman and Marston make the best of the accepted custom by closing an act with an allusion to the music to follow or by opening an act with a dumb show "during the song," one may infer that their artistic integrity has impelled them to attempt to weave such music into the fabric of the play. But one does not condemn a modern play on its overture or its entr'acte music, and there is no justification for applying a different standard to the drama of the seventeenth century.

Less common, but still noteworthy, was the later insertion of songs into occasional plays, presumably to increase their popular appeal but not necessarily in response to popular demand. As an aspect of the relationship between the songs and the early texts, this practice will be discussed in a subsequent chapter; but it may be remarked here that Heywood, for example, is generally censured for the songs in *The Rape of Lucrece,* whereas actually he may have had nothing at all to do with the presence of half of them.[8]

It must never be forgotten that the age of Shakespeare and Fletcher was a singing age and that the twentieth century is not. Mr. Petrillo seems bent on making it so, but as yet one cannot walk down a New York street singing cheerfully to oneself without drawing curious stares, and such industries as favor music for their workers usually have to supply it in recorded form. The point is that a modern critic is in no position to understand the extent to which song was part of the texture of everyday life three hundred years ago. To criticize the extraneous song is little less absurd than it would be to criticize the extraneous cigarette on the contemporary stage—the ubiquitous cigarette which is always being lighted coolly, inhaled thoughtfully, puffed nervously, or ground out angrily. The cigarette is seldom essential to structural unity, but an essay might be written on its contribution to characterization, atmosphere, and tempo.

Fifth and last, there has never been an adequate study of the background of the dramatic lyric. Wood, for instance, insists on the importance of the musical element in the medieval drama, both religious and secular, in determining the development of later dramatic singing. This influence obtains but should not be emphasized to the obscuring of the influence of the *cantici* of Plautus and Terence and the interpolated songs

6. See, for example, W. J. Lawrence, "Music and Song in the Elizabethan Theatre," *The Elizabethan Playhouse and Other Studies* (Stratford-upon-Avon, Shakespeare Head Press, 1912).

7. See, for example, Thornton Shirley Graves, "The 'Act Time' in Elizabethan Theatres," *Studies in Philology, 12* (July, 1915), 103–34, and above, p. 71.

8. See below, p. 103.

in the medieval and Renaissance romances.[9] A people accustomed to the presence of lyrics in writings varying in date and nature from Chaucer's *Troilus and Criseyde* to Dekker's prose works would have had the right to expect songs in its drama even had there been no continuity from the liturgical tropes. But if song was in the air, it was also in the specific sources used by the dramatists. The songs in a dramatization of Sidney's *Arcadia* owe their being, in part at least, to those in the original romance.[1] Jonson takes his character Hermogenes from Horace, and the banquet songs in *The Poetaster* are suggested by those at the synod of the gods in the *Iliad*.[2] Heywood's use of song in *The Captives* is clearly influenced by his source in Plautus.[3] Suetonius gives Massinger the hint for Domitia's song to torment her doomed husband in *The Roman Actor*.[4] This whole question of fidelity to sources deserves, in fact, a study of its own.

Considering the positive value of song to the dramatist and the forces, literary, historical, and social, behind its use—considering, too, the negligible proportion of songs unacceptable by modern critical standards or at least not explained by a sympathetic understanding of the seventeenth-century meaning of song—one dismisses the charges of extraneousness and wonders only why these playwrights used the dramatic lyric with such restraint.

It is a mistake, moreover, to think of the Stuart drama as "music-hall entertainment,"[5] with "many elements of the modern miscellaneous concert,"[6] and to suppose that the theater was the only place a man could go to hear good music. Granted, the boys had their overture concerts, the public theaters their jigs, and both their entr'acte music; but during the play the music was subordinate to the play. When it was not, the result was a masque, and the distinction between the masque and the legitimate play was perfectly clear-cut. Marston's merchants make an equally explicit distinction between the play and the concert:

> *Lion.*   Gentlemen, how shall wee spend this after-noone?
> *Four.*   Fayth lets goe see a Play.
> *Vel.*   See a Play, a proper pastime indeed: to heere a deale of prating to so little purpose.

9. Moore denies the influence (or, rather, the existence) of the *cantici* in his Harvard dissertation, "The Song in the English Drama to 1642," p. 126. A beginning toward a study of the importance of medieval influences is made by Frank Allen Patterson in "Shakspere and the Medieval Lyric," *Shaksperian Studies* (New York, Columbia University Press, 1916), pp. 431–52.

1. For example, Pyrocles' off-stage song in J. Shirley (?), *The Arcadia*, II, i.

2. Herbert S. Mallory, ed., *The Poetaster* (New York, Henry Holt, 1905), pp. liv–lvi, xxxiv.

3. Plautus, *Rudens;* but Heywood was familiar with other plays by Plautus.

4. William Lee Sandidge, ed., *The Roman Actor* (Princeton, Princeton University Press, 1929), pp. 13, 143.

5. Anonymous, "Song and Drama," p. 226.

6. W. Wright Roberts, "Music in Shakespeare," *Bulletin of the John Rylands Library* (Manchester), 7 (August, 1923), 480–93, at 480.

> *Vour.*　Why this going to a play is now all in the fashion.
>
> *Lyon.*　Why then lets goe where wee may heare sweet musick and delicate songs, for the Harmonie of musick is so Heavenlike that I love it with my life.
>
> *Four.*　Nay faith this after-noone weele spend in hearinge the Mathematickes read.
>
> *Vel.*　Why then lets to the *Academy* to heare *Crisoganus.*
>
> *Omnes.*　Content.[7]

A modern gentleman's range of choice could include little more except the opera, which, it is worth pointing out, was an importation from Italy, not an outgrowth of the English dramatic lyric.

If the songs seem to us to occupy an unduly important place in the Stuart drama, we might think of the importance of classical allusions and quotations in English prose writing a few generations ago. No modern prose writer would dare be equally erudite; at best he would not be understood, while at worst he would be damned for bookishness. People no longer are familiar with the classics. We understand, nevertheless, that when Lowell quoted Cicero, he did so not for the sake of the quotation itself but because Cicero, as a part of the idiom of cultured thought, had a communicative value. The case is the same with the dramatic lyrics, except that they cannot well be explained or translated in footnotes; we have lost the language of music from our intellectual and emotional equipment and consequently, failing to understand what a given song had to say to a Stuart audience, we conclude that it had nothing to say.

7. Marston, *Histrio-Mastix,* I, iii.

VII

The Songs and the Early Editions

THERE CAN BE no doubt that the Stuart dramatists looked upon song as a useful, almost an indispensable, tool, well adapted to their dramatic technique and, when handled skillfully, capable of effects of great power and almost infinite variety. It would be of considerable value to modern students to know further how these playwrights felt about the lyrics which they used—whether they considered song a necessary evil, a claptrap, suitable for the theater but not worth preserving in print, or whether they took an artist's pride in their lyrics as works of art complete in themselves, like the stained-glass windows in a cathedral. The first alternative is suggested by the great number of songs which are "blank," their texts irretrievably lost. On the other hand, the possibility that a hack writer may have been hired to supply songs for Blount's 1632 edition of six comedies by Lyly would indicate that song texts were sufficiently in demand to justify that expense. A re-examination of the evidence in the Blount case and in others involving textual irregularities in the early editions of the plays may throw new light on exactly what the song meant, not only to the dramatists but to the actors, stage managers, book-sellers, audiences, and reading public of the Stuart period.

1. The "Blank" Songs

As everyone knows who is at all familiar with the literature of the time, it is common to find in a Stuart play a stage direction calling for a song the text of which is missing. Such blank songs number in the scores, perhaps even in the hundreds. There are seventeen indicated in Shirley, twenty in the Beaumont and Fletcher canon, over thirty in Marston. These figures do not include cases of mere solmization, occasions when people sing to accompany their own dancing, the singing exits of drunken characters, and the like. They refer only to stage directions indicating formal and complete songs of the sort which the anthologists would like very much to have.

Only to the anthologists, however, do these songs represent a total loss. Frequently they are partly described in the stage direction or in the dialogue context: "a scuruie Dittie, to a scuruie tune";[1] "no light air

---

1. Massinger, *The Duke of Milan,* II, i.

. . . it carried some thing, methought, Of sorrow's descant; I heard love in't too";[2] "This was never penn'd at *Geneva,* the Note's too sprightly."[3] It is seldom difficult to tell from the circumstances what the nature of the song was, and even to imagine its content; the reader who has studied a few typical seduction songs, for example, could easily reconstruct an appropriate one. But the original texts are lost, no doubt irretrievably.

One can infer from the circumstances of these blank songs no common quality of type, literary merit, appropriateness, dramatic functionalism, or decency (or the lack of any of these) by which one might account for their omission. The practice of individual authors varies widely: thus the proportion of blanks to the total number of songs indicated is very high in Chapman, Marston, and Shirley; about average in Beaumont and Fletcher; and very low in Jonson and Ford. In fact, inconsistency frequently obtains within a single play, one song being blank and the next one being printed in full.[4]

The existence of these blank songs presents the intrinsic challenge of any puzzle; moreover, it offers a potential clue to the attitude held by seventeenth-century authors, audiences, and readers toward the dramatic lyrics as poetry. Thus it is not surprising to find that various theories have been advanced to account for the blank songs.

J. Q. Adams suggested to Bald that lyrics were often prefixed or appended to the "book" of a play, as they are to *The Shoemakers' Holiday,* and hence were easily lost.[5] Actually, the number of printed plays with songs appended is negligible.[6] But even were one to accept Adams' suggestion, one still would not know why the song texts were appended rather than printed in their proper place, and so would be little the wiser.

Reed aimed more directly at the heart of the problem. One of his conjectures supposes a common quality in the songs not printed: that they were simply appropriate ones lifted from the songbooks of the contemporary madrigal writers and lutanists, so that there was no need to put them into the manuscript of a play.[7] He gives in evidence the appearance in *Every Woman in Her Humour* of songs by Dowland, Bateson, and Robert Jones, and Brome's borrowing of a lyric by Campion for *The Queen and Concubine.* Other examples might be added. Schelling says that one of the songs in *A Jovial Crew* is "undoubtedly Campion's" and believes that some of the lyrics in Shirley's plays were written by

2. J. Shirley (?), *The Arcadia,* II, i.

3. Fletcher and Massinger, *The Elder Brother,* IV, iv.

4. E.g., Fletcher, *Bonduca;* songs and snatches are printed in IV, i, and v, ii, blank in II, ii, and III, i. There are many other examples.

5. Thomas Middleton, *Hengist, King of Kent; or The Mayor of Queenborough,* ed. R. C. Bald (New York and London, Charles Scribner's Sons, 1938), p. xxxiii, n. 3.

6. I have found 19 songs appended to 11 plays; see below, pp. 108 ff.

7. Reed, *Songs from the British Drama,* pp. 347-8.

Carew.[8] Webster, with a modesty (or disdain) perhaps unparalleled in his day, goes out of his way to disclaim authorship of a ditty in *The Duchess of Malfi*.[9]

All this is true, but is it significant? Reed's evidence from *Every Woman in Her Humour* cannot be admitted, because the songs he cites from this play are not performed as formal dramatic lyrics; instead, they are sung in brief snatches by a comic singing character Philautus. As we have seen, it is conventional for such characters to sing easily recognizable phrases from familiar songs and ballads. Philautus' taste in music is no more an indication that many of the blanks originally were filled from the songbooks than Merrythought's is an indication that they were filled from the current supply of popular ballads.

Unfortunately for Reed's theory, moreover, almost any internal evidence adduced in support of it automatically contradicts it. The examples just mentioned show, perhaps, that the songbooks occasionally furnished lyrics for the stage; but since all these examples are printed in full, or at least in part, in the plays named, they do anything but indicate that it was customary to exclude borrowed song texts from the printed quartos.

There is on the other hand good reason for believing that many of the lost songs were *not* borrowed. It is possible to make this statement on the evidence of ten songs which belong in plays by Beaumont and Fletcher, which are missing in the first (1647) folio and which are restored in the folio of 1679. One can hardly believe that songs like "Let the bells ring," which recapitulates a comic scene in *The Spanish Curate*,[1] were borrowed from the madrigalists and lutanists. They fit their settings too aptly not to have been written for the scenes in which they occur. Moreover, their appropriateness to context destroys their value out of context; considered as independent lyrics, they would seem meaningless or eccentric. No one has ever seriously questioned that they were written by Beaumont and Fletcher specifically for the plays to which they have been restored. Certainly they were not excluded from the 1647 folio because they had been borrowed.

Reed's generalization cannot be applied without reservation even to the use of popular songs—those which today would be defined as in the public domain. When such a song is meant to be sung in full but the text is not printed, it is very apt to be identified by title or by general description in the stage directions or dialogue. Thus one finds the ballads of John Dory and of Agincourt, "Fortune My Foe," "It was a lady's daughter," "The Soldier's Delight," "The Soldier's Joy";[2] and, more

8. Felix E. Schelling, *A Book of Seventeenth Century Lyrics* (Boston, Ginn, 1899), pp. 258, 231–2.
9. Webster, *The Duchess of Malfi*, III, iv.
1. Fletcher and Massinger, *The Spanish Curate*, III, ii.
2. Respectively, in Fletcher, *The Chances*, III, ii; Heywood, 1 *King Edward IV*

vaguely, "the old song," "a new song," "a Welsh song."[3] In some cases it is obvious that the author's purposes may be served by almost any song of a given type, and the final selection is left to the actor or the manager. Marston's direction "Enter a *Ballet singer,* and singes a Ballet"[4] is such an instance, as is the ballad sung and admired by Brome's Antipodean courtiers.[5]

These and a few comparable examples show Reed's suggestion to have some merit but indicate that acceptance of it must be qualified. It is safe to say that a song which can be identified by title or first line *may* not be printed in full, and that a song employed for the mere sake of the singing (rather than for its particular content) is very likely to be left blank. But the Beaumont and Fletcher recoveries already described, especially if they can be taken as a representative group, warn one to minimize the proportion of the blank songs to which this explanation applies, because only one of those ten songs can be accounted for in this way.[6]

Reed also suggested, as an alternate explanation, that after writing a song the playwright passed it over to one of the company's musicians, who set it to music and taught it to the actor who was to sing it. The text of the song then remained in the hands of the musician or the singer. Nothing but the cue for it would be needed in the prompter's book. Consequently, if the play were printed from the prompt copy (as many plays demonstrably were), the song would be missing there.[7] Unfortunately (again), we know of a few cases in which songs which are blank in printed plays have been found in full in promptbooks.[8]

Bald accepted Reed's first hypothesis substantially as it is modified here but improved on the second by suggesting that a song composed by the playwright and included by him in his manuscript probably would not be transcribed if a new copy were made for use as a promptbook, because there would be no occasion to prompt during a song; in fact, when the singing was done "within," the singer could hold both words and music in his own hands.[9]

These explanations are logical. They are supported, moreover, by evidence which neither Reed nor Bald mentions. There are occasional passages in Stuart plays where, although all the songs are present in the

---

(Pearson reprint, I, 52; part of the ballad is printed, the rest indicated by *"&c."*); Beaumont (and Fletcher?), *The Knight of the Burning Pestle,* v, iii; *ibid.;* Massinger, *The Unnatural Combat,* III, iii; Glapthorne, *The Revenge for Honor,* III, ii.

3. Respectively, in Brome, *The Court Beggar,* IV, iii; Brome, *The Queen and Concubine,* v, ix; Armin (?), *The Valiant Welshman,* II, i (cf. Shakespeare, I *Henry IV,* III, i).

4. Marston, *Histrio-Mastix,* II, ii.

5. Brome, *The Antipodes,* IV, vi; note also *The City Wit,* IV, iv, where two songs by Crack are blank but a third which is significant to Brome's plan is printed in full.

6. Higgen's third song, "He ran at me first," in Fletcher and Massinger, *Beggar's Bush,* III, i, seems to have formed part of a familiar ballad.

7. Reed, *op. cit.,* pp. 346-7.   8. See below, p. 98, n. 5, and p. 99, n. 6.

9. Bald, ed., *op. cit.,* p. xxxiii.

first edition, some minor confusion exists over the exact position of a song within its dialogue context. For example, in *Love's Cure* Piorato appeals to the Alguazier for permission to see his sweetheart Malroda:

> *Alg.* I'll call her to you for that.
> *Pio.* No, I will charm her. [*]

> *Enter* Malroda.

> *Alg.* She's come.
> *Pio.* My Spirit.
> *Mal.* Oh my Sweet,
> Leap hearts to lips, and in our kisses meet.

SONG.

> Pio. *Turn, turn thy beauteous face away,*
> *How pale and sickly looks the day.*[1]

Dyce, an alert and indefatigable editor, noted, "Qy. Ought not Piorato's song to follow immediately after this speech [here indicated with an asterisk]?"[2] Obviously it should; the song is Piorato's "charm" to summon Malroda.

Such a misplacement of a song could hardly have occurred if the compositor had worked from a perfect copy of the play; it can best be explained by the supposition that the text of the song was written on a separate sheet, so that the compositor had to use his own judgment about fitting it into the dialogue. Reed and Bald have shown why the songs might be on separate sheets rather than incorporated into the prompt-book text. If those sheets were lost, or if the publisher were too hurried or too careless to hunt them up, the play would be printed with its songs blank.

But before accepting unreservedly the theories advanced by Reed and Bald, one must realize that they leave unanswered some highly pertinent questions. Why is there so much variation among the practices of individual authors? Why should the percentage of blank songs be very high in Chapman, Marston, Shirley, and Massinger and very low in Jonson, Ford, and Suckling? The suggestion has been made that in plays presented by children's companies, the songs were simply selected from the boys' permanent repertoire.[3] Such a theory might account for the omissions in Marston and Chapman, but it has no bearing on Shirley and Massinger.

There is another possible explanation. Jonson prepared his own plays for the press,[4] Ford himself dedicated his, and Suckling's were edited

1. Massinger (?—revising Beaumont and Fletcher?), *Love's Cure,* III, ii.
2. Dyce, ed., *The Works of Beaumont and Fletcher,* IX, 149 n.
3. Moore, "The Songs of the Public Theaters in the Time of Shakespeare," p. 172.
4. Folio edition, 1616.

from his personal papers.[5] Would it be true, therefore, that a playwright might be expected to keep personal or file copies of his songs and so be able to supply the texts if they were not present in the promptbook copies from which his plays were printed? Not inevitably; there are too many blank songs in plays printed under the authors' own supervision. The two blank songs in Ford's work occur in plays carrying his dedications.[6] It is puzzling that an author preparing a play for the press should let it go imperfect to its patron or to the public. Even had he lost his own copies of the songs, one might expect him to remember them well enough to reproduce them or, failing that, to sit down and write new ones.

What does the existence of blank songs indicate as to the critical status of the dramatic lyric? Is it safe to assume, from the seeming indifference of both playwrights and booksellers to the absence of song texts from their printed plays, that the lyric was generally held in low regard? Not inevitably, again, because this indifference cannot be proved. Jonson, Suckling, and others evidently thought their songs worth the keeping and the printing, and we shall see that to the booksellers the presence of a new or a recovered song in a playbook was a selling point and was advertised accordingly.[7]

Why should some songs be blank and others in the same play be printed in full? This situation occurs frequently. It would hardly be probable that one singer needed prompting while another did not, or that the same singer needed prompting on one song and not on another. The Reed-Bald theories throw little light here.

The people best fitted to answer these questions, obviously, are the dramatists themselves—and one of them actually does give us an answer. That it seems to have been overlooked heretofore may be due to the fact that most previous students of the dramatic lyric have tended to underestimate the importance of the blank songs and that this happens to be part of the context of one.

The scene is a drinking bout in Glapthorne's *The Lady Mother*. The town waits have been invited to furnish entertainment; they play, and then a boy sings. The comments of the drinkers constitute a little extradramatic joke, because this play probably was performed at Whitefriars':

> *Crac.* Now on my life this boy does sing as like the boy at the *Whitefryers* as ever I heard: how say you Captain?
> *Suc.* I, and the Musicks like theires: come, Sirra, whoes your Poett?

5. Title page, *Fragmenta Aurea* (London, 1646): "A Collection of all the Incomparable Peeces, written By Sir John Svckling. And published by a Friend to perpetuate his memory. Printed by his owne Copies."

6. Ford, *Love's Sacrifice*, III, iii (choral singing); *The Fancies Chaste and Noble*, II, ii (wedding song).

7. See below, pp. 107–8.

Crac. Some mad wag, I warrant him: is this a new song?

Mus. Tis the first edition, sir: none else but we had ever coppie of it.

Suc. But you wilbe intreated to let a gent have it?

Mus. By no meanes; the author has sworne to the contrary, least it should grow so wonderous old and turne a Ballad.[8]

Sucket accepts the musician's answer unquestioningly, and we may safely do the same. The very ring of the phraseology suggests that Glapthorne's "Poett," in refusing to give out copies of his song lest it be sung to death, is behaving just as a real-life dramatic poet might have done. He has sworn not to let his song circulate "least it should grow so wonderous old . . ." We must remember that the seventeenth century had no recordings the sales of which could be stimulated by a radio hit parade; instead, the freshness of the songs was an inducement to attend a given play. The acting companies guarded their "books" jealously and were unenthusiastic about seeing their plays printed. On the other hand, pride of authorship might bring a poet to forestall or to correct by a supervised edition the bad impression made by a garbled pirated text of one of his plays. These same two impulses, from pride and pocketbook, would motivate the withholding of lyrics from the press, not only because they would be particularly vulnerable to memorization and repetition *ad nauseam* but because they represented a concentration of poetic effort on the author's part.

". . . and turne a Ballad." Now we can be sure that Glapthorne is thinking of actual conditions. Throughout the period a class-conscious distinction is drawn between the art song, an essentially aristocratic musical form, and the ballad, which is treated patronizingly as song of, by, and for the vulgar. Walker discusses the lowly position of the professional ballad-writer, ballad-singer, and ballad-seller.[9] Even more to the point are such passages as Venture's disparagement of his song in *Hyde Park* as a "very ballad"[1] and Brome's choice, as an illustration of the complete topsy-turviness of Antipodean life, of the incident of the courtiers who relish a ballad which in England would be appropriate to a carter.[2]

The supposition that a Stuart playwright might deliberately withhold dramatic lyrics from publication is supported, then, by the logic of both economic and personal motivation. Moreover, this explanation for the existence of blank songs offers a resolution of most of the inconsistencies that controvert other explanations. It premises in every dramatist a normal pride of authorship; but it conceives that pride to express itself in different ways—to impel one man to print his songs, another man to with-

8. Glapthorne, *The Lady Mother*, II, i.
9. Walker, "Popular Songs and Broadside Ballads," pp. 107 ff.
1. J. Shirley, *Hyde Park*, IV, iii.   2. Brome, *The Antipodes*, IV, vi.

hold his. It suggests why a song might appear in a promptbook and not in a printed copy of a play. It affords, too, a possible way of accounting for the presence in a single play of some complete songs and some blank ones, in that a dramatist who kept his best songs from publication might be willing to print others of which he was less fond. Perhaps this is what happened in *Bonduca,* where a trivial little catch and some ballad snatches are printed but a love song and the Druids' solemn hymn are left blank.[3]

One more argument for this theory is that it seems to be supported by the recovery of the Beaumont and Fletcher songs already mentioned. According to the publishers of the second folio, ten songs were supplied to them by a gentleman who had been intimate with both authors. He must have been a literate and intelligent gentleman, since he read over the texts of the plays and "Corrected several faults (some very gross) which had crept in by the frequent imprinting of them."[4] He sounds like the sort of person to whom a poet might have given copies of his favorite lyrics, knowing that they would meet with discerning appreciation and would not fall into the hands of the public. If this is what happened, the authors' confidence was justified, for this anonymous friend preserved his copies of the lyrics for fifty years, surrendering them only when their permanent value as literature had become evident.

This explanation is not offered as the ultimate and only solution to the problem of the lost songs. At most, it supplements the theories advanced by Reed and Bald. But it is significant, because the passage quoted represents apparently the only scrap of direct evidence to be found in the plays themselves. It is important, too, as a corrective to the tendency to assume that, because the dramatic lyrics are so often omitted from the printed plays, they were held in little esteem; it proves that the lyricists took pride in their work. And by implication it reveals that among the lost songs of the Stuart drama may be some of the finest lyrics of the period, the jealously protected favorites of the men who wrote them.

2. The "Unsuspected" Songs

In view of the probable high literary quality of the songs lost from the Stuart drama, it is distressing to be told that these losses are greater in number than is generally realized. But Reed believed that the plays under consideration originally contained a sizable body of dramatic lyrics the very existence of which is now unsuspected:

> The stage directions do not indicate all the lyrics we have lost; if by chance we could restore to the plays every song they call for, there would be still many a one missing. It not infrequently happens that

3. Fletcher, *Bonduca;* blank songs in ii, ii; iii, i; lyrics printed in iv, i; v, ii.
4. *Beaumont and Fletcher,* ed. Arnold Glover and A. R. Waller (Cambridge, Cambridge University Press, 1905–12), I, lx.

in the first edition of a play not merely a song, but all references to it were omitted; and only the fact that the play was reprinted in a more complete edition gives us the song or the allusions to it. . . . it is plain that we cannot appreciate the use of song by Tudor and Stuart dramatists from the texts of their plays.[5]

In support of this hypothesis Reed gives three examples: Desdemona's "willow" song and the lines immediately preceding it, omitted from the 1622 edition of *Othello* but present in the First Folio a year later;[6] the songs of Aspatia and Dula and their introductory dialogue in *The Maid's Tragedy,* missing from the 1619 quarto but present in that of 1622;[7] and a passage in *The Duke of Milan* where, although no stage direction indicates a song, one is predicable from a speech by the Duke.[8]

Moore contradicts this theory flatly, writing of it,

> The assumption that a vast body of original lyrics in the plays has been lost to us is contradicted by external evidence such as the limited time of afternoon performance, as well as by the internal evidence of the quartos. In the great majority of cases, the songs survive, or we at least know where they occurred and what they were meant to suggest.[9]

He does not elaborate on what he means by "the internal evidence of the quartos."

The resolution of this disagreement between the two foremost American students of the dramatic lyric obviously is important to the complete understanding of the Stuart drama. If there are grounds for suspecting that the dramatic use of song was much more widespread than is realized today, then the importance which we attach to song as a form of dramatic idiom and an aspect of play production must be weighted proportionally. It is impossible here to evaluate Moore's "external evidence"; the scholarship on the length and mechanical arrangement of a Tudor or Stuart dramatic performance constitutes an imposing literature in itself. But the internal evidence merits a re-examination in the light of a pertinent discovery made some years after Reed and Moore had issued their statements.

Technically speaking, such internal evidence as Reed's example from *The Duke of Milan* is inadmissible. If songs are conjecturable from the dialogue, even though there is no stage direction to call for them, they are not completely "unsuspected," nor do they indicate the quondam existence of any songs that cannot be conjectured from the surviving texts.

---

5. Reed, *op. cit.,* pp. 345–6.   6. Shakespeare, *Othello,* IV, iii.
7. Beaumont and Fletcher, *The Maid's Tragedy,* II, i.
8. Massinger, *The Duke of Milan,* I, iii.
9. Moore, "The Songs of the Public Theaters in the Time of Shakespeare," p. 202.

It is true, nevertheless, that the recognition of all the songs indicated by dialogue alone would add an impressive number to the total of songs known to be lost. Suggestions for some fifteen have been made by succeeding generations of editors; an equal number that apparently have not been noticed before can be postulated with some assurance. Most of these are listed in the Appendix as "probable" or "possible" blank songs. To describe and evaluate them all would make an unwieldy document, but a detailed analysis of one or two will establish an adequate basis for discussion.

Frequently the necessity for a song, though obvious when pointed out, does not become apparent unless the reader is looking for it. This accounts for the failure of so able an editor as Parrott to supply an essential stage direction in *Sir Giles Goosecap*. The comic subplot of this play (which is probably Chapman's) is almost devoid of real incident; its interest lies in the characterization and conversation of three comic figures, whose climactic scene finds them courting their respective ladies before an interested circle of friends. First, Sir Giles himself woos Penelope by displaying to her his skill at embroidery and explaining to her why he wants to marry her—so that he can join his friends on the married men's football team. Then Sir Cuthbert Rudesby, whose name is descriptive, courts Hyppolita with absurd bluntness and lack of tact. All now look expectantly at the third member of the comic triumvirate, Captain Foulweather:

> *Fur.*   Excellent Courtship of all hands, only my Captaines Court-shippe, is not heard yet, good madam giue him fauour to court you with his voyce.
> *Eug.*   What shood he Court me with all else my Lord?
> *Mom.*   VVhy, I hope madam there be other things to Court Ladies withall besides voyces.
> *Fur.*   I meane with an audible sweete song madam.
> *Eug.*   VVith all my heart my Lorde, if I shall bee so much indebted to him.
> *Foul.*   Nay I will be indebted to your eares Ladie for hearing me sound musicke.
> *Fur.*   VVell done Captaine, proue as it wil now.[1]

At this point the sudden arrival of a messenger ends the comic interlude.

The question is whether or not Captain Foulweather actually gets to sing his song. Structurally, it is necessary that he should: he deserves an equal share with his ludicrous colleagues in this, the last big comic scene of the play. His individual humor (he is a "french affected Trauayler") could hardly be displayed to full advantage in a spoken courtship, especially after Sir Giles's ingenuousness and Sir Cuthbert's bluntness; but

1. Chapman (?), *Sir Giles Goosecap*, v, i.

his climactic position as the third wooer would be justified and variety would be achieved if he could make the most of an opportunity to sing a comic love song. Moreover, the entire passage quoted above becomes a singularly pointless anticlimax if one assumes that the song is prevented by the arrival of the messenger.

One small change in the punctuation of the Captain's lines would clarify the whole passage. His speech should read,

> Nay I will be indebted to your eares Ladie for hearing me. Sound musicke. [*Song*]

This pointing changes the words "Sound musicke" from an unidiomatic excrescence into a direction to the unseen musicians to begin the accompaniment for the song—a sense in which this expression frequently is used.[2] The next speech, Lord Furnifall's "Well done . . . ," is a compliment to the Captain as he finishes his song and a recognition that the fate of the suitors now rests in the hands of the ladies.

One more illustration is justified because it proves that these suggestions for the restoration of stage directions calling for song are not just a game of wits. In Heywood's *The Golden Age* Jupiter, disguised as a peddler, gains entrance to Danae's tower and is given permission to sleep overnight in a corner. It is bedtime; a new scene begins:

> *Enter the foure old Beldams, drawing out* Danae's *bed: she in it.*
> *They place foure tapers at the foure corners.*
>
> *Dan.*   Command our Eunuch's with their pleasing'st tunes
> To charme our eyes to rest. Leaue vs all, leaue vs.
> The God of dreames hath with his downy fanne
> Swept or'e our eye-lids, and sits heauy on them.
> 1. *Bel.* Hey-ho, Sleepe may enter in at my mouth,
> if he be no bigger then a two-peny-loafe.
> *Dan.*   Then to your chambers, & let wakelesse slumbers
> Charme you in depth of silence and repose.
> *All.*   Good night to thee faire *Danae.*
> *Dan.*   Let musick through this brazen fortresse sound
> Till all our hearts in depth of sleepe be drown'd.[3]

Now Danae goes to sleep, and Jupiter enters at once.

It would seem rather foolish for Danae to keep calling for music if she is not intended to have any. A song here would be in the nature of a lullaby and would put her to sleep realistically. It would be true to life; and, if it lasted long enough, it might develop some suspense. But there is no stage direction to indicate music.

2. E.g., Marston, *Jack Drum's Entertainment,* v, i: "Come, sound Musick there"; *What You Will,* ii, ii: "So ends our chat, sound Musick for the Act"; Gough, *The Strange Discovery,* iii, ii: "Sound musicke then."
3. Heywood, *The Golden Age,* iv, v.

Some weeks after deciding that Heywood's scene demanded a song, I came upon Bullen's description of the British Museum's Egerton Manuscript 1,994 and found this passage:

> The next piece, entitled *Calisto* (leaves 74–95) . . . consists of scenes from Heywood's *Golden Age* and *Silver Age*. There are many variations from the printed copies, showing that the most active of the old playwrights found time to revise his works. Here is a song that was omitted in the printed copy. Its proper place in Pearson's *Reprint* of Heywood is vol. iii. p. 67 :—
>
> > Whether they be awake or sleepe,
> > With what greate Care ought Virgins keepe,
> >   With what art and indevor,
> > The Jewell which they ought to pryse
> > Above the ritchest marchandise,—
> >   And once lost lost for ever!
> >
> > Virginity is a rare gem,
> > Rated above a diadem,
> >   And was despised never:
> > 'Tis that at which the most men ayme
> > And being gott they count their game
> >   And once lost lost for ever.[4]

In addition to fulfilling the functions conjectured above, this song in praise of chastity would, under the circumstances in which it is sung, develop a mild but effective dramatic irony.

The gratifying thing about a discovery like this is that it proves that we are thinking along the same lines as the old dramatists. Not much is known of the history of Egerton MS 1,994—not enough for us to tell whether this song was sung as part of the original performance of *The Golden Age,* was written to supply the loss of the original song, or was an afterthought of Heywood's.[5] But its authorship has never been questioned. Consequently, its very existence proves that reconstruction of the sort proposed here is not mere guesswork and demonstrates the soundness of the principles laid down in the first five chapters of this study.

4. A. H. Bullen, ed., *A Collection of Old English Plays* (London, Wyman & Sons, 1883), II, 419. Bullen goes on to print from *Calisto* a song which he identifies as an inferior version of "Haile beauteous *Dian*" (Heywood, *The Golden Age,* II, iv [Pearson reprint, III, 27–8]); it seems more likely, however, that this is the exit song which is missing at the end of that scene.

5. For what is known, see, for instance, the introduction to *Edmond Ironside* (MSR, Oxford, Oxford University Press, 1927), p. ix. It is supposed that the manuscript is formed, at least in part, of the prompt copies used by an acting company performing in the provinces, and that it dates from before 1642. Note that, if this description applies to *Calisto,* we have a late promptbook containing song texts; see above, p. 90.

If these suggestions and the others noted in the Appendix are adopted, the total number of songs definitely lost is increased by nearly a fifth—a proportion high enough to deserve attention. Indirectly, by showing that song was used more widely than has been supposed, this list lends credibility to Reed's hypothetical body of songs to which all reference has been lost. But there is better evidence than this to support Reed's assumption.

Middleton's *Hengist, King of Kent; or The Mayor of Queenborough,* written about 1618 but not printed until 1661, was a play without songs. It contained at least two scenes (a religious procession in i, i, and a convivial party in iv, ii) where song would have been both appropriate and conventional, but in neither place was there any indication in stage directions or dialogue that singing was a part of the performance. This was the state of knowledge until 1938. But in that year Bald published a new edition of the play, based on a collation of the 1661 quarto with two previously unedited manuscript copies, apparently private transcripts from an annotated promptbook.[6] Both manuscripts contain not only the stage directions but the complete texts for two songs, which come exactly where one might have suspected they should be.

Although Reed wrote several years before this discovery was made, it is precisely the sort of thing he hypothesized. Bald shows that the two songs must have been part of the original text as Middleton wrote it,[7] yet the 1661 quarto contains no hint of their ever having existed. If songs could thus be missing from the first printed version of one play, they could be missing from others as well; and though he may make shrewd guesses from his knowledge of where song was conventional, the modern scholar has no earthly way of proving how often this very thing happened.

That it could happen rather easily is indicated, however, by the adventures of a song which was lost and found again in the succession of printed editions. In Massinger's *The City Madam* the first quarto contains a prompter's note printed in the margin at the beginning of Act v:

Musicians come down to make ready for the song at Aras.

There is no stage direction later to indicate exactly when the song was performed. Probably it belongs where Kirk puts it in his edition of the play,[8] in a scene where "Musick" is prescribed in connection with a sham-supernatural banquet. As we know, both banquet scenes and sham-super-

6. Middleton (ed. Bald), *op. cit.* The MSS are the Lambarde MS (at the Folger Library) and the Portland MS (at Welbeck Abbey). Note that, if Bald's identification of the MSS is correct, these two songs were present in promptbooks and yet were omitted from the first printed edition of the play; see above, p. 90.

7. Middleton (ed. Bald), *op. cit.,* p. xxxiii, n. 2.

8. Massinger, *The City Madam,* ed. Rudolf Kirk (Princeton, Princeton University Press, 1934), v, iii.

natural passages are likely to involve singing, but there is nothing here, either in the stage directions or the dialogue, to indicate that anything more than instrumental music is intended.

What makes this case important is the fact that all the eighteenth- and nineteenth-century editors of Massinger—Coxeter, Mason, Gifford, Coleridge, Cunningham, Symonds—failed to reproduce the prompter's marginal note. Without it there was no sign that song had ever been a part of this particular play. That information was available only in the none too accessible quartos; the song literally was lost for over two centuries, from Coxeter's edition to Kirk's.

If six editors, some of them good scholars, could omit a marginal note in reprinting a play, it stands to reason that a commercial printer of the early seventeenth century might have failed to print an occasional marginal note in a manuscript promptbook. If such a note happened to call for a song like the one in *The City Madam*, then that song's chances for historical survival depended solely, as Reed argued, on the appearance of a later more accurate edition or, as the Middleton songs show, on the preservation of a complete manuscript.

The example from *The City Madam* makes one wonder if there are other cases in which the stage direction "Musick" actually meant "Song." Moreover, the fact that both it and the Middleton recoveries occur in circumstances where song definitely was conventional suggests that other unsuspected songs (if there were others) probably followed the same rules, so that one may amuse oneself by guessing where some of them might have occurred. It is worth remembering, too, that songs may have been interpolated into particular performances, either by actors or even by stage managers.[9] These are largely matters of conjecture, of course. But the demonstration from Middleton and Massinger does have two practical results: it supports the restorations of songs predicable from dialogue and it verifies Reed's basic assumption, in that what has happened once may have happened often.

Since Reed's own evidence is rather questionable,[1] however, the existence of the two good examples in Middleton and Massinger is not enough to support the supposition that the body of song which has vanished without trace is a vast one. On the contrary, we may even have preserved in the quartos some songs which were never actually performed on the stage. Brome says of the printed text of *The Antipodes* that it is his own original version, not the cut one used by the actors.[2] It is possible that one or more songs were among the material cut. Another reason for the omission of a song from a performance is given by Richards, whose *The Tragedy of Messallina* contains this stage direction after a song which is printed in full:

9. See below, pp. 102 f.   1. See above, p. 95, and below, pp. 103 ff.
2. Brome, *The Antipodes,* note to the reader at end of play text in Q 1640.

After this song (which was left out of the Play in regard there was none could sing in Parts) Enter the Ghosts . . .[3]

Such statements as Brome's and Richards' are exceptional; but these considerations of time and talent must have bedeviled all the dramatists alike. Other dramatists must have shared, too, the vanity of authorship which led Brome and Richards to print material not used on the stage. Perhaps the thought is not too fantastic that occasional lyrics in the quartos may have a kinship with the gems of modern oratory which, though printed in full in the *Congressional Record,* are never delivered.

3. Interpolations, Recoveries, and Forgeries

The cases just presented from Middleton and Massinger indicate how interesting a challenge is posed by almost any textual irregularity involving a song. Normally such irregularities occur in two forms: the appending of a song text at the beginning or end of a play rather than in its proper place and the appearance in a subsequent edition of a song not included in the first printing of a play. It is noteworthy that a song once printed never disappears.[4]

Unfortunately, no single explanation seems to account for all the irregularities of either type. At least three theories have been advanced to explain the late appearance of songs not present in a first edition: that they are interpolations by the original author or another; that they represent a recovery of material not available to the first printer or somehow carelessly omitted by him; and that they have been written or selected purposely to fill obvious gaps caused by the loss of the original lyrics. It will be worth while to investigate whether any general principles exist by which one can determine what has happened in a given case.

A number of passages that would seem to be evidence of the practice of interpolating songs into plays must be thrown out as irrelevant or immaterial. Obviously, no play which has survived in only one edition or manuscript can offer anything more than grounds for conjecturing an interpolation. Whether such grounds are stylistic or structural, the supposition of a modern scholar that a particular scene is a late addition by the original author or by a hack is, in the final analysis, mere opinion and therefore inadmissible.[5] Alterations within a manuscript copy of a play

3. Richards, *The Tragedy of Messallina,* v, iv.
4. The serenade tribute to the condemned heroines of D'Avenant, *Love and Honor,* v, ii, is not present in the 1673 folio; but this entire scene appears to have been replaced on the Restoration stage and so is not actually a relevant case.
5. E.g., Thomas Marc Parrott, ed., *The Plays and Poems of George Chapman* (New York, E. P. Dutton, 1910), III, 757, n. 1, thinks that III, i, of *The Gentleman Usher* may have been added by a hack. Evans, *Ben Jonson and Elizabethan Music,* p. 45, thinks that Jonson himself interpolated Juniper's first song in *The Case Is Altered* in response to the manager's demand for opportunity to show off the musical talents of the Children. Neither idea is capable of proof.

must be shown to result from the adaptation of the play for the stage, not from a change in the author's plans during its composition, if they are to be admitted as proof of interpolation.[6] Even unquestionable interpolations are irrelevant here if it can be proved (as sometimes it can) that they were made on the Restoration stage.[7]

It is demonstrable, however, that interpolation occasionally was practiced. For example, the 1640 quarto of Middleton's *A Mad World, My Masters* contains an appended song labeled "The Catch for the Fifth Act, sung by Sir *Bounteous Progresse* to his Guests." This song is not present in the quarto of 1608, and there is nothing in the text of either volume to indicate why or precisely where it should be sung. The same song, with minor variations, had been printed in 1632 in Blount's volume of *Sixe Covrt Comedies* by Lyly,[8] and its authorship is a moot subject; in addition to Lyly and Middleton, it has been ascribed to Randolph[9] and perhaps to others. Since Middleton died in 1627, it is likely that he had nothing to do with the association of the song with his play but that some actor with a good voice first sang it at a revival of *A Mad World* in the 1630's.

Less guesswork is involved in an example from *A Fair Quarrel,* by Middleton and Rowley. First printed in 1617, this play was reissued later in the same year with a fresh title page, advertising "new Additions of Mr. Chaugh's and Trimtram's Roaring, and the Bauds Song. Neuer before Printed."[1] The three sheets bearing these additions were to be placed "at the latter end of the fourth Act"; they form what is Act IV, scene iv, in modern editions. This is an independent scene of extraneous comedy and would seem to indicate that the roaring sequences in the original version were sufficiently popular for Middleton or Rowley to try to capitalize by adding more. Such a practice would correspond to the revision that goes on during the tryout period of a modern stage production and even in a motion picture after audience reaction has been tested by means of sneak previews.

6. For example, the MS of J. Shirley (?), *Captain Underwit* (reprinted by Bullen, *op. cit.,* II), begins Act IV with the bare stage direction, *"A song ith taverne"*; a whole scene, including the text of this song, is added at the end of the play but, of course, cannot qualify as a late interpolation. Alterations in the MS of Marmion or Clavell, *The Soddered Citizen* (MSR), may represent preparation for performance, but the only change involving a song is the elimination of the reading of the text of one lyric (IV, vii). before it is sung.

7. For example, a second catch for the comic watch in D'Avenant, *The Wits,* v, ii, first appears in the 1673 folio. Passages in Pepys' *Diary* indicate that it was performed as early as 1667. James Maidment and W. H. Logan, eds., *The Dramatic Works of Sir William D'Avenant* (Edinburgh, William Paterson, 1872–74), II, 111–112. This catch and other new material were not printed in the 12mo copy of *The Wits* in 1665; evidently the additions were made between 1665 and 1667.

8. It is incorporated into the text of *Campaspe,* I, ii.

9. A. De Morgan, "An Old Song," *Athenaeum,* February 15, 1868, p. 254.

1. Alexander Dyce, ed., *The Works of Thomas Middleton* (London, 1840), III, 443.

But the most conclusive evidence of interpolation occurs in that curious play, Heywood's *The Rape of Lucrece*. The text of the first edition contains eleven songs and snatches; in addition, at the end there are appended two lengthy songs, with this prefatory explanation: "Because we would not that any mans expectation should be deceived in the ample Printing of this Book: Lo, (Gentle Reader) we have inserted these few Songs, which were added by the stranger that lately acted *Valerius* his part, in forme following." In the fourth quarto (1630) four more songs appear for the first time, three with brief introductory dialogue;[2] a fifth quarto introduces still five more lyrics, labeled "The first new Song," and so on.[3] In this fifth edition, as in the third and fourth, the songs appended to the first edition are still appended, still with the same explanation; apparently they were sung only by the first Valerius and never became integrated into the text as an accepted part of the play.

Reed has made much of one of the songs added in the fourth edition, the familiar "Pack clouds away," as an example of a song which was lost and subsequently found.[4] Moore, however, has demonstrated that this is highly unlikely and that, in fact, all nine of the late-appearing songs, like the two appended ones, probably were interpolated by successive actors "that lately acted *Valerius* his part."[5] *The Rape of Lucrece* is important, then, as supplying positive evidence that songs were sometimes interpolated and as explaining specifically how that interpolation might take place.

If the practice of interpolating songs is beyond doubt, so is the fact that a few songs have turned up long after the plays in which they belong were first printed. The best evidence here is the second folio edition of Beaumont and Fletcher, published in 1679, which supplies the texts of ten songs missing from the 1647 folio.[6] The recovery of these songs is mentioned on the title page as an advertising point. Better yet from the scholar's point of view, the editors explain in their preface how the recovery came about: the songs, with certain other material, were sup-

2. "The Gentry to the Kings Head," ii, iv; "The *Spaniard* loves his ancient slop," iii, v; "Packe cloudes away" and "Come list and harke," iv, vi.

3. "She that denies me, I would have," ii, iii; "Though the weather jangles," ii, iv; "O yes, roome for the Cryer," iii, iv; "On two white Collomns" and "I'de thinke my selfe as proud in Shackles," iv, vi.

4. Reed, *op. cit.*, pp. 289–90, 344.

5. John Robert Moore, "Thomas Heywood's 'Pack Clouds Away' and 'The Rape of Lucrece,' " *Studies in Philology, 25* (April, 1928), 171–7.

6. "Dearest, do not you delay me," *The Spanish Curate,* ii, v (ii, iv, in F 1679); "Let the bells ring," *The Spanish Curate,* iii, ii; "He ran at me first," *Beggar's Bush,* iii, i; "Merciless love," *The Chances,* ii, ii; "Welcome, sweet liberty," *The Chances,* iv, iii; "Come away," *The Chances,* v, iii; "Weep no more" and "Court ladies laugh," *The Queen of Corinth,* iii, ii; "Sit soldiers," *The Knight of Malta,* iii, i; and "A health for all this day," *The Woman's Prize,* ii, vi.

plied by "an ingenious and worthy Gentleman," an admirer of the drama, who "had an intimacy with both our Authors."[7] Although both authors had been dead for fifty years, the authenticity of these songs has not been questioned; Colman printed them in footnotes in his edition of Beaumont and Fletcher in 1778, but succeeding editors have always accorded them the dignity of their place in the text.

Reed was a firm believer in the authenticity of most late-appearing songs.[8] He noted those of the Beaumont and Fletcher folio, of course, and also cited the songs of Aspatia and Dula in *The Maid's Tragedy* as examples. These latter songs, with the dialogue introducing them, were first printed in the second quarto. Although Reed does not mention the fact, the same thing is true of the third lyric in the hymeneal masque in the same play.[9] It is important to understand that the circumstances here are not parallel to those of the recoveries by the second folio editors: of those songs, nine were demanded by stage directions in the first folio, and the tenth was clearly indicated by dialogue. In the first edition of *The Maid's Tragedy,* on the other hand, there is nothing to suggest that these three songs were intended. Reed's dismissal of the possibility that they were interpolations is somewhat cavalier; whereas one obviously cannot say with assurance that these lyrics were not part of the original plan, their dramatic effectiveness is the only good reason for thinking that they were. If Middleton and Rowley embellished a play after its first publication, Fletcher might have done the same thing at nearly the same time.

Moreover, there are logical grounds for suspecting the three songs of *The Maid's Tragedy* to be interpolated—grounds which Reed should have recognized, since they derive from his own theory about how songs became lost. This theory, as has been explained, was that the lyrics were written on separate sheets which were retained by the singer or the musician who composed the setting, and that it was unnecessary, therefore, to transcribe them at length in the promptbooks. The preservation of the separate sheets by the musician (or by a friend of the playwright's, if the songs were withheld in order to keep them from growing hackneyed) would of course account for their turning up later. But it is hard to understand why the introductory dialogue should be with the songs and not in the promptbook, where it ought to have been had it formed part of the play as originally acted. One can accept as genuine the songs recovered in the Beaumont and Fletcher folio without committing oneself to the belief that a song which became lost in the printing could take its context with it into limbo.

7. "The Book-sellers to the Reader," Second Folio; *Beaumont and Fletcher,* ed. Glover and Waller, I, lx.
8. Reed, *op. cit.,* pp. 343–5.
9. Beaumont and Fletcher, *The Maid's Tragedy,* I, ii: "To bed, to bed!"

If it is difficult to distinguish between songs which have been interpolated and those which have been lost and recovered, it is even more difficult to decide whether a particular "recovered" text is actually the missing original lyric or a literary forgery committed to fill an obvious gap in a play text. Fortunately, this latter question has been raised in connection with only one group of songs—which, however, have inspired much scholarly controversy. Stage directions and dialogue in the quarto editions of the plays of John Lyly indicate about thirty-one lyrics to be missing; texts for twenty-one of these songs were first printed in Edward Blount's volume of *Sixe Covrt Comedies* by Lyly in 1632. Doubts that these were actually the originals they purported to be were expressed at least as early as 1868;[1] their authenticity became a real issue in 1905 when W. W. Greg made a full-scale attack on Lyly's claim to them.[2] Since that time at least five scholars have defended the position that the songs are Lyly's;[3] Greg and Moore have argued that Blount hired a hack writer, perhaps Dekker, to supply lyrics to fit into the gaps;[4] and a splinter group maintains that the Earl of Oxford composed the songs as a sort of preconditioning for writing Shakespeare's plays.[5]

Many of the arguments advanced have been from vocabulary and style. These are available in the works noted here; they are too long and involved for recapitulation, and some of them seem inconclusive and even subjective.

More promising as clues are two songs which appear also in other plays of the Stuart period. One of these already has been mentioned: the drinking song appended to the 1640 edition of Middleton's *A Mad World*.[6] Its appearance there eight years after the publication of Blount's book cannot be considered as proof that Lyly did not write it.

The other lyric is a bird song; printed in Blount's edition of *Campaspe*, it occurs also, in ruder form, in Dekker and Ford's *The Sun's Darling*, printed in 1656 but written in 1624.[7] Lawrence and Moore debated the

1. W. Carew Hazlitt, "John Lyly: the Songs in His Plays," *Notes and Queries, 38* (December 12, 1868), 558; A. De Morgan, *op cit.,* p. 254.

2. W. W. Greg, "The Authorship of the Songs in Lyly's Plays," *MLR, 1* (October, 1905), 43–52.

3. W. J. Lawrence, "The Problem of Lyly's Songs," *TLS,* December 20, 1923, p. 894; Reed, *op. cit.,* pp. 266–7; G. W. Whiting, "Canary Wine and *Campaspe*," *MLN, 45* (March, 1930), 148–51; R. Warwick Bond, "Lyly's Songs" and "Addendum on Lyly's Songs," *Review of English Studies, 6* (July, 1930), 295–9, and 7 (October, 1931), 442–7; M. Hope Dodds, "Songs in Lyly's Plays," *TLS,* June 28, 1941, p. 311.

4. W. W. Greg, "Lyly's Songs," *TLS,* January 3, 1924, p. 9; John Robert Moore, "The Songs in Lyly's Plays," *PMLA, 42* (September, 1927), 623–40. Albert Feuillerat also expresses doubt that the songs are authentic in *John Lyly* (Cambridge, Cambridge University Press, 1910), p. 403 n.

5. E.g., Percy Allen, *The Case for Edward de Vere 17th Earl of Oxford as "Shakespeare"* (London, Cecil Palmer, 1930), pp. 47–66; J. Thomas Looney, *"Shakespeare" Identified* (New York, Frederick A. Stokes, 1920), pp. 276–84.

6. See above, p. 102.   7. Dekker and Ford, *The Sun's Darling,* II, i.

tangential issue of whether this song was present in the 1624 version of
The Sun's Darling or was interpolated there as a borrowing from *Campaspe* between 1632 and 1656; Moore shows conclusively that it was present in 1624. But that fact matters little if the song had been written many years before. Greg claimed in 1905 that the Dekker version of the song was the original; although this point is a key to the whole problem, no one has raised any real protest against Greg's judgment.

Greg's reasoning is, in brief, that the *Campaspe* version of the song is more artistic than the Dekker version and that it is, therefore, a revision of the Dekker version. Thus, for one particular couplet Blount's text reads,

> Braue prick song! who is't now we heare?
> None but the Larke so shrill and cleare;[8]

Dekker's has a different second line:

> Brave prick-song; who is't now we hear!
> 'Tis the Larks silver leer a leer:[9]

This is Greg's comment: "Surely it was the onomatopoeic 'leer a leer' that determined the rimes for the couplet. The reviser kept the first line, but Dekker's grammar was open to criticism, and he felt constrained to alter the second in order to obtain a personal consequent to 'who.' "[1] With regard to Greg's psychology, unless the imitation of a given sound has become so conventionalized as to admit no alternative, there is no easier way to evade a problem of rhyme than to coin a meaningless onomatopoeic rhyme-word—as anyone knows who has heard or read a little child's attempts at verse. The argument from grammar is no less specious. Had some Stuart purist been offended by the disagreement of the personal pronoun and the impersonal consequent, it would have been simpler for him to substitute "what" for "who" than to compose a new second line for the couplet. Moreover, it should be remembered that Greg inclined to the belief that Dekker himself wrote the doubtful songs for Blount; this leaves Greg arguing that Dekker found his own grammar unbearable. The questions of rhyme and grammar, and the whole relationship between these couplets, become clear if one thinks of the Dekker version as a reconstruction from inaccurate memory of the Lyly version, which Dekker could have heard sung by some of the old Paul's Boys who had played in *Campaspe*.

Other internal evidence adduced against Lyly's authorship of the songs and in support of their being interpolations is textual, dealing with minor misplacements of the lyrics, misattributions of parts, and inappropriatenesses. If weighed carefully, however, most of these are seen to

8. *Campaspe* (ed. Blount), v, i.   9. Dekker and Ford, *The Sun's Darling*, ii, i.
1. Greg, "The Authorship of the Songs in Lyly's Plays," pp. 49–50.

prove only that the lyrics were supplied from some source other than that of the plays proper. This fact was known already; Blount printed the plays from the latest quarto editions, which omitted the songs.[2] That the song texts were on separate sheets would be true whether they were recovered or forged.

Specific evidence being so inconclusive, there is left a double foundation for hypothesis: human nature and the general publishing practices of the period. Lawrence objected to the idea of a literary forgery because it would imply Blount to have been dishonest;[3] but he may have been. Bond objected that Dekker would have been more interested in receiving full credit for writing the songs than in the money for keeping quiet about them and added that Jonson would have detected and exposed any fraud;[4] this argument is pure supposition based on Bond's own conception of the character of those men. The only indubitable fact is that Blount was a business man, expecting to make a profit on his volume. Would he have considered the trouble and expense of commissioning substitute songs an investment which would make his book more salable?

Between 1630 and 1635 many a new play was published without some of its song texts—and this although presumably it would have been easy for the printers to get the songs from the authors, who were living and in some cases actually supervised the publication of their works.[5] It would seem that in 1632 the printers recognized no irresistible public demand that the texts of all dramatic lyrics be printed in full. Blount may, of course, have felt that the fact that the Lyly plays were old-fashioned and no longer on the boards would call for a promotional stunt like the forgery of some songs; but in that case he would have advertised them, either on the title page or in his dedicatory epistle. At least, that is what other publishers did when they expected to capitalize on hitherto unprinted songs. For instance, the 1638 edition of *The Rape of Lucrece,* which interpolates five songs almost certainly not by Heywood, makes this brazen claim: "The Copy revised, and sundry Songs before omitted, now inserted in their right places."[6] The second printing of Middleton's *A Fair Quarrel* calls attention to "new Additions of Mr. Chaugh's and Trimtram's Roaring, and the Bauds Song. Neuer before Printed."[7] The

---

2. R. Warwick Bond, ed., *The Complete Works of John Lyly* (Oxford, Clarendon Press, 1902), II, 305, and elsewhere.

3. Lawrence, "The Problem of Lyly's Songs," p. 894.

4. Bond, "Addendum on Lyly's Songs," pp. 444–5.

5. E.g., Massinger, *The Roman Actor* (Q 1629), 2 songs, both blank; *The Renegado* (Q 1630), 1 song, blank; Middleton, *A Chaste Maid in Cheapside* (Q 1630), 3 or 4 songs, 1 or 2 blank; D'Avenant, *The Cruel Brother* (Q 1630), 2 songs, 1 blank; J. Shirley, *Love Tricks* (Q 1631), 3 formal songs, 1 blank; *The Bird in a Cage* (Q 1633), 5 songs, 1 blank; Ford, *Love's Sacrifice* (Q 1633), 1 song, blank.

6. That no scandal seems to have arisen from this claim might indicate that survivors from Lyly's original audiences or even from his original acting company would be unperturbed by similar misrepresentations by Blount.

7. Cf. also the exaggeration on title page and in preface of the recovery of 10 genuine

psychology of selling has not changed much through the centuries; and since Blount did not call attention to the songs which he had acquired, it is hard to believe that he had spent money for them. Moreover, it seems peculiar that a literary forger would not do a thorough job by filling all the blanks, rather than only two-thirds of them.

Blount's songs must be either recovered originals or else forgeries; there is no question of his having found some songs to fit, because these lyrics are too obviously designed for their contexts to have been written for any other purpose. The Beaumont and Fletcher folio recoveries demonstrate that songs could be and occasionally were preserved independently of the plays for which they were composed; the folio also explains one way in which such preservation could take place—through a friend of the author. A second possibility, that songs might survive in the memory of an actor, has already been suggested here. On the other hand, there is no proof that any Jacobean or Caroline printer ever hired anyone to write songs to replace ones missing from an earlier edition; the interpolations which we have examined all were made as additions, not to fill gaps in earlier texts. In other words, the choice of what to believe about Blount's songs is one between something that occasionally *did* happen and something that *might* have happened. There seems to be little prospect of a more definite solution.

4. The Appended Songs

The last of the major textual problems involving the Stuart dramatic lyrics is the question why, in certain plays, songs are either prefixed or appended instead of being incorporated into the text. There are some nineteen of these songs, affixed to eleven plays.

The two songs appended to Heywood's *The Rape of Lucrece* are, as we are told frankly, interpolations by an actor; the one appended to Middleton's *A Mad World, My Masters* (1640 edition) can almost certainly be explained in the same way; a song by Campion is affixed to both *Philotus* and *The Queen and Concubine;* and another song prefixed to *The Queen and Concubine* had been printed ten years earlier in its place in the text of Quarles's *The Virgin Widow.* On the basis of about a third of the evidence, then, the problem of appended songs seems to have solved itself: Stuart dramatists and editors would appear sporadically to have been motivated by a sense of textual integrity to set borrowings and late interpolations apart from the genuine work of the playwright. Some such explanation seems called for also by the four songs appended to Massinger's *The Fatal Dowry.* The first is wholly inappropriate, the second

---

songs in the 1679 edition of Beaumont and Fletcher; this case is parallel but does not constitute ideal evidence because of its much later date and the consequent changes in attitude toward the prewar drama.

does not fit the introductory dialogue, and there is confusion as to the identity of the singers of the remaining pair and their position in the theater. Not one of the four songs contains any internal reference to the circumstances evoking it, and it is quite possible that none of them was written especially for this play.

Unfortunately, the rest of the evidence contradicts the theory that all appended songs are borrowed or interpolated. It does not seem to be true of any of the remaining nine songs: several of them fit particular contexts too well not to have been designed for those contexts; they have not turned up elsewhere; and they have not aroused the suspicions of successive generations of editors. Moreover, too many borrowed and interpolated songs have been integrated into play texts, and there is too much reworking and imitating of older material in general, to allow us to believe that any of the Stuart play-makers ever thought much about textual integrity.

On the evidence now available to us, therefore, it seems impossible to explain why these few songs are appended or prefixed to their respective plays. The authenticity of such songs may be suspect, but the mere fact that they are not printed in their proper places is not in itself proof that they are either borrowed or interpolated.

It is possible, however, to discredit one preposterous theory about the appended songs. Wright assumes that their segregation from the text of the play means that at least some of them were intended to be sung at any time during the performance that the actors thought the attention of the audience might be wandering.[8]

Now, eleven of the appended songs are intended for definite locations where they are called for by specific stage directions. A twelfth, the welcome to the forest queen in *The Guardian,* could be sung nowhere but at the entrance of the outlaws at the beginning of Act v. Three more, those appended to *A Mad World, My Masters* and *The Rape of Lucrece,* are interpolations by actor-singers and, as such, indicate little or nothing about the theories of dramatists or booksellers. *Philotus* is almost certainly a closet drama; the song from Campion appended to it may have been included as a sort of bonus for the purchaser but could hardly have been intended to recapture an audience's attention. Wright's particular targets are the remaining three: the appended song for the second act of *The Late Lancashire Witches* and the two songs prefixed to *The Shoemakers' Holiday.*

Of the first of these, Wright says, ". . . the place of insertion is indefinite. Evidently the song could be put in at the beginning, end, or between the scenes of the second act, wherever the players wished."[9] The song

8. See below, n. 9, and p. 110, n. 3, for two specific references.
9. Wright, "Extraneous Song in Elizabethan Drama," p. 272.

in question is an invitation by a witch or witches to four familiars; it begins,

> Come *Mawsy,* come *Puckling,*
> And come my sweet *Suckling,*
>   My pretty *Mamillion,* my Ioy,
> Fall each to his Duggy,
> While kindly we huggie,
>   As tender as Nurse over Boy.
>   Then suck our blouds freely, and with it be jolly,
>   While merrily we sing, hey Trolly Lolly.[1]

In the first scene of the second act of the play, this passage occurs:

Enter 4. Witches: (*severally.*)

> *All.*   Hoe! well met, well met.
> *Meg.*   What new devise, what dainty straine
> More for our myrth now then our gaine,
> Shall we in practice put.
>   *Meg.* [*sic*] Nay dame,
> Before we play another game,
> We must a little laugh and thanke
> Our feat familiars for the pranck
> They playd us last.
>   *Mawd.* Or they will misse
> Vs in our next plot, if for this
> They find not their reward.
>   *Meg.*   'Tis right.
>   *Gil.*   Therefore sing *Mawd,* and call each spright.
> Come away, and take thy duggy.

Enter foure Spirits.

> *Meg.*   Come my *Mamilion* like a Puggy.
> *Mawd.* And come my puckling take thy teat,
> Your travels have deserv'd your meat.[2]

It is hard to see why Wright would suppose the song to have been sung between the scenes or anywhere else when it is so patently demanded by this dialogue.

Wright is even more positive about the floating nature of the Dekker songs: "Since the songs were not related directly to the play, they could be sung at any point where the players thought they might be needed to renew the interest of the spectators."[3] It is true that there is little in the

---

1. Heywood, *The Late Lancashire Witches,* "Song. II. Act." (appended after Act v; Pearson reprint, IV, 261).
  2. *Ibid.,* II, i.   3. Wright, *op. cit.,* p. 265.

play itself to indicate precisely where these songs are to be sung. But it is very unlikely that they could be sung whenever the players saw fit. In fact, it is possible by applying what we have learned in the first half of this study to tell exactly where they belong.

Of the conventional occasions for song, three occur in *The Shoemakers' Holiday:* there are a morris dance (III, v), a wedding procession (v, ii), and a party (v, iv, v). The title of the second prefixed song, indicating that it is to be sung at the latter end of the play, suggests the possibility of an epilogue song. Dekker has a trick of presenting craftsmen and servants who sing at their work;[4] Eyre's whole crew of shoemakers are shown happily at work in IV, ii. Finally, in III, i, Mrs. Eyre comments acidly on Firk's singing.

There are in the play, then, six possible loci for song. Two can be eliminated at once. Neither of the prefixed songs would be at all appropriate for a wedding procession. When Mrs. Eyre rebukes Firk for singing, Hodge is present, but there is no one on hand to take the third part of a three-man song. Neither is there any necessity for supposing a formal song intended; the journeyman may give Mrs. Eyre cause for anger merely by chirping cheerfully to himself.

Now, the first three-man song is a summery, outdoor lyric:

O the month of Maie, the merrie month of Maie . . .

A country-sports song, it must belong in the morris-dance scene. The other is harder to place. It is a drinking song, and the title says that it is "to be sung at the latter end." Its content would suggest that it was meant for the new Lord Mayor's feast, the title that it should be sung either during the feast or as an epilogue. But there is no real opening for a song at the party; and although Dekker uses epilogue songs elsewhere,[5] he would hardly be guilty of the anticlimax of having one here immediately after a formal closing speech by the King. However, Act IV, scene ii, begins,

> *Enter Hodge at his shop boord, Rafe, Firke, Hans, and a boy at worke.*
> *All.* Hey downe, a downe dery.

Through the banter, gossip, and shop-talk which follow, Firk keeps on repeating this refrain at intervals. Three pertinent facts are apparent. First, this scene takes place on the inner stage, the actors being revealed at their work by the drawing of the curtain; it has been shown above that song frequently was used on such occasions to give the effect of

4. E.g., Janicola's household in *Patient Grissill,* ii (A4v, B1r); Barnaby Bunch in *The Weakest Goeth to the Wall,* ii (B2r, v); Roger in 1 *The Honest Whore,* II, i; Boniface in *Westward Ho,* II, i.

5. E.g., *Old Fortunatus* (followed by spoken epilogue); *Westward Ho.*

continuing action behind the traverse.[6] Second, all five workmen actually are singing at their work—as good conventional craftsmen were expected to do.[7] A kind master like Eyre had no objections to the use of the "iolly Nut-browne boll" during working hours.[8] Third, the refrain sung first by all, then repeatedly by Firk, is very like two lines in the second three-man song, which is, in its references to Saint Hugh, peculiarly a shoemakers' song.

By a logical process of elimination, then, one can assign the first three-man song to the morris-dance scene in III, v, and the second to the beginning of IV, ii, the scene in Eyre's shop. The latter assignment requires a liberal interpretation of the words "at the latter end," though of course IV, ii, is past the middle of the play.

There is interesting confirmation of this reasoning in a note published long ago by the Shakespeare Society.[9] The author, who. called himself Dramaticus, reported that a friend of his possessed a copy of *The Shoemakers' Holiday* with the actors' and singers' names supplied in seventeenth-century handwriting. According to this information, the first three-man song was performed by Firk (Robert Wilson), Lacy (Charles Massey), and Hodge (John Singer) ;[1] the second was given to Hodge (Singer), Firk (Wilson), and "the boy."[2] Dramaticus thought the second song might have been sung as an epilogue but had no theory as to the place of the first.

Dramaticus' ascriptions of the songs to particular characters are wholly plausible, whether or not one accepts his assignments of roles to actors.[3] Firk and Lacy both sing independently, and singing boys are legion in the Stuart drama. Firk, Lacy, and Hodge are all on hand for the morris dance. The characters on stage in the working scene are "Hodge at his shop boord, Rafe, Firke, Hans, and a boy." The boy has no spoken lines

6. Above, p. 70. (n. 6)   7. Above, pp. 42–3. (n. 7)
8. In fact, he has already sanctioned its use: *The Shoemakers' Holiday*, II, iii.
9. "Dramaticus," "The Players who acted in 'The Shoemakers' Holiday,' 1600, a Comedy by Thomas Dekker and Robert Wilson," *The Shakespeare Society's Papers* (London, 1849), IV, 110–22.
1. *Ibid.*, p. 119.   2. *Ibid.*, p. 120.
3. Of the Dramaticus letter, Chambers says that Fleay and Greg "unite in condemning this communication as a forgery, but I rather wish they had given their reasons." E. K. Chambers, *The Elizabethan Stage* (Oxford, Clarendon Press, 1923), III, 292. Greg's undocumented judgment that the letter is "an obvious forgery, and a very clumsy one" (W. W. Greg, ed., *Henslowe's Diary* [London, A. H. Bullen, 1908], II, 203) may be based merely on the fact that it assigns parts to some actors whose names are not encountered elsewhere. In regard to the three named here, however, the biographical data presented by Chambers (*op. cit.*) and by Gerald Eades Bentley (*The Jacobean and Caroline Stage* [Oxford, Clarendon Press, 1941]) indicates Dramaticus' assignment of roles to Massey and Singer to be quiet probable; it is not impossible that the Robert Wilson described by Chambers should have played Firk or even that there might have been two Robert Wilsons. At any rate, Dramaticus' letter shows too accurate a knowledge of the personnel of the Admiral's Men in 1599 to deserve Greg's condemnation as a "very clumsy" forgery. (For Greg's probably unjustified suspicions of forgery in another instance, see above, pp. 105–8.)

in this scene; there is no reason for his presence except to bear a part in the song. If it be objected that Hans (Lacy), being a singer and on stage, might be expected to take a part also, the answer is probably that he was a baritone or a bass and that the musical setting called for a tenor; the latter part of the conjecture, at least, is true, because one of the textual cruces of the second three-man song is whether the words "Close with the tenor boy" were sung or represent an instruction to the singers.

Both these songs, of course, are used by Dekker to underline the carefree holiday mood of the play, and the above analysis is rewarding in that it shows that they are used in accordance with the accepted techniques for song. A further benefit appears in the correcting of editions of the play which have inserted these songs either at points where there are no appropriate characters on stage to sing them or in scenes where, though they do no harm, they do no particular good either.[4]

5. Summary

In view of the fact that the material treated in the preceding pages is involved and contains some apparent contradictions, it may be helpful to review what conclusions seem worthy of belief and what these conclusions imply about the critical status of the dramatic lyric.

The many lost songs in the Stuart drama are of two types. The texts of some were excluded from the promptbook copies from which the quartos were printed either because they were familiar and could be identified by title or first line, or because within broad limits any song would serve the ends of the dramatist, who therefore left the actual selection of a suitable lyric to the actor-singer or the stage manager. Other songs were missing from the promptbooks because they had been written on separate sheets which remained in the possession of the singer or the composer, or which were deliberately withheld from publication by the author to prevent their being sung *ad nauseam* by the vulgar. In addition, song texts occasionally may have been omitted as unnecessary when a promptbook was recopied, the old one having worn out.

It is certain that song was used more widely in the Stuart drama than is now generally realized. Meager evidence indicates that this body of unsuspected song was not large, however; in fact, some of the printed lyrics do not appear to have been performed on the boards. But a considerable number of songs can be conjectured from dialogue and a few more, with less certainty, from the nature of particular scenes in which the use of song was conventional.

4. E.g., Ernest Rhys, ed., *Thomas Dekker* (The Mermaid Series. New York, Charles Scribner's Sons, n.d. [1894?]), pp. 46–7, 79–80. Rhys places the first song in III, v, before the arrival of the morris dancers, when there are no likely singers on stage, and the second song in v, iv, at the banquet, just before the return of Lacy and Rose from the church.

On occasion, songs were interpolated into plays some time after the original performance. A few original lyrics have been rediscovered long after the publication of editions which left them blank. It has been suggested, too, that enterprising booksellers may sometimes have commissioned the forgery of lyrics to fill obvious gaps in the texts of plays which they were reprinting. There is no proof that this last practice ever really took place; rather, there is presumptive evidence against it.

Although unquestionable examples exist of both interpolation and recovery, there is no blanket rule by which one can determine which explanation accounts for any single late-appearing song; each case must be decided on an individual basis. If such a song brings its introductory dialogue with it out of nowhere, however, that song is likely to be an interpolation; one can account for the omission of a song text from the promptbook but not for the omission of all the spoken lines introducing it.

In some eleven plays certain song texts are appended or prefixed, rather than printed in their proper places. There seems to be no general rule explaining this practice, but one theory advanced may be discarded: that such songs could be sung at any time during the performance that the attention of the audience seemed to be wandering.

The knowledge that song was used more freely by the Stuart dramatists than is manifest from the early texts requires an upward revision of our appraisal of its importance as a dramatic technique. But its importance was esthetic as well as utilitarian. The phenomenon of blank songs in the quartos is not evidence that the dramatists held their lyrics lightly; rather, such blanks and the occasional printing of lyrics not actually sung on the stage are diverse manifestations of the authors' genuine pride in their songs. That is not to say that these men considered all their work to be great literature—the additions to *A Fair Quarrel* show that to some extent they thought of themselves as being in the entertainment business—but they were proud of their serious lyrics.

At least a few actors apparently enjoyed singing and looked on a song as a chance to steal the show. That songs were popular with the audiences is proved (if proof is needed) by the fact that the stage managers allowed these actors to interpolate irrelevant ditties as they saw fit.

An astute bookseller provided his customers with what was available to him, without discriminating between original and interpolated material. He usually represented the result as the acting version of the play. He would hardly go to great expense or trouble to acquire substitute lyrics or even to seek out missing original songs, for although the reading public welcomed song texts, it did not insist on having them; consequently, until the closing of the theaters new plays continued to be printed with occasional songs left blank.

VIII

The Human Element and the Dramatic Lyric

WHILE THE PUBLIC'S DEMAND for what it wanted in the acted and printed plays was an external factor exerting an influence on the amount (but not the presence) of song in the Stuart drama, an equally influential factor operated internally. This might be described as the personalities of the dramatist, the actor, and the acting company, making themselves felt individually or in combination. The term "personality" applies most accurately to the dramatist, but it is not wholly inappropriate as applied to the policy and tradition of an acting company. The importance of the individual player depended simply on his possession or lack of a good singing voice. There was, necessarily, an interplay among these influences; but for convenience in discussion they may be treated separately.

1. The Dramatist

Of the various ways in which the personality of the dramatist influences the extent to which song is used in his plays the most direct, probably, depends on his fondness for music and the fecundity of his lyrical talent. Shakespeare and Dekker obviously loved music; Beaumont and Fletcher turned out charming lyrics as easily, one feels, as they breathed; Middleton and Brome were inferior as poets, but to them, too, song was a natural form of expression. On the other hand, Massinger was uncomfortable in the lyric vein; Shirley does not seem to have been particularly fond of music; Heywood, alone among his contemporaries, on one occasion speaks almost slightingly of song, and that in his own person.[1] Such

---

1. Heywood, *The English Traveller*, Prologue:

> A Strange Play you are like to haue, for know,
> We vse no Drum, nor Trumpet, nor Dumbe show;
> No Combate, Marriage, not so much to day,
> As Song, Dance, Masque, to bumbaste out a Play;
> Yet these all good, and still in frequent vse
> With our best *Poets* . . .

Heywood goes on to explain that, although he *can* use these devices, this play represents an experiment:

> He onely tries if once bare Lines will beare it . . .

In his prologue to *The Doubtful Heir*, J. Shirley warns that it will contain "No bawdry, nor no ballads," but he seems to mean "ballads" literally, not to be disparaging song in general.

predilections are necessarily reflected in the plays which these men wrote : the music-lovers and the facile lyricists used song freely, easily, and naturally ; the others used it sparingly and with constraint.

This difference seems to have been purely a reflection of the tastes of the playwrights themselves, not a response to the current demands of the public. Heywood abjured song at a time when Shakespeare, Marston, Chapman, and Jonson were using it freely ; Shirley and Massinger employed it grudgingly even while Brome, Glapthorne, and others were capitalizing on it. In general, there appears to be little correlation between date and the amount of song in the drama.[2]

A second respect in which a dramatist's personality makes itself felt through the presence or absence of song depends on his individual ideas of propriety—specifically, his sense of what is proper to the different types of drama.

Broadly speaking, there is not much distinction among the major dramatic types—tragedy, comedy, and tragicomedy—so far as the use of song is concerned ; the individual lyrics are adapted to their places in the total scheme of the play, of course, but song itself occurs indifferently in all three types. It is perceptibly less common in chronicle histories and in domestic tragedies—not, certainly, because the use of song was regarded as inimical to verisimilitude, but perhaps because the subject matter of these realistic types brought them within the experiential range of the audience and eliminated the need for much artificial stimulation of the proper emotional responses. On the other hand, the more exotic genres like the pastoral, the moral masque, and certain kinds of satirical comedy ordinarily have a very high song content.

This pattern, it must be emphasized, is the general one. But some authors set their own standards. Jonson, for instance, never uses a song in a Roman tragedy (unless, as is barely possible, he intended the choruses in *Catiline* to be sung ;[3] but those could hardly be called dramatic lyrics). Chapman uses very little song in his tragedies of French history, none in *Caesar and Pompey* (if it be his). Both Jonson and Chapman, of course, were classical scholars, and their ideas of propriety probably derive from their acquaintance with classical critical doctrine. The result is a difference in technique from writers like Shakespeare, Heywood, Nabbes, and May, who humanized their ancient Romans by attributing to them the seventeenth-century audiences' own love of song.[4]

A third side of the playwright's personality which may exert an influ-

---

2. This statement, referring to the amount of song and not to the spirit in which it is used, is not incompatible with the observations made below, pp. 130–1.

3. See *Ben Jonson*, ed. C. H. Herford and Percy Simpson (Oxford, Clarendon Press, 1925–47), II, 115, for this suggestion.

4. E.g., Shakespeare, *Antony and Cleopatra*, II, vii, and *Julius Caesar*, IV, iii ; Heywood, *The Rape of Lucrece, passim;* Nabbes, *Hannibal and Scipio*, I, iii ; II, v ; IV, v ; May, *The Tragedy of Cleopatra*, I, ii.

ence on the amount of song in his plays is the development of his dramatic technique. Willa Evans has attempted to trace and explain such a development in Jonson. She sees four stages in his use of song. The first is a period of lack of lyric skill, as exemplified by the "feeble song of the cobbler" in *The Case Is Altered*.[5] Then comes a period of apprenticeship in song writing, in the plays written for the Chapel Children—an apprenticeship perhaps forced upon Jonson by the manager's insistence upon opportunities for his little troupers to display their musical talents.[6] Third is a period of mastery marked by a businesslike division of materials, with the bulk of the songs going into the masques—this because Jonson could use his entire lyrical output there and because he chose to entrust his songs to the excellent voices available for court masques rather than to "squander them upon the harsh voices of the Children or upon badly trained adults."[7] Finally, Miss Evans sees in the songs in *The Staple of News* a conclusion of Jonson's interest in song-writing and a decline in his lyric power.[8]

This theory seems strangely uncomplimentary to Jonson. Even allowing for Miss Evans' tendency to bracket the terms "best" and "most elaborate,"[9] one must protest her using songs designed to be appropriate to a clownish shoemaker and a ridiculous poetaster[1] as evidence of lack of lyric ability on Jonson's part, and her disregard of the good songs in the very late plays *The New Inn* and *The Sad Shepherd*.[2] The hymn to Cynthia is certainly not the work of an apprentice song-writer. The two plays for the Chapel company, *Cynthia's Revels* and *The Poetaster,* are full of songs, but not necessarily because some manager demanded them; these two plays are Jonson's only attempts at comedy in the Aristophanic manner,[3] and Jonson would have been more amenable to the suggestions of Aristophanes than to those of the manager of the Children. And to the thesis that during his period of lyric mastery Jonson had to allot most of his lyrics to his masques there are at least three objections. First, only three of his legitimate plays during this period are without songs, and two of them are Roman tragedies.[4] Second, there is no good reason for supposing that Jonson could not write as many lyrics as he felt he needed for both his dramatic fields. And, third, it is hard to imagine why Miss Evans thinks that the children's voices were harsh and that the adult singers were badly trained.[5a]

5. Evans, *Ben Jonson and Elizabethan Music*, p. 74.   6. *Ibid.*, pp. 45, 48, 75.
7. *Ibid.*, p. 66; see also pp. 61, 74–5.   8. *Ibid.*, p. 72.   9. *Ibid.*, p. 76.
1. Respectively, in *The Case Is Altered*, I, i, and *The Staple of News*, IV, ii.
2. Jonson, *The New Inn*, IV, iv (song read), and *The Sad Shepherd*, I, v. At least one more song was projected in the latter play.
3. Alexander Corbin Judson, ed., *Cynthia's Revels* (New York, Henry Holt, 1912), pp. lxv–lxvi.
4. *Sejanus* and *Catiline;* the third is *The Alchemist*.
5a. Perhaps she took seriously the burlesque of the "ignorant critique" in the Induction to *Cynthia's Revels:* "And then their *musicke* is abominable—able to stretch a

A protest against Miss Evans' theory of a qualitative and quantitative curve in Jonson's use of songs does not imply, however, that such curves may not exist in the lyric work of other dramatists. For example, Heywood's dramatic production falls into two periods: up to 1612 and after 1623. On any basis of comparison Heywood's use of song doubles after the eleven playless years—even including the very exceptional *The Rape of Lucrece,* which alone accounts for a third of the songs in the earlier period. It was during the early period, too, that Heywood had glanced at song as an expedient "to bumbaste out a Play."[6] Something happened to make him change his mind; whatever it was, it was an external influence operating through the personality of the playwright to affect the frequency of song in his plays.

Dekker may be another case in point. His playwriting career is broken, like Heywood's, into two periods, with a blank between 1611 and 1619. Among the later plays attributed to him in full or in part, only *The Sun's Darling* (1624) makes much of song. Did Dekker's long imprisonment deprive him temporarily of his lyric gift? Or did advancing age dull it? Unless he did turn out lyrics as before, only to have them lost in the printing, some personal element is involved here, too. It would be interesting to know what it was, but the significant fact is that the personal life of the dramatist could and did so definitely influence his use of song.

The last and most amusing of the four ways in which an author's personal tastes or interests are likely to be reflected in the songs in his plays results from the temptation for a playwright who was also a player to tailor roles to his own particular talents. The combination in one man of gifts for writing, acting, and singing was not common, but it did occur. Thus, Baldwin and Bentley agree that the "line" of William Rowley was that of a fat clown.[7] Although it is not certain that Rowley acted in all his own plays, there are fat clowns in all eight of the plays which he either wrote or helped to write, and six of these clowns are called upon to sing. Armin, another famous comedian, wrote and acted in *The Two Maids of More-Clacke,* probably doubling in two roles both of which afford opportunity for comic singing. From our own day we may remember the care of Noel Coward the writer to display all the varied talents of Noel Coward the entertainer. The practice simply combines good business with ordinary human nature.

It is essential to realize that the influences on song just discussed all operate within the patterns of dramatic functionalism described in the earlier chapters of this study. The personality of the author—his love of

---

mans eares worse then tenne—pillories, and their ditties—most lamentable things, like the pittifull fellowes that make them—Poets . . ."

6. See the Prologue to *The English Traveller,* quoted above, p. 115, n. 1.

7. Thomas Whitfield Baldwin, *The Organization and Personnel of the Shakespearean Company* (Princeton, Princeton University Press, 1927), p. 214; Bentley, *The Jacobean and Caroline Stage,* II, 556.

music, his lyric ability, his sense of dramatic propriety, his technical development, the accident of his being an actor-singer—is likely to affect the amount of song in his plays; but it does not affect the way in which he uses song. In that respect he abides by the unwritten rules, because those rules are based on sound psychology.

2. The Player

If the idiosyncrasies of the author could affect the amount of singing in any given Stuart play, so could the vocal abilities or inabilities of the individual actors for whom that play was designed. This fact has been recognized but has not always been treated with complete objectivity. Thus Wright, urging the extraneous quality of much of the song in the drama, has implied that many lyrics were included solely to display the talents of an actor with a good singing voice, their dramatic functionalism being of little moment.[8] Reed thought it was less of a problem for the dramatists to supply songs for their singers than to find singers for their songs, and gave much attention to techniques which he considered makeshifts to permit the assignment of song to a particular character even when the actor playing that role had no vocal ability.[9] There are elements of truth in the arguments of both men; the aim of this section is to find the safe middle ground between their positions.

The best way to determine the importance of the individual singer is to set down in chronological order the plays performed by a single acting company and to list the singing roles in them. The King's Men make an ideal subject for the experiment for several reasons: they alone had a continuous history from before 1600 to 1642; their repertoire of well over 130 plays affords ample material for study; they used song more freely than the rival adult troupes; and, as Shakespeare's company and one for which, sooner or later, most of the major dramatists wrote, they transcend their rivals in interest to present-day students.

Baldwin has shown that the organization of a Tudor or Stuart acting company was permanent and rigid, and that therefore "the play had to be cut to the company and not the company to the play."[1] The result was the establishment of a more or less fixed "line" of parts for each of the principal actors of the company. After tabulating the actor-singers in the plays of the King's Men and eliminating those named characters whose singing amounts only to a merry or drunken snatch requiring no genuine vocal ability, one can distinguish certain singing lines which correspond to and frequently coincide with the acting lines pointed out by Baldwin.

8. Wright, "Extraneous Song in Elizabethan Drama," p. 270 and *passim*.
9. Reed, *Songs from the British Drama*, pp. 349–50.
1. Baldwin, *op. cit.*, p. 307 and *passim*. I accept Baldwin's broad conclusions without subscribing to all his assignments of roles.

Clearly, in 1610–16 the troupe was well supplied with singing "actresses":

1610	The Maid's Tragedy	Aspatia, Dula
	A Winter's Tale	Dorcas, Mopsa
1612	The Captain	Frank, Clora
1613	The Two Noble Kinsmen	Gaoler's Daughter
1615	More Dissemblers besides Women	"Page"
	The Witch	Isabella
1616	The Widow	Philippa, Violetta

During this time a singing group made its appearance, headed by a principal actor who usually played the comic-adventurous role of a gay young soldier:[2]

1613	Bonduca	*Junius, Petillius, Decius, Demetrius
1615	More Dissemblers	*Gypsy Captain, Dondolo, gypsies
1616	The Widow	*Latrocinio, thieves
1617	The Mad Lover	*Stremon
	The Queen of Corinth	"six men"
1618	The Loyal Subject	*Ancient, several other soldiers
	The Knight of Malta	the guard
1619	The Bloody Brother	three servants
	Barnavelt	the executioners (?)

As this singing group broke up two comic lines took its place. One singer was small and seemingly effete—qualities which he could turn to advantage in either sympathetic or unsympathetic parts:[3]

1619	The Little French Lawyer	La-Writ
	The Fatal Dowry	Aymer
1620	Women Pleased	Lopez (?)
	The Duke of Milan	Graccho
1621	The Wild-Goose Chase	Pinac (?)
1622	Beggar's Bush	Higgen (?)
1625	The Chances	Vecchio
	The Nice Valor	Passionate Lord (?)
	The Staple of News	Peniboy Canter (?)
1628	The Lover's Melancholy	Cuculus (?)
1629	The Northern Lass	Widgin
1632	The Weeding of Covent Garden	Cockbrain
	The Soddered Citizen	Brainsick

2. Asterisks indicate the principal actor, whom Baldwin (ibid., chap. viii, tables) identifies as William Eccleston.

3. Question marks indicate comic roles probably but not necessarily belonging to this line. For example, Baldwin gives the role of Lopez to Eccleston.

There were also a few singing roles which belonged properly to a fat clown:

1623	*The Lover's Progress*	Host's Ghost
	The Maid in the Mill	Bustofa
1625	*The Nice Valor*	Base (?)

From 1625 to 1635 there was another decade of good parts for singing "women"; about 1635 the company must have acquired a new singer whose role was usually that of a lighthearted young cavalier; and other singing lines are distinguishable through the period.

It would be possible, combining this material with Baldwin's, to extend his assignment of roles and perhaps to emend it occasionally. For example, he gives the parts of La-Writ and Pinac to Thomas Pollard;[4] the manuscript of *The Soddered Citizen,* one of the few contemporary sources of information about acting assignments to which he does not refer, proves that Pollard played the role of Brainsick.[5] It might not be amiss to assign to Pollard most or all of the similar comic singing parts occurring between 1619 and 1632. Baldwin, dating *The Chances* in 1615, names Nicholas Tooley as the original Vecchio;[6] if Harbage's date of 1625 is more nearly right, Pollard may have had that role.

William Rowley was probably the fat clown who played Bustofa in *The Maid in the Mill.* Baldwin suggests that his role in *The Lover's Progress* was that of Lancelot.[7] But Rowley's singing would find an outlet in the part of the Host's Ghost, and his bulk would be appropriate there as well. Actually, there is no reason why Rowley could not have doubled in the two parts; their scenes not only do not coincide but allow time for the two quick changes of costume that would be necessary.[8]

Intriguing though such conjectures as to identities may be, they are merely the by-product of a demonstration the chief import of which is this: the existence of clearly defined singing lines is a reaffirmation of what Baldwin proved—that the Stuart dramatist wrote his plays with one eye on the people who were to act in them. If he knew that a certain vocal talent was available and had won the approval of the public, he was very likely to provide an opportunity for the displaying of that talent. To this extent Wright's position is sound.

But the negative evidence must not be overlooked, as so often it has been. It is significant, of course, that between 1613 and 1619 seven plays demand a combination of singing and acting ability in one major figure and several associates, and that two more plays may allow the group to

4. Baldwin, *op. cit.,* p. 215.
5. Marmion or Clavell, *The Soddered Citizen* (MSR, 1936), Dramatis Personae.
6. Baldwin, *op. cit.,* p. 212.
7. *Ibid.,* p. 214; Baldwin is somewhat hesitant about making this assignment.
8. Lancelot does not appear between III, ii, and IV, iv. The Ghost's only scenes are III, v, and IV, ii.

sing in isolated scenes. But it is no less significant that during those seven years at least eleven plays were produced which do not require songs by this group. Although, from La-Writ to Brainsick, there are thirteen plays calling for a singing clown, there are forty plays which do not call for him. The only possible conclusion is that the playwright was completely independent in the use he chose to make of the musical talent at his disposal. If his plan allowed singing by Pollard, well and good; but the play was the thing, and if the dramatic plan did not allow a song by Pollard, then Pollard did not sing. The presence in the company of an actor with a good voice was a resource to be exploited intelligently, not blindly; it seems highly doubtful that any Stuart dramatic lyric has as its primary function the mere exhibition of a fine voice.

On the opposite side of this question, Reed thought that the playwrights frequently were vexed with the problem of what to do in a situation calling for a functional song when the proposed singer had no vocal ability. He distinguished three ways of getting around this difficulty: to make the character go off stage for the song and return after it (thus allowing a professional vocalist, unseen, to do the actual singing); to have him declaim the song rather than sing it; and to let him sing vicariously by commanding his page or some musician to "sing the song I made."[9]

There is no denying the fact that all these devices occur in the Stuart drama, and occur fairly often; but it is questionable whether they occur always for the reason that Reed names. For instance, as introduction to a song which Reed conjectures in *The Duke of Milan,* Sforza says,

> Command the Eunuch
> To sing the Dittie that I last compos'd,
> In prayse of my *Marcelia.*[1]

This is what Reed calls "vicarious singing." But it would be a strange breach of decorum to handle this song in any other way. The occasion is a state banquet in celebration of Marcelia's birthday; no monarch with any sense of dignity would himself give a public performance under such circumstances as these. Sforza is, after all, a tragic hero of sorts. The characterizing values of the song are achieved sufficiently by having him acknowledge the words as his own and command the performance; to allow him to sing it himself would only make him ridiculous.

Again, in Massinger's *The Renegado* Donusa orders the eunuch Carazie to sing a ditty she has composed upon her "love-sick passion."[2] During the song Vitelli is to enter and be seduced. Obviously, Donusa cannot conveniently do this song herself—it would tie her hands, so to speak. Sung by Carazie, it supplies the conventional erotic stimulus aimed at Vitelli, leaving Donusa free to concentrate on her intended victim. This is

---

9. Reed, *op. cit.,* pp. 349–50.   1. Massinger, *The Duke of Milan,* I, iii.
2. Massinger, *The Renegado,* II, iv.

vicarious singing, it is true—but dictated by dramatic fitness, not necessarily by Donusa's inability to sing. Quite possibly she could sing, for that matter: that same year, the Lady Elizabeth's Men were producing such tuneful plays as *The Captives* and *The Sun's Darling,* both of which require songs by "women."

Mention of Carazie's song suggests something it should be hardly necessary by now to point out—that the importance of a character's spoken role has no bearing whatsoever on the functionalism or extraneousness of his songs. Carazie has a very minor speaking part, but a nameless boy or even a professional musician off stage would serve the purpose equally well in this scene. Donusa wants the song for its psychological effect on Vitelli, and Massinger wants it for its psychological effect on the audience; provided it is introduced realistically and performed adequately, the identity of the singer is of absolutely no consequence.

As in these examples, so in general it is true that vicarious singing by musicians or boys is governed by rules of decorum or propriety. The man or woman who has someone sing to or for him is a man or woman who would do the same thing in real life, whether or not he was able to sing himself. It is possible that in a few instances this technique was used, as Reed says, to get around the fact that the actor who should have sung was unable to; but much more often propriety explains the usage.

Reed's second evasive device is to have a song declaimed rather than sung; he cites the dirge in *Cymbeline,* which Arviragus and Guiderius chant because, as they say, their voices are changing and they no longer can sing.[3] Undoubtedly this would be a clever way to gain the effect of a song by two boy actors in just that plight; a background of instrumental music would provide the emotional impact which, even more than the words, dictated the use of the song. But what of the dirge in *Antonio's Revenge*?[4] Feliche's body is being buried; Antonio wants a dirge sung, but Pandulpho demurs and himself declaims "an honest antick rime." The significant point here is that a page assists with the burial and that it is he whom Antonio asks to sing. The boy who played the page certainly was not cast for his acting ability. Here, then, are both an opening for a song and an available singer; the fact that the dirge is declaimed can mean only that Marston wanted it declaimed. But if Marston valued the dramatic effect of a declamation, Shakespeare may have valued it, too. The proportion of cases in which the declamatory technique was forced on the poet is smaller than Reed implies, at any rate.

Reed's example of a song sung "within" by a major character is a passage in Fletcher's *The Spanish Curate* where Leandro goes off stage to sing in the hope of attracting the attention of Amaranta.[5] The little

3. Shakespeare, *Cymbeline,* IV, ii.   4. Marston, *Antonio's Revenge,* IV, ii.
5. Fletcher and Massinger, *The Spanish Curate,* II, v (II, iv, in F2).

scene of mutually bashful eagerness which follows could be handled just as well, probably, with Leandro on stage and Amaranta peeping in, and Reed's interpretation seems reasonable. On the other hand, if William Eccleston played Leandro, as Baldwin thinks,[6] he needed no professional musician to do his singing for him, off stage or on.

It is easy to demonstrate that not all off-stage singing by major characters is attributable to the necessity for having ghost voices perform the songs. For instance, in *The Chances* both Constantias sing off stage.[7] Since other characters confuse their voices it is possible that the same musician did the singing for both. But the main reason for keeping the singers off stage is that each song is the basis of a comic passage built around the mistaking of the invisible singer for someone else—mistakes which could not occur if the singer were in sight.

If one accepted Reed's reasoning here, it would be hard to know where to limit its application. Thus Miss Evans suspected that Volpone's song to Celia was actually sung by a professional musician backstage and that the actor playing Volpone merely "gestured with his lips."[8] The idea is not utterly fantastic; but it is extremely difficult to achieve such an effect on the legitimate stage, and the difficulty increases in inverse proportion to the size of the auditorium. In the Stuart theater the trick would be possible only in scenes utilizing the inner or the upper stage, where the ghost singer could be concealed close behind the supposed singer. Such a deception is always dangerous from the producer's point of view because, unless it is very skillfully done, the effect is ludicrous. It is a device which no wise stage manager would be eager to try on a house full of irreverent groundlings.

It seems probable that people like Reed and Richmond Noble exaggerate the difficulty of presenting song on the stage.[9] A man does not need to be a trained musician to sing acceptably and even pleasingly. Any good actor who is not tone deaf (if a good actor *can* be tone deaf) has the two qualities essential to dramatic singing: he knows how to project his voice, and he has a stage presence which commands attention—which "sells" the song. He may not be able to read music but he can put his song across merely by *acting* a singer. Anyone who follows a small stock company through a season can observe this for himself; occasionally it can be seen on Broadway. Walter Huston was not a singer but *Knickerbocker Holiday* did not suffer.

All this is not to deny the existence of any truth whatsoever in what Reed and the others have to say; it is simply a caveat against taking them too seriously. On rare occasions all three of Reed's tactics probably were

---

6. Baldwin, *op. cit.*, pp. 211, 376.   7. Fletcher, *The Chances*, II, ii, and IV, iii.

8. Evans, *op. cit.*, p. 65.

9. Noble is inclined to forgive modern stage managers for omitting the songs from productions of Shakespearian plays because of the difficulties inherent in providing a suitable voice and accompaniment (*Shakespeare's Use of Song*, pp. 16-17).

employed to mask the inability of excellent actors to sing. But those devices could be and very often were employed for entirely different reasons, so that their importance as evasive tactics cannot be weighed by the number of times they occur in the plays. After all, there was one infallible recourse in the lack of an actor to sing a particular song, and it sometimes was resorted to : the song could simply be left out.[1]

The dramatists had up their sleeves another trick which Reed overlooked : they could convey the impression that a particular character was a good singer without ever letting him sing a note. There are dozens of characters in the Stuart drama who enjoy musical reputations of this sort. Constanza in *The Spanish Gypsy* is mentioned several times as a singer but does not sing alone.[2] Septimius, in *The False One,* is characterized as a singer of scurrilous ballads but he never performs one; the characterization is built entirely on what he says about himself and what other people say about him.[3] One has to think twice to remember that Anne Frankford does not actually sing in *A Woman Killed with Kindness.*[4]

The influence exerted by the individual actor and his talent or lack of it, then, while a genuine influence, is secondary to the aims of the playwright in its effect on the use of the lyric. The dramatic function determines whether song is to be used and to a great extent how it is to be used. The availability or nonavailability of good singers may affect the amount of singing or the details of production, but the actors' versatility and stage experience usually were sufficient to take care of any problems involved in getting a particular song sung.

3. The Acting Company

Third among the human factors influencing the amount of singing in the Stuart drama is the make-up and policy of the individual acting company. Traditional opinion is that song was the particular forte of the children's companies, that the dramatic lyric owed its ultimate importance to its almost accidental emphasis by these companies, and that the use of song by the adult troupes was forced upon them by their competition with the "little eyases." A final analysis of the effect of the child actors upon the development of the dramatic lyric would have to take into consideration the entire Tudor drama and so is precluded by the limits of this study ; but light can be thrown on some aspects of it. It can be shown, moreover, that the frequency of song depended to some extent upon the company for which particular plays were designed.

1. E.g., Richards, *The Tragedy of Messallina,* v, iv: "After this song (which was left out of the Play in regard there was none could sing in Parts) Enter . . ."
2. Middleton, *The Spanish Gypsy,* I, v ; III, i ; v, i.
3. Fletcher and Massinger, *The False One,* I, i ; IV, iii.
4. Heywood, *A Woman Killed with Kindness,* v, ii, iii.

A comparison of the use of song by different companies must of necessity involve statistics, but statistical precision in regard to the songs is almost impossible. Most of the difficulties arise in definition. Where should the line be drawn between formal songs and informal snatches? How can one tell whether a given lyric passage is meant to be sung or declaimed if neither dialogue nor stage directions make the author's intention clear? When should a conjectural song be allowed and when not? One cannot defend one's judgment in every questionable case—not, at least, in a single volume. But for a preliminary investigation it may be sufficient to say, without defining or defending my standards, that I have tried to apply them impartially to all doubtful cases. The body of material is so large and the facts are so clear that almost any other reasonable set of standards would give substantially the same results as does the set I have used.

Of 132 plays which, according to Harbage, were performed by the King's Men between 1601 and 1642, almost exactly 75 per cent call for song. There is a perceptible curve of distribution, the bulk of the plays without song occurring before about 1611 and after about 1635. This curve is at least partly determined by the principal poets of the company. Shakespeare is the only consistent exponent of song in the first decade of the century; then come Beaumont and Fletcher, whose fluent lyrical gifts were appreciated not only by the public but by a school of imitators who continued to produce for some years after Fletcher's death. Here is another factor undermining the accuracy of statistics. It is less significant in the case of the King's Men, where the body of plays is large, than it is in the case of, say, Queen Anne's Men, many of whose surviving plays were written by Heywood during the period when he simply did not use song. All the investigator can do is to recognize clearly this and the other factors which may distort his results and then to go ahead with his study hoping that the trends indicated will be marked enough to warrant at least generalized conclusions.

It is unfortunate that there is no other single company with an active career lasting throughout the Stuart period to which the King's Men might be compared; it is unfortunate, too, that the plays surviving from the repertoires of some of the other companies are too few in number to afford an accurate index to their dramatic practices. But despite all these difficulties it will still be possible to learn something from an examination of what material is available.

The first decade of the seventeenth century saw two children's companies enjoying popularity. The one known successively as the Children of the Chapel, of the Queen's Revels, and of Blackfriar's preserved a reasonably distinct entity between 1600 and 1613. Of 29 plays which it performed during those years, about 72 per cent employ formal song, with an average of approximately 2.4 songs per play. During the same period 39 titles acted by the King's Men average about 1.4 songs per play, with formal songs present in about 49 per cent of the plays. The incidence of song is even higher in the plays produced by Paul's Boys than in those done by the Queen's Revels company.

In general, though the children's plays do not show many singing lines, they make more exacting demands than the adults' in the way of actor-singers. Jonson's *Cynthia's Revels* is an extreme case; in it singing is required of the actors who portrayed Echo, Prosaites (and possibly Gelaia and Cos), Hedon (who also must play on the lyra), Amorphus, Hesperus, Phantaste, Asotus (a snatch only), and, if Gifford's assignment of the final song be accepted, Crites and Mercury[5]—between five and eleven people who must both sing and act. More commonly only two or three are required; *The Knight of the Burning Pestle,* for example, calls for five named characters to sing, but two of them do so "within."[6] In comparison, the most demanding play done by the King's Men during the same period is *The Tempest,* which requires songs of Ariel, Juno and Ceres in the masque, and Stephano and Caliban (who sing drunkenly and need have no real ability in music).

Certainly the conclusion is justified that during this decade song was used much more widely by the children's companies than by the adult ones. The qualification "during this decade" must be stressed, however, for during the eleven years from 1615 to 1625 the King's Men performed 38 new plays, 89 per cent of which contain songs; the average content is 2.8 songs per play. In other words, during these years the King's Men used song more freely than had the Children of the Chapel at the peak of their career. In six plays which Middleton wrote for Paul's Boys, the average incidence of song is 1.67 per play; in six plays which he wrote later for the King's Men, the average is 3.5 songs per play. This latter comparison is significant because it is not affected by the personalities of different authors.

It is to be emphasized, then, that the extensive use of song was by no means limited to children's companies. The directors of the children saw its advantages first, indeed, but when the King's Men realized its dramatic value they made the most of it.

The King's Men used song more than most of the rival adult troupes. Of 32 plays performed between 1602 and 1623 by the company known successively as Worcester's, Queen Anne's, and the Red Bull (Revels), only about 38 per cent call for song, and the average content is about 0.8 songs per play. During the same years the King's Men acted 69 plays, of which

5. The early editions give no indication who is to sing the song. Gifford's assignment apparently was made on grounds of dramatic propriety; but neither Mercury nor Crites sings elsewhere, and there is no real reason why Amorphus and Phantaste, who have just sung the palinode, should not do this song as well.

6. Merrythought, Jasper, and Luce sing on stage, as does at least one anonymous boy; Michael and Venturewell sing "within."

about 69 per cent call for song, the average content being about 2.1 songs per play. Even allowing for the fallibility of the statistics, one is safe in concluding that the King's Men used song about twice as lavishly as Queen Anne's Men.

The same partiality to song is characteristic of the King's Men in later years. Queen Henrietta's company, during its career from about 1625 to 1636, acted about 34 plays, of which 47 per cent contain formal songs; the King's Men did 40 plays, with 78 per cent containing songs. The plays acted by Queen Henrietta's Men average about 0.9 songs per play, those of the King's Men about 1.85 songs per play. Once again, the statistics may not be accurate, but a difference of 100 per cent allows plenty of room for error and still shows convincingly that the King's Men were a singing troupe compared with their major rivals. In fact, only the two metropolitan companies which played under the name of the Lady Elizabeth's Men seem, during their brief careers, to have given the King's Men much competition in the use of music.

Identical conclusions can be reached by other methods. For example, of the eleven plays which Massinger wrote for the King's Men, only one is without a song; of six plays which he wrote for other companies, only one contains a song. Brome used slightly more song in his plays for the King's Men than in the plays he wrote for Beeston's Boys, a company which contained an unusually high proportion of children, supposedly good singers.[7]

These statistics warrant two conclusions. Compared to its longest-lived rivals, the group known as the King's Men was a highly musical one; its use of song may have been a factor in its continued success, along with its superior stables of actors and poets. More generally, the "personality" of an acting company exerted a definite effect on the amount of singing in its plays.

Comparing the children's companies with the adult ones, one must grant that during the lifetime of Paul's and the Queen's Revels the children did make more use of song. Traditional opinion is corroborated to that extent. But after the demise of the children's companies, the adults used song fully as much as the children had before. There is probably no single explanation for this phenomenon. Perhaps the public had become accustomed to song by 1613 and, with no children's companies to supply it, the adults were forced to do so. Perhaps Richmond Noble is at least partly right in thinking that among the writers for the adult companies only Shakespeare at first recognized the dramatic potentialities of song and that it took some time for his pioneering and the technical experimen-

---

7. The later King's Revels was another such company. Oddly enough, it was from one of its plays, Richards' *The Tragedy of Messallina*, that a song had to be omitted "in regard there was none could sing in Parts." Evidently the later "boys'" companies were less musical than the children's troupes of a generation before.

tation of Chapman and Marston to find acceptance on the public stage.[8] In some cases (this is true at least of the first Lady Elizabeth's Men), as the children grew up and were absorbed into adult companies, they took their musical ability with them.[9]

It seems certain, however, that there is no qualitative difference between the songs of the children's plays and those of the adults'. Moore thought otherwise. He argued that "the songs of the Children tended to be, from first to last, decorative rather than dramatic in character."[1] His reasons, as I understand them, are that the children sang polyphonic music, that there are in their plays no extant songs "comparable in dramatic poignancy" with Ophelia's or with "Hark, hark, the lark," and that most of their songs are blank, whereas those of the adults are usually intact.

Whatever may be said of the Tudor drama, these arguments do not apply to the children's companies of the seventeenth century. In the first place, it has been shown above that the psychological effect of song derives essentially from the music rather than from the words, so that, under the right conditions, a polyphonic song may be fully as dramatic as an "ayre." But Moore may overestimate the amount of polyphonic singing that went on in the children's plays: much of their song was solo work, and it is difficult for one person to sing polyphony.[2] "Here they sing prick-song" is a unique stage direction and occurs in an adults' play.[3] Moore's second test is inconclusive: where else even in the adult drama can one find songs comparable in dramatic poignancy to Shakespeare's best? As for the third point, it has been demonstrated already that a song's being "blank" and its dramatic functionalism are quite unrelated matters. Moore says elsewhere that "the earlier plays . . . of Marston are without songs."[4] But Marston's first four plays (according to Harbage's chronology) contain directions calling for twenty-eight songs and about seven brief snatches.[5] All these songs cannot be called decorative simply because most of their texts have been lost. To prove to oneself that the songs of the children's plays were functional, one need only glance through the notes for the earlier chapters of this study and see how fre-

8. Noble, *op. cit.*, p. 12.

9. Frederick S. Boas, *An Introduction to Stuart Drama* (Oxford, Oxford University Press, 1946), p. 11.

1. Moore, "The Songs of the Public Theaters in the Time of Shakespeare," p. 172.

2. E.g., in Marston's *Antonio and Mellida* there are 7 formal songs, of which 3 are probably, 3 more are indubitably, solos. The stage directions for the former 3 are uniformly "Cantant," but the contexts indicate each to be by a single voice. Only one song can, with any assurance, be called polyphonic.

3. Middleton, *More Dissemblers besides Women,* v, i; the prick-song is part of a singing lesson.

4. Moore, "The Function of the Songs in Shakespeare's Plays," p. 80.

5. *Antonio and Mellida* (1599), 7 formal songs; *Antonio's Revenge* (1599), 6; *Histrio-Mastix* (1599), 8; *Jack Drum's Entertainment* (1600), 7. This is more songs than are contained in all Marston's other plays together.

quently the children's plays of Marston, Chapman, and Middleton are cited in illustration of dramatic techniques.

In fact, if the development of the dramatic lyric owes a special debt to any single man within the period covered by this study, that man probably is Marston, who wrote only for the children. Reed is right in saying that Shakespeare did little to enlarge the range of song in the drama;[6] but Marston was an innovator, and a highly ingenious one. He used almost every song situation that was to become important later; he was particularly skillful with the technique of reversal developed so tellingly by Fletcher. Perhaps the effectiveness of the later dramatic lyric is due to the fact that it had a joint parentage, with Marston's uninhibited originality and Shakespeare's contribution toward beauty, poignancy, and fitness merging to make the song a flexible and powerful instrument in the hands of the best playwrights even while it became a technical device so conventionalized that the less able writers could hardly go wrong with it.

4. The Changing Times

The mechanical process of arranging in chronological order the plays of the Stuart period and their songs makes clear a trend which cannot easily be presented in charts or footnotes but which suggests a critical generalization that may be worth expressing despite its subjective nature.

Not only in the plays of the King's Men but in the Stuart drama in general, the songs of the earlier playwrights are an easy, natural form of expression to the characters who sing them. This truth is manifested particularly in the free use of song snatches—bits of familiar songs and ballads, quoted, adapted, or paraphrased. These characters sing as though song were part of their normal, everyday life and as though that life were an unsophisticated but a cheerful, busy, ebullient one—the sort the Elizabethan life is usually represented to have been. As the decades pass, however, the easy snatches gradually disappear and the set songs tend toward ever greater formality. The later dramatists polish their lyrics and set them up as showpieces which, while they continue to fulfill some of the old dramatic functions, reflect more and more the somewhat stilted nature of the love-and-honor drama. A few derivative writers, like Brome and Glapthorne, retain the old zest and vitality; the other dramatists— Ford, Shirley, D'Avenant—display occasional flashes of it, but in general they take care that their good manners show.

If the drama of the Caroline years is decadent, surely that decadence is symbolized by this change in the use of song. It is a matter of getting away from the vitality of real life, a sort of embarrassment at the unin-

---

6. Reed, *op. cit.*, pp. 352–3. Reed's statement has consistently enraged Shakespeare-lovers who have not stopped to consider exactly what it means.

hibited display of the normal, hearty emotions of normal, hearty people. Something like it is taking place on the modern stage and has already taken place in the cinema. In the Caroline drama the effect was a careful sifting of the passions represented, the ideal being to portray not those of everyday life but only the artificial, conventionalized ones of a high society faced perpetually by dilemmas of love and honor. In the twentieth century the effect is apparent not so much in the subject matter as in the acting; it is a far cry from the emotion of the silent films to the deadpan screen acting of today, and some of the more thoughtful critics are even now warning against the underacting which insidiously is usurping the legitimate stage.[7] In either case the cause is the same—a fear of honest emotion; and although the symptoms are different, the end must be the same, too—the strangulation of any truly vital drama.

It is easy to see why the dramatic lyric should be a peculiarly sensitive mirror of developments such as these. The earlier chapters of this study have demonstrated that song was essentially the spontaneous outpouring of the basic emotions of joy, grief, or love, and that it was the most effective instrument for inducing in the audience an empathic response to these emotions as represented on the stage. But when the Caroline audiences no longer found intellectual satisfaction in the dramatic presentation of these emotions and no longer wanted to be made to feel them deeply, then the real function of the song was destroyed. Although formal lyrics still occurred in the situations where song had become conventional, the core of genuine emotion in these situations was largely forgotten, and the song took on the empty superficiality of any convention which has outlived the conditions which first gave it meaning. But when one is tempted to lament the end of a glorious period, one must remember to be grateful that the period existed and that it has left a heritage of incomparable plays whose vitality owes no small debt to their incomparable lyrics.

7. E.g., Kurt Pinthus, "A Plea for More Expressive Acting," *New York Times,* Theater Section, Sunday, February 1, 1948, x and x3. John Gielgud had expressed a similar opinion two weeks earlier in an interview with Murray Shumach: "British View of Our Audiences," *New York Times,* Theater Section, Sunday, January 18, 1948, x and x3.

AFTERWORD

IT IS APOLOGETICALLY that one adds a few hundred pages to the mountains of scholarship on the Tudor and Stuart drama. The burrower in those mountains is likely to be overwhelmed by double endings and anagrams, by opinion and dissent—to lose his sense of values and to forget the very fact he should remember : that he is dealing with a corpus of plays to which ordinary people went for enjoyment. Enjoyment should even today be the reason for turning to these plays.

If there is justification for a study such as this, it lies in the fact that enjoyment is to some degree dependent on understanding. As a dramatic idiom becomes obsolete, our understanding of the plays in which it is used is narrowed, and our enjoyment of those plays is correspondingly reduced. The dramatic lyric is such an idiom. We can admire it as pure poetry, but it does not mean to us what it meant to its original audience. The rediscovery of that original meaning should increase our understanding of the plays exploiting it and, in consequence, our enjoyment of them. We may be able to regain some of the zest of a Stuart audience if we can visualize their drama as produced rather than as printed, and if we can transport ourselves in imagination into their theater. At the same time, a different kind of pleasure is gained from the ability to contemplate intelligently the craftsmanship of the Stuart dramatists. Finally, there is still a fourth kind of satisfaction in fitting together a piece or two of the broken urn—in contributing, no matter how little, to the restoration of a given play text to what it was originally. These are the ends toward which this study has been aimed.

APPENDIX

Explanatory Note

THE FOLLOWING information is appended for two reasons: it may be useful as reference material for other students of the dramatic lyric and it presents most of the evidence supporting the conclusions of this study. There are, of course, frequent instances of the use of instrumental music under precisely the same "rules" as those for the song;[1] occasionally, too, a song will be proposed under significant circumstances but not actually performed.[2] These passages would corroborate the evidence of the songs proper, but considerations of space prevent their inclusion.

The songs are listed by author and play to provide a partial index to the text. Page references are to the text above. An italicized page reference indicates detailed discussion of the song in question; other symbols used in this appendix are as follows:

* indicates a snatch or fragment, not a formal and complete song.

t after a page reference indicates that the discussion concerns textual rather than literary matters.

ANONYMOUS
Claudius Tiberius Nero
 "Can Livia still participate this air?" xxvi; N2r, v
 A seven-stanza lyric of the "come sweet Death" order, either sung or declaimed by Livia just before she leaps to her death to become the fifteenth corpse in this play.
The Country Girl [by "T. B."]
 Wordless singing ii, i
 Gillian, pleasurably excited, sings to accompany her own dancing; this is an exit device.
 Blank song v, ii; p. 6 n.
 "Applied to my Ladyes melancholie" over the plight of her lover, who is in hiding after supposedly killing a man in a duel, this song combines elements of the complaint and the therapeutic song.
Every Woman in Her Humour
 Solmization (attributed wrongly [?] to Servulas) i; A4v; pp. 37, 88–9
 "Here's none but only I"* i; B1r; pp. 37, 88–9
 "Sleep, wayward thoughts"* i; B1v; pp. 37, 88–9
 "All hail to my beloved"* i; B2r; pp. 37, 88–9
 "Sad despair doth drive me hence"* i; B2v; pp. 37, 88–9

1. E.g., the instrumental serenade provided by Deliro for his wife Fallace in Jonson, *Every Man Out of His Humour,* iv, ii.
 2. E.g., the drinking song demanded of Britannicus in May, *The Tragedy of Julia Agrippina,* iv, iv.

"For I did but kiss her"* iii ; D3v, 4r ; pp. 37, 88–9
"Sister, awake, close not . . ."* iii ; D3v, 4r ; pp. 37, 88–9
"Coll her and clip her, and kiss her too"* iii ; D3v, 4r ; pp. 37, 88–9
"The friar was in the . . ."* and solmization v ; E1v ; pp. 37, 88–9
"And then to Apollo, hollo trees hollo"* vii ; G1r ; pp. 37, 88–9
"Here's none but . . ."* vii ; G1r ; pp. 37, 88–9
"Fortune my foe"* (attributed to Graccus) vii ; G3r ; pp. 37, 88–9

Philautus is a singing character who is constantly bursting into snatches of identifiable songs, some but not all of which are noted by Reed. The dozen snatches listed are probably all his. Reed transfers "Fortune my foe" to him from Graccus, and the solmization would be more appropriate to him than to Servulas. "All hail" and "Sad despair" are first lines but may not actually be sung. Reed identifies as another song snatch (I think wrongly) Philautus' question on B1v, "Is it not now most amiable and fair?"

Probable blank catch v ; E1v

A drinking catch by Philautus, Graccus, and Acutus is required by the dialogue.

"My love can sing no other song" viii ; H2r

Philautus, arrested, is pardoned when he sings this song, apparently in full, though not quite two lines are printed.

"Chaunt birds in every bush" viii ; H2v

This song, part of a comic hymeneal masque at the end of the play, is sung by the Host, Cornutus, and others; Reed seems in error when he attributes it to Philautus.

The Faithful Friends

"Hark, oh, hark, you valiant soldiers" i, ii ; p. 56

A drinking song by Bellario and the impressed artisans; only the first three lines are printed.

Blank song ii, iii ; p. 56

A catch by Bellario and his artisan-soldiers as they buy a drink from the sutler.

"Then farewell the drum, pike, gun, and the fife" iv, v ; p. 56

A comic mock-ritual song by Bellario as the artisan-soldiers hang up their arms in the temple of Mars, vowing never to go to war again.

The Ghost

Wordless singing iv, iv ; p. 33 n.

Philarchus sings to accompany his own dancing, which is indicative of wantonness and amorous anticipation.

"Come, Cloris, hie we to the bower"* v, i

This song is demanded by Philarchus as a sexual stimulant and is sung by the bawd Erotia; but since the same song has been selected as a recognition signal by Engin and Valerio, to be used during a scene in a dark cave with several characters in disguise, its performance results in comic confusions of identity.

The Honest Lawyer [by "S. S."]

"Even as the bird, which we chameleon call" III, i ; E4v

Nice, defending drunkenness caused by poetry as preferable to drunkenness caused by liquor, probably sings a comic "sonnet" intended later for his mistress.

"Mun tut, &c"* v, ii; I2r

Bromley apparently sings in drunkenness or anticipation of drunkenness. Cf. Brome, *The Northern Lass*, III, ii.

The Knave in Grain

"And ever he gave her a bob" III, ii

Stultissimo apparently sings a quatrain in joy, elation, and amorous anticipation.

"Clink, boys, drink, boys"* III, v

"In ample stories written 'tis" III, v

Lodwick, Thomaso, and Stultissimo sing a fragment of a catch as they begin a drinking party in a tavern; later a fiddler and "Rupert's noise" perform a song for their entertainment.

"Then three merry men, and three merry men be we"* IV, vii

Julio, arrested by two sergeants, apparently sings an ironic snatch.

Solmization v, i

Stultissimo, for no apparent reason.

Note that in I, iii and iv, Stultissimo projects a love song to be sung to Dulciflora; this song is not sung, however, because Fub, the intended singer, is hoarse.

Look about You

"All alone, making moan"* G2r

Block, a clownish servant, may sing an internally rhymed line in a facetious mood.

Possible blank song H2v; p. 76 n.

Prince Richard, an unsuccessful suitor to the Lady Marian, here brings musicians to sing her a song; though a stage direction is lacking, it seems likely that they actually sing it, for a moment later Robin Hood enters, disguised as Marian, to ask that the music be dismissed.

The Merry Devil of Edmonton

"Poor Milliscent" II, iii

The comic servant Bilbo has a doggerel comment on Milliscent's entering a nunnery; if he sings it, as Oliphant for one thinks he does, the snatch is comic and covers his exit.

Narcissus

"Gentles all" Induction

An overture song by a group of wassailers come to entertain the Twelfth-night company; this group then presents the play proper.

"Hark, they cry, I hear by that" vi; p. 72 n.

A hunting song by Narcissus and his friends. There is nothing in the scene but the song; it evidently is meant to stand for the entire hunt after which Narcissus is so thirsty as to drink from the fountain.

Nero

Blank song III, iv; p. 43

Nero sings in evil exultation as Rome burns.

The Partial Law

Blank song III, iii

Three servingmen sing a catch in comic rehearsal of a song to be used later in courtship.

Philotus

"Were Jacob's sons more joyful for to see" stanzas 161–4

Sung by the "foure Lufearis" as a joyful sort of hymeneal song which amounts almost to a finale; interesting as occurring in what seems to be a closet drama.

"What if a day or a month or a year" (appended) pp. 108, 109

This song, appended in Q 1603 but missing from Q 1612, is identified by the editor as Campion's; cf. Brome, *The Queen and Concubine*.

The Return from Parnassus, I

"Now listen, all good people" II, iv

Luxurio sets up as a ballad-maker and -seller; this song, by his boy, is his advertisement: a realistic song, an exit song, and a parody of the ballad to match an earlier parody of Shakespeare.

The Return from Parnassus, II

"How can he sing whose voice is hoarse with care?" v, i

Philomusus combines an expression of private grief with a rehearsal of his disguise as a strolling musician. Cf. Wild, *The Benefice,* IV, i.

The Second Maiden's Tragedy

"If ever pity were well placed" IV, iv

A dirge sung by a boy while Govianus mourns at the tomb of the Lady. There is possible irony in that the Tyrant has removed her body from her tomb; the song may also help to prepare for the entrance of the Lady's ghost a moment later.

"Oh, what is beauty that's so much adored?" v, ii

A song, half dirge and half macabre serenade, as the Tyrant stands looking at and kissing the hands of the dead body of the Lady.

Swetnam the Woman Hater

"Whilst we sing the doleful knell" IV, iii

A dirge as Leonida is led ceremonially across the stage to be executed.

The Two Merry Milkmaids [by "J. C."]

"For he did but so, so . . ."* I, ii; p. 75 n.

A snatch in ridicule of Dorilus' love-making by the madcap Julia.

"The maids they went a milking" I, ii

An entrance snatch: Frederick's comic way of disclosing that he has overheard the girls' plan to disguise as milkmaids and that his silence will have to be bought.

"Fortune my foe, why dost thou frown on me"* III, i

A comic-rueful entrance snatch by Frederick, under sentence of banishment with his family.

Blank song v, i; p. 81 n.

Act V of this play is pure vaudeville; this song is part of the entertainment but ostensibly is performed to allow time for the contestants in a comic rhyming contest to compose their verses.

The Two Noble Ladies

Blank song v, ii

A supernaturally provided song designed by the scholar-magician Cyprian as part of his attempt to seduce Justina.

Two Wise Men and All the Rest Fools

Wordless singing VII, i; p. 37

Insatiato sings to accompany his own dancing. This is a stock method of characterizing an empty, frivolous courtier; cf. Jonson's Asotus, Shirley's Startup and Volterre.

The Wit of a Woman

Probable wordless singing v; CIv

The Doctor may sing briefly in the grip of amorous excitement or amorous imaginings.

"Sir snuff with your huff"* ("Farewell Signor Snot"?) xv; G3v

"I am as you see, sir"* xv; G3v

These are rhymed bits by two servants; if sung, they indicate drunkenness and general impudence. For the first, cf. Dekker, *Northward Ho,* I, iii.

ARMIN, ROBERT

The Two Maids of More-Clacke p. 118

Possible blank song AIv

A song would be appropriate for the wedding procession of Mrs. Humil and Vergir and may be indicated by the dialogue. This situation is ironic: Humil, an Elizabethan Enoch Arden, watches and comments on the "solemne shewe of the marriage."

"And was not good King Solomon"* (also "Tom Tyler"?) C3v

Disjointed snatches by the feeble-minded John of the Hospital. Solmization by boy C4r

"A maiden sitting all alone" C4v

An aspect of Toures's disguise as a drunken tinker, which he assumes in order to see his sweetheart Mary; the boy sets the pitch, evidently, and Toures sings the song.

"Mortal down, thistle soft"* ("Mary Ambree"?) D3r

A clown snatch in veiled ridicule of the jilted lover Filbon

The Valiant Welshman

Blank song ("a Welsh song") II, i; pp. 60 n., 74 n., 90

A conventional wedding-masque song, followed by a Fletcher reversal: the summoning of the groom to war.

BARRY, LODOWICK

Ram-Alley

"And three merry men, and three merry men"* II, i

A snatch by Will Smallshanks in exultation over the success of a trick, self-satisfaction.

Probable blank song v, ii; p. 20 n.

The dialogue demands a conventional serenade by musicians for a ridiculous and unsuccessful suitor; it is marked by comic irony, develops comic suspense, and is followed by an absurd reversal.

Blank song v, iii; p. 71 n.

The concluding speech calls for "an old song"; although there is no stage direction for it, there obviously must be an epilogue or finale song.

BEAUMONT, FRANCIS, and FLETCHER, JOHN

Beggar's Bush

"Cast our caps and cares away" ii, i; p. 56

A mock-ritual song celebrating the coronation of Claus as king of the beggars.

"Have ye any work for the sow-gelder, ho?" iii, i; pp. 68 n., 74 n., 82 n.

"Take her and hug her" iii, i; pp. 68 n., 74 n., 82 n.

"He ran at me first in the shape of a ram" iii, i; pp. 68 n., 74 n., 82 n., 90 n., 103 n.

Obscene comic songs, sung by the amiable outlaw Higgen, disguised as a sow-gelder, to several boors drinking in a tavern, by way of preparation for picking their pockets a few moments later.

"Bring out your coney-skins, fair maids, to me" iii, i; p. 68 n.

A cry-song like the first by Higgen, this is sung by a boy accompanying Claus, who is also in disguise.

The Bloody Brother

"Drink today and drown all sorrow" ii, ii

Four comic servants rehearse a drinking song for the banquet to celebrate the newly sealed friendship between Rollo and Otto; a few lines later Latorch enters and persuades them to poison Otto's food and drink.

"Come, Fortune's a whore, I care not who tell her" iii, ii; p. 76

The servants pause on their way to the gallows to sing their own "hanging ballad."

"Take, oh, take those lips away" v, ii; pp. *28*, 71 n.

Edith, planning to murder Rollo, provides a seduction song to arouse his lust and thus ensure the damnation of his soul.

Bonduca pp. 88 n., 94

Blank song ii, ii

Junius, hopelessly in love with Bonduca's daughter, sings a love complaint, which is burlesqued behind his back by Petillius.

Blank processional singing and blank song iii, i

Pagan ritual singing by the Druids at a sacrifice.

"Smooth was his cheek" iv, i

Four young Roman officers enter singing a catch in high spirits at Junius' escape from death and his liberation from his love for Bonduca's daughter.

"She set the sword unto her breast"* v, ii

"It was an old tale, ten thousand times told"* v, ii

Petillius has fallen in love with the manner in which Bonduca's eldest daughter has committed suicide, and Junius proceeds to pay back Petillius' earlier ridicule of his love. Dyce identifies the first snatch as adapted from the ballad "Little Musgrave and Lady Barnard."

The Captain

"Tell me, dearest, what is love" II, ii; p. 83 n.

Frank and Clora sing an essentially undramatic duet.

"Away, delights, go seek some other dwelling" III, iv; pp. *49–50*

Lelia, seeking to win back her estranged suitor Julio, provides a "sad song" to soften him up emotionally before she talks with him.

"Come hither, you that love, and hear me sing" IV, v; IV, iv, in FF; p. *50*

A song provided by Lelia as part of her preparations for her attempt to seduce a tough old man. Since the man she has chosen turns out to be her father, the situation is ironic and turns into a reversal.

The Chances

"Merciless Love, whom nature hath denied" II, ii; pp. *76*, 103 n., 124

Constantia No. 1, her love affair apparently thwarted, sings a love complaint; comedy is achieved when two servants mistake her voice for that of a devil. This song is part of the build-up to the comedy of errors in IV, iii.

Blank song (the ballad of "John Dory") III, ii; pp. 37, 89

Antonio, wounded, insists on being "opened" to the warlike tune of "John Dory"; this situation characterizes Antonio and burlesques the conventional therapeutic song.

"Welcome, sweet liberty, and care, farewell" IV, iii; pp. 6 n., *76*, 103 n., 124

Possible blank song IV, iii; pp. 6n., *76*, 124

Constantia No. 2, a courtesan, sings during a drinking party; her song is overheard by the Duke, who mistakes the voice for that of the pure Constantia No. 1 and racks his brain to reconcile the nature of the song with the character of the supposed singer.

"Come away, thou lady gay" v, iii; pp. 103 n., 121

A sham-supernatural song, part of the hocus-pocus by which the conjurer Vecchio restores Constantia No. 1 to the Duke.

The Coxcomb

Possible blank song I, ii

The dialogue demands a song by Maria to entertain her party guests; Sympson, Weber, Dyce, and others thought that this song was actually sung.

"Thou art over long at thy pot, Tom, Tom" I, vi

"Then set your foot to my foot, and up tails all"* I, vi

A drunken catch by Ricardo and his three friends, sung at their entrance and exit, and a drunken snatch by Silvio.

Cupid's Revenge

"Lovers, rejoice! your pains shall be rewarded" I, ii; pp. *53–4,* 60

A pagan ritual song in Cupid's temple, followed by a Fletcher reversal.

Possible blank song v, iv; p. 6 n.

The dialogue indicates a song by Urania to soothe and cheer the depressed and sleepless Leucippus; the need for this song seems to have gone unnoticed by editors of Beaumont and Fletcher. If sung, it makes possible an effective reversal.

The Custom of the Country
Blank song I, ii; p. 61

A "sad epithalamion": Zenocia is married to Arnoldo, but the tyrannical governor Clodio demands the observance of an old custom giving him the right to the first night with every bride. The mood is reversed almost immediately by the escape of the bridal couple.

Blank song III, ii

A "lusty song" forming part of Hippolyta's attempt to seduce Arnoldo.

The Double Marriage
Possible blank song II, i; p. 6 n.

The Gunner calls for a song to "shake the Duke from his dumps," but there is no stage direction to indicate that one was actually performed.

The Elder Brother
Blank song IV, iv; p. 88

A "sprightly" song is part of Brisac's attempt to seduce Lilly, the wife of his servant.

The Fair Maid of the Inn
Blank song v, iii; pp. 59–60

Performed as guests gather for the wedding of Mentivole and Clarissa, this is presumably a hymeneal song. It leads into a reversal when Alberto and Cesario burst in a few moments later to forbid the ceremony.

The Faithful Shepherdess p. 81
"Sing his praises that doth keep" I, ii

A pagan ritual song, part of a shepherds' ceremony in honor of Pan.

"Come, shepherds, come" I, iii; p. 32 n.

A "sung soliloquy" giving frank expression to the wantonness of Cloe, the lustful shepherdess.

"Do not fear to put thy feet" III, i

A love song to Amoret by the God of the River, an unsuccessful suitor.

"All ye woods and trees and bowers" v, v

A pagan ritual song to Pan, serving also to clear the stage and amounting almost to a finale.

The False One
"Look out, bright eyes, and bless the air" I, ii; p. 71 n.

A cheering serenade arranged for the captive Cleopatra by her faithful servant and guardian Apollodorus; it develops an impressive first entrance for her, and her response to it has characterizing value.

"Isis, the goddess of this land" III, iv

"Come, let us help the reverend Nile" III, iv

"Here comes the aged river now" III, iv

"Make room for my rich waters' fall" III, iv

These four songs are part of a masque arranged by Ptolemy to make Caesar forget Cleopatra temporarily; it succeeds, but it also, by its display of the wealth of Egypt, arouses Caesar's covetousness and so helps to motivate the later action.

Four Plays in One

"Martius, rejoice! Jove sends me from above" "Triumph of Honor"

A sham-supernatural song accompanying the removal of the rocks (this play uses the plot of Chaucer's Franklin's Tale).

Three blank songs "Triumph of Time"

Indians sing around Plutus; Simplicity and the other friends of Anthropos "sing the world's shame"; Jupiter has singers perform in honor of Anthropos.

Blank song or singing "Triumph of Death"

The villain Lavall's evil spirit reminds him of all his crimes, sings his "knell," and leaves him to be killed by Gabriella.

Note that "singing" is called for also as part of the triumphal processions of Love, Death, and Time.

The Honest Man's Fortune

Blank song III, i; pp. 60, 83 n.

A "sad song" by Veramour to soothe the unhappy Duchess; this song leads into a Fletcher reversal on the entrance of Montague, fainting, his sword drawn, as the music ends.

The Humorous Lieutenant

"Rise from the shades below" IV, iii

"I obey, I obey" IV, iii

The first song is sung by a magician who is conjuring up spirits to help him prepare a love philter; the second is the spirits' response.

The Island Princess

Probable blank song II, i; p. 43

The dialogue requires the captive King of Tidore to show his fortitude by singing in prison; Dyce noted this passage.

Blank singing II, viii

Boys sing for joy in the triumphal procession celebrating the liberation of the captive King.

The Knight of Malta

"Sit, soldiers, sit and sing, the round is clear" III, i; pp. 56, 103 n.

A drinking song by the military watch.

"See, see the stain of honor, virtue's foe" V, ii; p. 56

"Fair child of virtue, honor's bloom" V, ii; p. 56

Ritualistic songs, accompanying the ceremonies of the degrading of a Knight of Malta and the investiture of another.

The Knight of the Burning Pestle pp. 81–2, 127

"Nose, nose, jolly red nose"* I, iv

"But yet, or ere you part (oh, cruel!)"* I, iv

"Heigh-ho, farewell, Nan"* I, iv

"When earth and seas from me are reft"* I, iv

"When it was grown to dark midnight"* ("Fair Margaret and Sweet William") II, viii

"I am three merry men, and three merry men"* II, viii

"Troll the black bowl to me"* II, viii

"As you came from Walsingham"* II, viii

"Why, an if she be, what care I"* II, viii

"He set her on a milk-white steed"* ("The Douglas Tragedy" and other ballads) II, viii

"Down, down, down they fall"* II, viii

"She cares not for her daddy, nor"* II, viii

"Give him flowers enow, palmer, give him flowers enow"* II, viii

"Was never man for lady's sake"* ("The Legend of Sir Guy") II, viii

"If you will sing and dance and laugh"* III, v

"Go from my window, love, go"* III, v; p. 75 n.

"Begone, begone, my juggy, my puggy"* III, v; p. 75 n.

"I come not hither for thee to teach"* III, v

Cf. Brewer, *The Love-Sick King,* II, i, and Jonson, *The New Inn,*
IV, ii.

"You are no love for me, Margaret"* III, v

"Who can sing a merrier note"* IV, v

A round in Ravenscroft's *Pammelia.*

"I would not be a servingman"* IV, v

"For Jillian of Berry, she dwells on a hill"* IV, v

"Ho, ho, nobody at home"* IV, v

Ravenscroft, *Pammelia,* No. 85.

"Come no more there, boys, come no more there"* v, iii

"Sing we and chaunt it"* v, iii

Morley, *First Book of Balletts,* No. 4.

"Oh, the Mimon round"* v, iii

"Why, farewell he"* v, iii

"Thou art welcome from Stygian lake so soon"* v, iii

"And where is your true love, Oh, where is yours"* v, iii

"With hey, trixy, terlery-whiskin"* v, iii

"What voice is that that calleth at our door"* v, iii

"And some they whistled and some they sung"* ("Little Musgrave and Lady Barnard") v, iii

"If such danger be in playing"* v, iii

"With that came out his paramour"* v, iii

The foregoing thirty-four songs (so identified by Dyce, probably correctly) are sung in snatches of one to five lines by the comic singing character Merrythought; pp. 42–3, 80, 89

" 'Tis mirth that fills the veins with blood" II, viii

This self-characterizing soliloquy by Merrythought may be either declaimed or sung.

"Tell me, dearest, what is love" III, i; pp. 23 n., 68 n.

A love duet by Jasper and Luce, probably used to compress the dramatic statement of their love for each other. Cf. *The Captain,* II, ii.

"Come, you whose loves are dead" IV, iv; pp. 24, 60

A dirge by Luce over the bier of Jasper, culminating in a reversal when the supposed corpse sits up at the end of the song.

"It was a lady's daughter" v, iii; p. 89

"Fortune my foe" v, iii; p. 89

Merrythought forces Mick and then Venturewell to sing before he will admit them into his house.

"Better music ne'er was known" v, iii

This is apparently an epilogue song or finale, suggested by Merry-thought.

The Laws of Candy

Blank song III, iii; p. *20*

A serenade by musicians to Erota, for Philander, an eventually successful suitor who just at this point meets with a rebuff vigorous enough to constitute a reversal.

The Little French Lawyer

"Come away; bring on the bride" I, i; p. *59*

A hymeneal song as Lamira and Champernel return from the church; a reversal follows when the wedding procession is rudely interrupted by Dinant.

"He struck so hard, the bason broke"* II, iii; pp. *39–40*

La-Writ, victorious in his first duel, allows his joy and exultation to bubble over in scraps of song from the ballad "The Noble Acts of King Arthur."

"This way, this way come, and hear" IV, vi; p. *64* n.

This is a Pied Piper song arranged by kidnapers; the intended victims mistake it for a compliment being paid them by a tenant or a client and follow the music into the woods, where they are captured.

The Lover's Progress

"Adieu, fond love! farewell, you wanton powers" III, iv; pp. *6* n., *67*

A Novice sings the "farewell to love and women" of Lydian, who is turning hermit; the song has a plot function in that its heavenly effect determines Clarangé to become a friar, and so it begins the resolution of the subplot.

" 'Tis late and cold; stir up the fire" III, v; p. *121*

The Host's Ghost sings off stage before appearing to Cleander; this is unusual in being a humorous supernatural song.

Love's Cure

"Turn, turn thy beauteous face away" III, ii; pp. *20* n., *81*, *91* t

Piorato, developed as a singing character, sings to summon his sweetheart Malroda to an interview.

The Loyal Subject

"All you that are witty"* (a possibly sung snatch) II, i

Blank song II, i

The Ancient sings to show his contempt for the efforts of Borosky to win the affections of the army away from Archas—in this case by the bribery of double pay.

"The good old woman on a bed he threw"* III, ii; pp. *8–9*

An apparently sung snatch by Theodore in incredulous amazement at his father's blind loyalty.

"Broom, broom, the bonny broom" III, v; pp. *68* n., *82* n.

"The wars are done and gone" III, v; pp. *68* n., *82* n.

"I have fine potatoes" (a mere cry) III, v; pp. *68* n., *82* n.

" 'Will ye buy any honesty? come away" III, v; pp. *68* n., *82* n.

"Have ye any crack'd maidenheads to new-leech or mend" III, v; pp. 68 n., 82 n.

"If your daughters on their beds" III, v; pp. 68 n., 82 n.

These songs by the Ancient and his men have, among other purposes, the unsubtle satirizing of the immorality of the court; but the main reason for the singing of cry-songs is that it is part of the Ancient's plan to gather a striking force of soldiers together inside the city without arousing the suspicions of the citizens.

The Mad Lover

"Orpheus I am, come from the deeps below" IV, i

"Charon, O Charon" IV, i

These two songs by Stremon (assisted in the second by a boy) are done in an elaborate attempt to cure, or at least to soothe, Memnon in his madness.

"O fair sweet goddess, queen of love" v, i; p. 60

A processional pagan ritual song sung when Calis visits the temple of Venus. This song reverses an obtaining mood of low comedy and establishes a solemn tone for the serious scene which follows.

"Arm, arm, arm, arm! the scouts are all come in" v, iv

Stremon again sings to calm Memnon, mad.

The Maid in the Mill

"Come follow me, you country lasses" II, i; p. 64 n.

A seductive Pied Piper song aimed to draw Bustofa and, through him, Florimel to the country sports, whence she is to be kidnaped.

Blank song II, ii

Part of the country sports already mentioned, and indirectly part of a reversal, since the song and dance are followed by the kidnaping of Florimel, which is taken at first to belong to the action of the masque.

"Now, having leisure and a happy wind" v, ii; pp. 32, 82 n.

"How long shall I pine for love" v, ii; pp. 32, 82 n.

"On the bed I'll throw thee, throw thee down" v, ii; pp. 32, 82 n.

"Think me still" v, ii; pp. 32, 82 n.

"The young one, the old one" v, ii; pp. 32, 82 n.

Florimel, kidnaped and fighting to preserve her honor, gains time which eventually saves her when she cools the ardor of Otrante by feigning wantonness; these five songs are part of the pretense.

"It was a miller and a lord" v, ii; p. 121

The clown Bustofa sings for the comic effect of a smutty song, which, incidentally, gets him off the stage.

The Maid's Tragedy

"Cynthia, to thy power and thee" I, ii; p. 60

"Hold back thy hours, dark night, till we have done" I, ii; p. 60

"To bed, to bed! Come, Hymen, lead the bride" I, ii; pp. 60, 104

These songs are part of the masque in celebration of the marriage of Evadne to Amintor; the masque is followed subsequently, in Act II, by a Fletcher reversal.

"Lay a garland on my hearse" II, i; pp. 25 and n., 66, 95, 104

"I could never have the power" II, i; pp. 95, 104

Aspatia "sings for sorrow"; Dula sings to lighten the effect of gloom cast by Aspatia's song.

Monsieur Thomas

"And wilt thou be gone, says one" III, i

Thomas, Hylas, and Sam sing a catch in triumphant ridicule of Francisco's physicians.

"The Merchant's Daughter"* (title) III, iii; pp. 56 n., 77 n.

"Oh, what is that to you, my fool"* III, iii; pp. 56 n., 77 n.

"The twelfth of April, on May-day"* III, iii; pp. 56 n., 77 n.

"O damsel dear"* III, iii; pp. 56 n., 77 n.

"My man Thomas/Did me promise"* III, iii; pp. 56 n., 77 n.

"Come up to my window, love"* III, iii; pp. 56 n., 75 n., 77 n.

"The love of Greece, and it tickled him so"* III, iii; pp. 56 n., 77 n.

"And climbing to promotion"* III, iii; pp. 56 n., 77 n.

"All young men, be warned by me"* III, iii; pp. 56 n., 77 n.

These songs, mostly familiar ballads or adaptations of ballads, are sung in full or in part in the riotous scene in which Thomas serenades Mary. Comedy comes both from the burlesque of the traditional serenade and from the patness of the snatches to the situation on the stage.

"If this be true, thou little tiny page"* IV, ii

Sebastian, in half-incredulous joy, sings a snatch from "Little Musgrave and Lady Barnard"; cf. Lord Feesimple in Field, *Amends for Ladies,* IV, ii.

Blank singing V, iv; V, iii, in F

Off-stage choral singing sets the scene and mood as outside a Christian nunnery.

The Nice Valor (The Passionate Madman)

"Thou deity, swift-winged love" II, i; p. 38 n.

The mad Passionate Lord sings in his love fit.

"Oh, turn thy bow" II, i

Part of a short masque designed to soothe and please the mad Lord.

"Hence, all you vain delights" III, iii; p. 38 n.

"A curse upon thee for a slave" III, iii; pp. 38 n., 76

The mad Lord sings in his melancholy and his angry fits; the latter song provides the comedy of incongruity in that the Lord beats Lapet in time to the music.

"Oh, how my lungs do tickle! ha, ha, ha" V, i; p. 38 n.

Joined by Base, the mad Lord sings in his laughing fit.

The Night-Walker (The Little Thief)

Blank singing of ballads III, iv; p. 65

Lurcher and Alathe, disguised as peddlers, give free ballads to the servants of Justice Algripe; the servants gather in an outhouse to try out the ballads, and under cover of the noise of their singing, Lurcher and Alathe bind and rob the Justice. This is a good example of the completely dramatic use of song.

The Pilgrim

"One, two, three, and four"* III, vii; III, vi, in FF

If sung, this is a snatch in madness by the "English Madman."

Blank song III, vii; III, vi, in FF

A song provided by the keeper of the madhouse to soothe the fit of the English Madman.

"He called down his merry men all"* IV, ii

A snatch paraphrased from "The Knight and Shepherd's Daughter" by Alinda, feigning madness.

Possible blank singing V, iv

If there is off-stage singing here, as suggested by Dyce, it is apparently either supernatural or is provided by Alinda and Juletta to implement their disguise as sibylline hags.

Possible choral singing or response V, vi

If there is singing here, as suggested by Dyce, it is an aspect of Christian ritual; at least, there is instrumental music and a shift into octosyllabic couplets.

The Prophetess

Blank song II, iii

Delphia causes a supernatural song at the investiture of Diocles; the Romans take the music to be the gods' expression of their pleasure in the action.

Blank song V, iii

Delphia pleases Diocles with a supernatural song which incidentally joins with other factors to enhance an idyllic pastoral scene.

The Queen of Corinth

Singing "to a horrid music" II, i

Six accomplices of Theanor go through fantastic hocus-pocus involving song, apparently to confuse Merione's memory of her rape by Theanor.

"Weep no more, nor sigh, nor groan" III, ii; pp. 6 n., 103 n.

"Court-ladies, laugh and wonder; here is one" III, ii; pp. 6 n., 103 n.

Contrasted songs, both aimed to cheer Merione from the despondency into which she has been plunged by her rape.

Rule a Wife and Have a Wife

Probable blank song III, i; p. 32 n.

The dialogue and the presence of a boy on the stage indicate the singing of a song as an expression of Margarita's wantonness and, perhaps, self-satisfaction; Dyce notes the need for this song.

The Spanish Curate

"Dearest, do not you delay me" II, v; II, iv, in F2; pp. 103 n., *123–4*

A serenade of sorts which breaks the ice between Leandro and Amaranta.

"Let the bells ring, and let the boys sing" III, ii; pp. 78 n., 89, 103 n.

A song of rejoicing provided by the parishioners when Lopez and Diego promise not to leave them.

The Tragedy of Sir John Van Olden Barnavelt

Blank song IV, iv

A merry song which is part of a Kermiss celebration and a tribute to Barnavelt's lady; at the same time, its being overheard by Orange reminds him of the danger inherent to the yet unsteady government in the popularity of Barnavelt and so helps to seal Barnavelt's death warrant.

Blank song v, ii ; p. 78 n.

A song by or for three executioners, used apparently for its comic or grotesque effect.

The Two Noble Kinsmen

"Roses, their sharp spines being gone" I, i; pp. *59, 71*

A processional wedding song, leading directly into a Fletcher reversal.

"Urns and odors bring away" I, v

A processional funeral song bringing the three black-clad queens on stage for a very short scene dealing with the burial of their husbands.

"For I'll cut my green coat, a foot above my knee"* III, iv; p. 38 n.

"The George alow came from the south"* III, v; p. 38 n.

"May you never more enjoy the light"* IV, i; p. 38 n.

"Oh fair, oh sweet"* IV, i; p. 38 n.

Sidney's *Arcadia* (ed. 1598), p. 474.

"When Cynthia with her borrowed light"* IV, i; p. 38 n.

"I will be true, my stars, my fate"* IV, iii; p. 38 n.

These six songs are sung in full or (as is more likely) in snatches by the Gaoler's Daughter in her madness; cf. Ophelia.

Valentinian

"Now the lusty spring is seen" II, v; II, iv, in FF; pp. *27,* 65

"Hear, ye ladies that despise" II, v; II, iv, in FF; pp. *27,* 65

Seduction songs provided by Valentinian and aimed at Lucina.

"Care-charming sleep, thou easer of all woes" v, ii; p. 60

A therapeutic lullaby for Valentinian, dying of poison; the emperor's violent outburst afterward may achieve a Fletcher reversal in contrast with the peace of the song.

"Honor, that is ever living" v, viii; pp. 56, 68 n.

"God Lyaeus, ever young" v, viii; pp. 56, 68 n.

Ritualistic songs, part of the ceremony of crowning Maximus. After the former, he is crowned with a poisoned wreath; the latter, a formalistic drinking song, allows the poison time to take effect, and sounds a note of tragic irony.

A Wife for a Month

"Come, you servants of proud love" II, vi; p. 62

This lyric probably is a song, an invitation to the dance in a masque celebrating the marriage of Evanthe and Valerio; cf. the very similar masque and general situation in *The Maid's Tragedy,* I, ii.

Blank song III, i

Apparently choral singing of a funeral song; it is intended to please and soothe the melancholy-mad Alphonso but also creates a mood blending the elements of pathos and religious solemnity.

The Wild-Goose Chase

One, probably two blank songs II, ii; p. 32 n.

A probable song by a boy to support Lillia-Bianca's pose as a merry, possibly light, woman; plus a song, probably done for comic effect, which Lillia-Bianca demands of Pinac.

"My Savoy lord, why dost thou frown on me?" III, i

Mirabel sings in elation at exposing a trick being practiced upon him.
"From the honored dead I bring" v, vi; p. 68 n.

This song by a singing boy is part of Oriana's elaborate masquerade to trick Mirabel into marriage; presumably she uses the song for its effect of exotic pomp, as well as for its pathetic effect on Mirabel. The text of the song is incomplete.

Wit at Several Weapons
Humming i, i
Sir Gregory hums in pretended nonchalance, to cover embarrassment.
Humming (of "Loath to depart"?) ii, ii
Pompey hums in elation, possibly in comic amorousness—if this phrase is a title and not part of a stage direction.
"Fain would I wake you, sweet, but fear" iii, i; p. 19 n.

An *aubade* sung by a boy to the Niece for the ridiculous suitor Sir Gregory Fop; the Niece is pleased with the music until she learns who has provided it.

Wit without Money
"The fit's upon me now" v, iv
Valentine sings, apparently in reckless excitement.
Probable blank song v, v; p. 53 n.
The dialogue demands a song, presumably a hymeneal song, at the very end of the play, as a sort of epilogue.

The Woman-Hater
"Come, Sleep, and with thy sweet deceiving" iii, i; pp. 21 n., 46
Oriana burlesques the traditional serenade by singing to the unappreciative woman hater Gondarino.

The Woman's Prize
"The wind and the rain"* ("Begone, begone, my juggy, my puggy") i, iii; p. 75 n.
Jaques sings a pat snatch to inform Petruchio that his bride is going on strike.
"A health, for all this day" ii, vi; pp. *56*, 103 n.
A drinking song by the women militant—a comic development from the conventional soldiers' drinking song.
"An every buck had his doe"* iv, i
A snatch by Bianca in impudent defiance of two old men.

Women Pleased
"If she die upon the same"* ii, iv
Dyce thinks he recognizes a song couplet; if sung, it is done merely for the comedy of vulgarity.
"Oh, fair sweet face! Oh, eyes celestial bright" iii, iv; pp. 21 n., 47 n.
Lopez, the comic cheated husband, sings this love song to his sleeping wife, thus creating comic suspense and developing a Fletcher reversal in an explosion which the audience know is bound to follow shortly.
"Silvio, go on, and raise thy noble mind" iv, ii
Belvidere apparently counts on this song, sung off stage, to prepare Silvio to accept her, in her disguise as a hag, as a sibyl upon whose advice he can rely; cf. *The Pilgrim*, v, iv.

Blank singing IV, iii; p. 77 n.

A French chimney sweep sings continuously through a comic "gag" scene involving the discovery of a lady's lover hiding in a chimney.

BERKELEY, WILLIAM
The Lost Lady

"Where did you borrow that last sigh?" IV, ii

A sort of love complaint, sung by Phillida for the unhappy Hermione and probably intended in part to cheer the latter. The text of the lyric is incomplete.

BREWER, ANTHONY
The Love-sick King

"Begone, begone, my juggy, my puggy"* II, i; p. 75 n.

"I come not hither for thee to teach"* II, i

Apt snatches (the first an entrance snatch) by the singing peddler Thornton; cf. Autolycus, Tawneycoat.

BROME, RICHARD
The Antipodes

"Domine, domine duster"* II, ix; p. 76

The schoolboy chant of the Antipodean senile schoolboys, developing the comedy of incongruity.

Blank ballad IV, vi; pp. 76, 90, 93

More incongruity; the Antipodean courtiers relish a ballad which in England would appeal only to clowns and carters.

"Health, wealth, and joy our wishes bring" IV, x

A ceremonial hymeneal song accompanying the "betrothal" of mad Peregrine to his own mad wife, the whole elaborate show of the Antipodes being a device to restore these two to sanity.

"Come forth, my darlings, you that breed" V, x; p. 46

"Come Wit, come Love, come Wine, come Health" V, xi; p. 46

Contrasted songs by Discord and Harmony in an allegorical masque, actually an excrescence on the play but presumably intended by Brome as a summary of the whole action.

The City Wit

"He took her by the middle so small"* II, ii

"The young and the old mun to't, mun to't"* II, ii

"Oh, she is, she is a matchless piece"* II, ii

"Along, along, where the gallants throng"* II, ii

"Now, fair maids, lay down my bed"* II, iii

"Then let us be friends, and most friendly agree" III, i

These are all apt snatches, adaptations, or songs by Crack, who, like Merrythought, converses largely in song.

Blank song IV, ii

This is a curative-consolatory song intended to soothe Sneakup's jangled nerves; but it is mistaken for some form of sex music by Sneakup's wife when she finds her husband lying with his head in a lady's lap while it is sung to him.

Two blank songs IV, iv; p. 90 n.

"Then shall a present course be found" IV, iv; p. 90 n.

Crack, threatened with whipping unless he will tell where the "Widow Tryman" is, delays through two blank songs and then indicates in the third one that he knows where she is. This is a comic scene with some plot function.

"Io Hymen, Io Hymen, Io Hymen" v, i; pp. 56, 66 n.

Crack sings a wry, ambiguous hymeneal song to celebrate the "marriage" of Toby and the "Widow Tryman," who is really a man.

The Court Beggar

Blank catch II, i

The wits sing over their bottles, off stage, to pass the time.

Probable blank catch IV, ii

The dialogue and a stage direction are confused but seem to indicate the singing of a catch to humor the supposed madman Ferdinand.

Blank song IV, ii; p. 66 n.

The Doctor is threatened with gelding by a supposed sow-gelder, who sings a song ostensibly to prevent the patient from feeling pain. This song thus combines comedy, comic suspense, a sort of realism, and a burlesque of the therapeutic qualities of song.

Blank singing IV, iii; p. 90

Ferdinand sings in a vain attempt to support his pretense of madness.

Blank singing v, ii; p. 77 n.

This comic scene, representing preparation for impromptu revels, is constructed around a confusion of fiddling, singing, dancing, whistling, and so on.

The Damoiselle

"Youth, keep thy money fast" I, i

"Thou shalt not woo my daughter, sir" III, i

Quatrains sung by Dryground, a merry and eccentric old man; the second may be partially in feigned wantonness or irresponsibility.

"Diana and her darlings, dear, dear, dear"* v, i

An exit snatch by Magdalen in drunken elation.

The English Moor

"She made him a bed of the thistledown soft"* I, iii; p. 32

"Go to bed, sweetheart, I'll come to thee"* I, iii; p. 32

"There was a lady loved a swine"* I, iii; p. 32

Millicent sings these snatches feigning wantonness in the hope of disgusting her repulsive old bridegroom and so saving herself from having to go to bed with him. Cf. Beaumont and Fletcher, *The Maid in the Mill*, v, ii.

"Down Plumpton-Park . . ."* III, ii

Exit singing by Buzzard, drunk.

Blank song IV, iii

Lucy provides a "mournful song" to comfort her brother Theophilus over the reported death of his beloved Millicent.

"Hay toodle loodle loodle loo"* IV, v

Buzzard, feigning feeble-mindedness, bursts out some thirteen times into variants of this meaningless song phrase; in addition to its psychological implication, this repetition has a cumulative "gag" effect.

"Hay diddy daddy, come play with thy baby"* v, iii

If sung, this snatch also is part of Buzzard's impersonation of feeble-mindedness.

A Jovial Crew

"From hunger and cold who lives more free" i, i; p. 7 n.

"Come, come away; the spring" i, i; p. 7 n.

These two songs by the beggars establish the atmosphere of the whole play as a comic-opera one and demonstrate that the beggars themselves are sympathetic, amiable outlaws. The second is also an exeunt song.

Wordless singing ii, ii

"There was an old fellow at Waltham Cross" ii, ii

A snatch and a song by Hearty, characterizing him as a Caroline Merrythought. The snatch covers his entrance; the song is an attempt to cheer the depressed Oldrents.

Confused singing off stage ii, ii

Explained as the gypsies' way of drowning out the cries of a woman in labor.

"Here, safe in our skipper, let's cly off our peck" ii, ii; p. 74 n.

A canting drinking song by the gypsies, explained as part of their "gossiping" feast.

"This is bien bowse, this is bien bowse" ii, ii; p. 74 n.

Another canting drinking song, this one performed by a drunken old woman as a token of the gypsies' gratitude to their benefactor Oldrents. This song is relatively extraneous comedy.

"I care not if I have her, I have her or no"* iv, i

Tallboy, jilted, sings through his sobs in a ludicrous attempt to "feign some mirth."

"A round, a round, a round, boys, a round" ("Old sack and old songs") iv, i; p. 76

A drinking catch, creating the comedy of incongruity in that the singers, Oldrents' servants, are all graybeards.

Confused singing off stage iv, ii

Explained as emanating from the wedding of a gypsy couple.

Wordless singing v, i

Justice Clack sings in tipsy good humor; there is comedy of incongruity in his singing at all.

"Old sack and old songs"* v, i

One of the beggars impersonates Hearty in a play-within-a-play by singing a snatch from Hearty's identifying song. Cf. *The Weeding of Covent Garden*, iii, i.

The Love-Sick Court

Blank song iii, iii; pp. 26 n., 68 n., 72 n.

A therapeutic lullaby for the distressed Eudina, this song puts her to sleep and covers a prophetic dumb show representing her dream.

Blank song v, iii; p. 66 n.

This would be a funereal song; it is sung over the body of the supposedly dead Philargus. It covers some necessary stage business in dumb show and has a suspensive effect.

A Mad Couple Well Matched
"O, she's a dainty widow"* IV, i
A possibly sung snatch by Careless.

The New Academy
Blank song IV, ii
This is part of a demonstration of the arts taught at the "New Academy"; the entire demonstration is nonessential.

The Northern Lass
"You say my love is but a man" II, iii; p. 31 n.
A love complaint by Constance, this song is mistaken (with comic effect) by Anvile for brothel entertainment.

"Nor love nor fate dare I accuse" II, vi
A love complaint sung by the disappointed Constance as a part of a hymeneal masque for Sir Philip; the masque itself has a plot function.

"A bonny bonny bird I had" III, ii; pp. 24 n., 38 n.
"But he is gone, alas, he's gone"* III, ii; pp. 24 n., 38 n.
"I wo' not go to't, nor I mun not go to't"* III, ii; pp. 24 n., 38 n.
"Mun toot, mun toot . . ."* III, ii; pp. 24 n., 38 n.
A song and snatches by Constance, mad for love; cf. Ophelia and the Gaoler's Daughter, and note that these songs stress both the purity of Constance's character and the cause of her madness. For the last, cf. Anonymous, *The Honest Lawyer,* v, ii, and Brome, *The City Wit,* II, ii.

"Hey down down . . ."* III, iii, p. 77 n.
"He that marries a scold, a scold" III, iii; p. 77 n.
This song, by Widgin, is the central structural element in a riotous comic scene; the snatch, by Howdee, apparently is intended to set the pitch for Widgin.

"Peace, wayward bairn, O cease thy moan" IV, iv
"Marry me, marry me, quoth the bonny lass"* IV, iv
"As I was gathering April's flowers" IV, iv
Songs and snatch by Hold-up, impersonating Constance in her madness; note Hold-up as a singing courtesan, and note that her songs contrast in character with Constance's.

"O what a delight she gave me"* v, vi
Snatch by Widgin in elation combined with sexual satisfaction.

The Novella
Blank song I, i
A serenade provided by Horatio and Francisco for the Novella, perhaps indicating the serenade in general to be as much sexual as romantic.

Blank song II, ii; p. 31
The Novella plays and sings on her balcony; she is a singing courtesan (a sham one, actually), and her song is a form of advertisement.

"Let not the corrupted steam" III, i
A song first read by Horatio, then sung by Jacconetta, to Victoria, apparently as an act of courtship.

The Queen and Concubine

"What if a day or a month or a year" IV, iii; pp. 72 n., 88, 108

Song by a pupil of the deposed Eulalia; it shows that Eulalia is serving out her sentence that she earn her living (by teaching singing), and the text sums up the lesson of her experience. Note that this song is borrowed from Campion and is prefixed to the text of the play.

"How blest are they that waste their wearied hours" V, iv; pp. 72 n., 108

Another song by pupils of Eulalia, this one a tribute to the new queen Alinda; the text of the song and the mere fact that it is sung both characterize Eulalia. This, too, is a prefixed song.

Blank song V, ix; pp. 66 n., 90

Described as "a new song," this seems to be a suspensive curative song, covering the awakening of Alinda from her long trance.

The Weeding of Covent Garden

Blank song I, i; p. 31

Dorcas, a novice courtesan, sings and plays on her balcony; cf. *The Novella,* above.

Humming of a Psalm tune ("How happy . . .") II, ii

By Gabriel to stall for time; the Psalm tune is part of the characterization of him as a Puritan.

"Away with all grief, and give us more sack" III, i; p. 75 n.

"To prove the baton the most noble to be" III, i; p. 75 n.

Cockbrain, in disguise, is forced to sing two extemporaneous songs as tavern entertainment. The first, the text of which is prefixed to the play, is in praise of sack and seems to be a fuller version of Hearty's song in *A Jovial Crew.* The second has an indirect plot function in that the secret exit of certain characters under cover of it ultimately helps to motivate the denouement.

CARLELL, LODOWICK

The Fool Would Be a Favorite

Solmization I, iii

By Young Gudgen, a gull who wants to become a court favorite, in greeting his singing teacher.

CARTWRIGHT, WILLIAM

The Lady Errant

"To carve our loves in myrtle rinds" I, iv

A consolatory complaint, vicariously sung by Eumela to please two ladies unhappy over the absence of their husbands at the wars.

"Wake, my Adonis, do not die" III, iv

A soothing complaint, to divert the "anxious fear" of one of the same ladies. This song develops some suspense and is followed by a mild reversal.

"Apollo, who foretell'st what shall ensue" V, viii; p. 72 n.

A song of half-religious, half-secular ceremony, amounting to a grand finale.

The Ordinary

"Come, O come, I brook no stay" III, iii

The maid Priscilla sings a wanton, seductive song for Meanwell's benefit; there is comedy (and possibly also suspense) in his mistaking the singer and attributing the song to his chaste love Jane.

"Then our music is in prime" III, v

An "eating song" by four comic characters.

"My name's not Tribulation"* IV, i

An entrance snatch by Credulous, in possibly tipsy merriment.

"Whiles early light springs from the skies" IV, v

"Now thou, our future brother" IV, v; p. 74 n.

These are comic epithalamia (here, serenades to the newly wed couple), the comedy being complicated by misunderstandings and mistaken identities. The second song is a satire on the Puritans.

The Royal Slave

"A pox on our gaoler, and on his fat jowl" I, i

A drinking song, sung as a curtain raiser by prisoners and so achieving complex characterizing and mood-setting values.

"Come from the dungeon to the throne" I, ii

A pagan ritual song, which incidentally covers some necessary stage business.

"Come, my sweet, whiles every strain" II, iii; p. 28

A seduction song, sung in an attempt to turn the thoughts of the scapegoat king Cratander from virtue and military conquest to ease, luxury, and pleasure.

"Now, now, the sun is fled" III, i

A drinking song, performed by professional fiddlers as entertainment for the participants in a drinking party. This song seems aimed at a Fletcher reversal and is, in fact, reminiscent of *The Bloody Brother,* II, ii.

"Thou O bright sun who seest all" v, vii; p. 66 n.

"But thou O sun mayst set, and then" v, vii; p. 66 n.

These pagan ritual songs, which are highly suspensive, are an integral part of the action in this, the climactic final scene of the play.

The Siege

"Strew we these flowers as we go" II, vii; p. 66 n.

A pathetic and suspensive ritualistic song, sung as Leucasia is being conducted to the tyrant Misander, a sort of sacrifice by which the peace and safety of Byzantium will be assured.

"Seal up her eyes, O sleep, but flow" III, v; p. 66 n.

A therapeutic lullaby for Leucasia, who has accidentally been stabbed; the song develops some suspense and possibly aims at a Fletcher reversal.

"See how the emulous gods do watch" v, iii; p. 66 n.

A therapeutic song to bring peace to Leucasia, this time supposed poisoned; the song develops pathos and suspense.

"Be thou, Hymen, present here" v, viii

"Awake out of this senseless trance" v, viii

The first is a pagan ritual song symbolizing an actual wedding ceremony; the second is the invitation to the dance in a hymeneal masque.

CHAMBERLAIN, ROBERT

The Swaggering Damsel

"Be not so cruel, fairest boy" II, iii

A love song, almost a love complaint, sung by a waiting-woman to soothe her melancholy mistress **Sabina**.

"Farewell this company" IV, iii

"Joy, health, and pleasure wait upon" IV, iii

Hymeneal songs after a marriage complicated by a double confusion of identities. The first is also a drinking song and an attempt to cheer the company; the second is performed by tavern fiddlers.

CHAPMAN, GEORGE

All Fools

Blank singing II, i; p. 69 n.

Gazetta sings at her sewing; this is a realistic device almost peculiar to Chapman.

Blank song II, i

Comedy: Valerio is coaxed into singing by his friends, who then proceed to ridicule his voice and his vanity; this incident motivates the entire subplot.

The Blind Beggar of Alexandria

"Health, fortune, mirth, and wine" iii; p. 24 n.

Leon (Irus) sings a combination serenade and drinking song directly to Samathis in a banquet-betrothal scene.

The Gentleman Usher

Solmization I, ii

By a page, practicing for a masque.

Blank singing I, ii; p. 70 n.

Coming to court Margaret, the Duke stages a theatrical masque-like arrival, which is heralded by an "enchanter," with "spirits singing." This procedure is of course an act of courtship.

Two blank songs II, i

Entertainment provided for the Duke includes a masque, during which two songs are sung: "Broom-maid and rush-maid" (possibly a cry-song) and a "Bugs song" (presumably a grotesque song, a part of the anti-masque).

Blank inter-act song Before III; pp. 71 n., 101 n.

Though referred to in the initial stage direction, it apparently has no dramatic function but is merely a detail of production.

"Let all the world say what they can" (*"Belle piu"*) v, i; pp. 61–2.

Bassiolo sings in self-admiration as he guards two young lovers from the Duke; since the Duke is watching from concealment, this scene is one of comic irony.

May-Day

Blank song I, i; pp. 69, 71

This play opens with a nondramatic overture of singing and dancing by a chorus of youths, which does, however, set the May-day mood and from which the opening soliloquy by Lorenzo is very smoothly developed.

"Maids in your smocks, set open your locks" III, i

Lorenzo sings this cry-song as part of his impersonation of the chimney sweep Snail; cf. Marston, *The Dutch Courtezan*, IV, v.

"He took her by the lily-white hand"* III, iii; IV, i

Wordless singing IV, i

"O noble Hercules, let no Stygian lake"* IV, i

These snatches by Quintilliano are part of his characterization as a *miles gloriosus* going home slightly tipsy from the tavern; they may also represent a working of inter-act music into the action.

The Revenge of Bussy D'Ambois

Blank song I, ii; p. 5 n.

Tamyra sings her grief in a sad song over Bussy's grave.

Sir Giles Goosecap

Blank song I, iv

This song, by musicians for Clarence, seems intended to help to characterize him as a Platonic music-lover and a Platonic man in general.

Blank singing II, i; p. 69 n.

Wynnefred and Anabell enter and sing at their sewing.

Blank song III, ii; p. 45

Clarence here explains Platonically his love of music; the song, performed for him by a musician while he writes a letter, helps to characterize him further and to create a sympathetic, unrealistic mood.

Probable blank song V, i; pp. 96–7 t

Captain Foulweather, a ridiculous and unsuccessful suitor to Eugenia, almost certainly sings her a comic love song as part of the last big comic scene of the play.

"Willow, willow, willow" V, ii; pp. 53 n., 71 n.

A willow song for the one unsuccessful suitor, Foulweather, and a hymeneal song for the three happy couples, this constitutes a concluding, perhaps an exeunt song at the very end of the play.

The Tragedy of Byron

Blank song II, i

Part of a masque celebrating the reconciliation of Henry IV's queen and his mistress.

The Widow's Tears

Blank singing and dancing V, i

Tharsalio chortles over the fulfillment of his prediction that his sister-in-law's fidelity would not long survive her husband's life.

CHETTLE, HENRY

Hoffman

"By my troth I am sleepy too; I cannot sing" III, i

This passage, printed in italics, may be spoken in soliloquy but may possibly be sung; in the latter case it is a lullaby which puts two characters to sleep, and it develops a Fletcher reversal in that violence and murder follow immediately afterward.

"Down, down a down . . ."* V, i

"Lo, here I come wooing my ding, ding"* V, i

Snatches sung by Lucibell, mad for love; cf. other mad girls who sing, and note these snatches as suggested by conversation and action.

COKAYNE, ASTON

The Obstinate Lady

"Sweet Diana, virtuous queen" I, i

A sung soliloquy by Lucora, stressing her lack of interest in love.

"Of six shillings' beer I care not to hear" I, i

A comic anti-Platonic drinking song by Lorece, which possibly emphasizes Lucora's coldness.

"All that about me sit" III, ii; p. 73 n.

Jaques, a drunken old servingman, sings this song for rather extraneous comedy.

"Say, boy, who are fit to be" IV, iii

This song is part of a somewhat comic hymeneal masque presented in celebration of the betrothal of Lorece and Vandona by the latter's servants.

"The spheres are dull, and do not make" v, i

Polidacre, a senile amorist, has his musicians perform this song in praise of Antiphila at a banquet which he gives for her.

Trappolin Supposed a Prince

"Since in my orb I shined fair" II, ii

Part of a hymeneal masque presented to Lavinio and Isabella.

" 'Tis idleness that is the cause" III, ii

Mild comic suspense: Mattemores soliloquizes on his love for Hipolita, then hears her sing this song against love, but in the ensuing dialogue persuades her to change her mind.

"Vienca wine and Padua bread"* v, i

An exit snatch in elation by Trappolin at having been successful in his masquerade as the Duke and at having got a kiss from the Duchess.

COOKE, JO.

Greene's Tu Quoque

Wordless singing iv; C2r

The courtesan Nan Tickleman bursts into wordless song as a result of the combination of wantonness and wine.

COWLEY, ABRAHAM

The Guardian

"Why dost thou frown, thou arrant clown"* II, ix

"And all our men were very very merry"* II, ix

Blade, thinking he has been poisoned and has just an hour to live, apportions half of it to drinking with his friends; this snatch and catch show his plan being put into execution. Note the comedy of incongruity.

"And what dost thou mean, old man?" II, x

A catch sung in ridicule of an unwelcome intruder; cf. *Monsieur Thomas,* III, i.

"Come to my bed, my dear" v, vi

By pretending to be converted to Puritanism, Cutter has won Tabitha in marriage; this salacious little song, combined with wine, he uses to break down her resistance to the pleasures of the world and the flesh, his victory being symbolized when Tabitha herself takes up the song. It combines elation, amorous anticipation, the seduction element, and finally slight tipsiness on Tabitha's part.

Love's Riddle

"Rise up, thou mournful swain" I, i, and *passim;* p. 70 n.

Alupis sings this song or snatches of it (particularly the refrain, "For 'tis but a folly . . .") 26 times in all, often on making an entrance or exit. The song is Alupis' trademark, and characterizes him as a merry man.

"The merry waves dance up and down, and play" I, i

" 'Tis better to dance than sing" I, ii

These also are sung by Alupis; they are expressive of his philosophy of life but are not particularly dramatic.

"It is a punishment to love" IV, i

Bellula sings a sort of complaint in a triangular love scene reminiscent of *As You Like It,* v, ii.

DABORNE, ROBERT

The Poor Man's Comfort

Possible blank song II, i

Urania, following her husband in disguise, finds service with the music-loving courtesan Flavia; she offers to, and may actually, sing a love complaint to her husband, who does not recognize her.

DANIEL, SAMUEL

Hymen's Triumph

"Had sorrow ever fitter place" I, i

Thirsis, a supposedly bereaved lover, has his boy sing a conventional complaint.

"Eyes, hide my love, and do not show" IV, ii

This song, composed as a love song, is sung by a friend to the heartbroken Thirsis as a consolatory lullaby.

"Love is a sickness full of woes" After I

"Desire that is of things ungot" After II

"From the temple to the board" After III

"Were ever chaste and honest hearts" After IV

"Who ever saw so fair a sight" After v

Each act of this play is followed by a choral song; four of these are appropriate to the state of the action, but nondramatic. The third choral song is dramatic: with a "show," it represents an actual wedding ceremony which is a complicating factor in the plot, though the principals in it appear nowhere else in person.

D'AVENANT, WILLIAM

The Cruel Brother

Blank song II, i

Lucio hears Corsa sing off stage during her music lesson and is enamored of her voice; this scene seems intended to justify D'Avenant's highly condensed treatment of the courtship and betrothal of this couple.

"Weep no more for what is past" v, ii; p. 71 n.

A boy sings this consolatory song to the wronged Corsa; its pathetic effect allows a Fletcher reversal when her brother enters immediately afterward, tells Corsa that this song has been her dirge, and kills her.

The Fair Favorite

Blank song II, iii

Eumena, the unwilling favorite, has her boy sing her a "song of jealousy"; though it is relatively extraneous, characterizing values can be read into it.

The Just Italian

"This lady, ripe and calm and fresh" v, i; p. 71 n.

Two boys sing a consolatory song to Alteza, who believes she has lost Altamont's love and expects to be killed at any moment; the song is suspensive and permits a Fletcher reversal when immediately after it Mervolle enters with the unexpected news of Altamont's death.

Love and Honor

"She was of Paris properly"* ii, iii

A probable snatch by Vasco.

"With cable and thong he drew her along" iii, iii

Altesto sings derisive encouragement to Vasco in his courtship of the ancient widow.

"No morning red and blushing fair" iv, ii

Altesto provides a satiric *aubade* for the comic newlyweds Vasco and the ancient widow.

"O draw your curtains and appear" v, ii; pp. 5 n., 101 n.

This is an unconventional serenade performed as a tribute to the heroic but doomed girls Evandra and Melora; Evandra calls it a swan song. It sets a mood of sadness and nobility for the rest of the scene.

News from Plymouth

"O thou that sleep'st like pig in straw" iii, iii

A comic *aubade* sung by Captain Topsail to Lady Loveright, intended partly as an apology and peace offering for his bad manners in her presence the night before.

"Thrice happy he who, cares laid by" iv, iii

The widow Carrack, trying to trap the marriage-shy Cable, masquerades as a courtesan and provides this stimulative seduction song as part of her campaign.

The Spanish Lovers

"None but myself, my heart did keep" ii, ii; pp. *21–2,* 67 n.

A serenade provided by Orgemon to Claramante; it and the reversal which follows it are basic plot elements.

Blank song ii, iii; pp. *21–2,* 67 n.

A "mock-song, to a ballad tune"—a comic serenade by Orco to Amiana; it and its totally unexpected effect are basic plot elements.

The Unfortunate Lovers

"You fiends and furies, come along" v, v; pp. 31 n., 66 n.

The tyrant Heildebrand has sent for Amaranta to appease his lust. As he waits, he hears this song, which he takes to be preparative or stimulative music. Actually, it is a supernatural warning of his own doom, which overtakes him immediately after the song.

The Wits

"Then Trojans, wail with great remorse"* iv, i; p. 47 n.

Pallatine Senior has been tricked into allowing himself to be locked in a chest; he sings this snatch apparently in wry self-derision. His singing may be preparation for his conversion to more sympathetic behavior.

"With lantern on stall, at Trea Trip we play" v, ii

The comic watch sing over their ale; though essentially comic padding, the song has some suspensive effect.

DAVENPORT, ROBERT

The City Night-Cap

"She that in these days looks for truth" i, ii

Francisco, posing as a singing master in order to make love to Dorothea, may recite but probably sings this song; Dorothea's overvirtuous response is immediately evident as a pose, and her husband Lodovico's approval of her conduct stamps him as a born cuckold. This song, then, combines plot function with characterization.

King John and Matilda

"Look what death hath done! here laid" v, iii

A dirge accompanying the processional entrance of Matilda's funeral cortege; this reverses the mood of rejoicing on stage over the reconciliation of King John and the barons.

"Matilda, now go take thy bed" v, iii

This dirge covers the processional exit of the cortege, clears the stage, and serves as a finale.

DAY, JOHN

Humour Out of Breath

Blank song i, i; pp. 45–6

Florimel sings as a climax to a speech in praise of "heavenly music"; essentially undramatic, the song is part of a scene in which Octavio turns his sons' humor from war to love.

"Peace, peace, peace, make no noise" iv, iii

Florimel has spirited Aspero out of prison; the comic old jailer Hortensio, thinking that the two have merely slipped into the next room for some quiet swiving, sings a song to enhance their pleasure and to warn them to come out. His error is comically ironic, and his song creates comic suspense.

The Isle of Gulls

"An ambling nag and a down a down," etc.* v, i

Demetrius apparently sings two or three inarticulate snatches in elation over winning the girls and (he thinks) spiriting them away safely from their parents and guardians.

Law Tricks

Blank song iii, ii

The Countess, divorced and ruined, supervises the sewing of several young gentlewomen; at their work they sing a song "sad sorrow to beguile."

Blank song iv, iii

A funeral song is sung as the funeral procession of the Countess crosses the stage; it transpires later that she is really alive, and the audience's surprise at that discovery owes somewhat to this scene and song.

DEKKER, THOMAS

The Honest Whore, Part i

Blank singing ii, i; p. iii n.

Roger sings the "ends of old ballads" while he goes through some clown pantomime with his mistress' cosmetics.

"Cupid is a god as naked as my nail"* II, i

"Down, I fall down and arise"* II, i

"Well met, pug, the pearl of beauty"* II, i

"Sing, pretty wantons, warble"* II, i

Bellafront sings snatches as she dresses; they are part of the characterization of her as a courtesan who is perfectly satisfied with her way of life. For the fourth, see also Heywood, *The Fair Maid of the Exchange*, II, 32–4.

"The courtier's flattering jewels" III, iii

This "sung soliloquy" is the third of four statements of Bellafront's complete reformation.

The Honest Whore, Part II

Solmization IV, i

Matheo sings to himself in satisfaction at having a new suit of clothes.

"There you may have her at your will"* V, i

Lodovico is telling Hipolito, rather crudely, that the latter's love Bellafront is in prison at Bridewell; he *may* sing this snatch in the process.

Blank singing V, ii

Dorathea Target, a prostitute in Bridewell, sings as a final touch in her cartoon-style characterization; she is unrepentant about the past, unconcerned about the future, and defiant of the Duke.

If This Be Not a Good Play

"The fit's upon me now"* V; III, 302

"My dove, my love"* V; III, 303

Bartervile *may* sing these tags in exultation at having learned a new way to avoid having to pay a just debt.

"Will you have a dainty girl? Here 'tis" xiii; III, 332; p. 28

A supernatural Italian zany sings this salacious song as the climax of the devil Shacklesoul's attempt to seduce the Subprior away from the paths of virtue.

Lust's Dominion

Blank singing III, ii

Fairies warn Maria of her impending doom and dance offstage, singing.

The Noble [Spanish] Soldier

"O sorrow, sorrow, say where dost thou dwell" I, ii; p. 26 n.

A dialogue song sung to soothe the deserted Onaelia; it is followed by a double reversal.

Northward Ho

"Methought this other night I saw a pretty sight" IV, iii; p. 73 n.

A mad bawd in Bedlam sings this song apropos of nothing; it is appropriate to both her calling and her condition.

Blank singing IV, iii; p. 73 n.

A mad musician, also in Bedlam, also sings.

"O hone, hone, hone, o nonero"* V, i

Greenshield may sing briefly in derision of the supposed cuckold Old Maybery.

"No, no, you fled me t'other day"* v, i

The dialogue indicates that Kate sings in impudent defiance of her husband.

"O hone, ho ho na ne ro"* v, i

The tables turned, Bellamont returns upon Greenshield the latter's own scornful snatch.

Old Fortunatus

"Fortune smiles, cry holiday" i, i

"Virtue's branches wither, virtue pines" i, iii

"Virtue stand aside; the fool is caught" iv, i

"Virtue smiles, cry holiday" v, ii; p. 111 n.

These songs introduce or accompany nearly every occasion on which the action leaves the human level and enters the supernatural, or morality, level of Fortune, Virtue, and Vice.

Possible blank song iii, i

Solmization iii, i

Orleans does some solmization to show how little he cares about anything but Agripyne. It is possible that he has a boy sing a love complaint to him at his entrance in this scene.

Blank singing iii, ii; p. 62 n.

The servant Shadow enters singing in general satisfaction with life, which is dashed immediately by the discovery that the magic purse of his master Andelocia has been stolen—a Fletcher reversal.

Patient Grissill

"Art thou poor, yet hast thou golden slumbers" A4v, B1r; pp. *42–3*, 111 n.

Janicola and his family sing at their trade of basketmaking; their song characterizes them as contented in the face of poverty and adversity.

Blank singing, solmization D4v

The comic servant Babulo enters singing contentedly but is dashed a moment later by the discovery that Janicola's family have been banished from the court. Cf. Shadow in *Old Fortunatus;* this is a favorite trick of Dekker's.

"Golden slumbers kiss your eyes" H1v

Janicola sings a genuine lullaby to Grissill's twins; this quiet mood is shattered a moment later by the arrival of Furio to take the babies away from their mother.

"Beauty, arise, show forth thy glorious shining" K3r, v; p. *7*

The Marquess forces Janicola to sing a wedding song to greet the supposed successor to Grissill.

The Shoemaker's Holiday

"O the month of May, the merry month of May" (prefixed) pp. 88, 109, *110–13* t

"Cold's the wind, and wet's the rain" (prefixed) pp. 88, 109, *110–13* t

These are probably a country-sports song belonging in iii, v, and a working-drinking song belonging in iv, ii; see text for a complete discussion.

"Der was een bore van Gelderland" ii, iii; p. *74* n.

Lacy enters, singing in Dutch as a part of his disguise. His song characterizes him, and their response to it characterizes Hodge and Firk, as lighthearted and as sympathetic to lightheartedness.

"Hey downe, a downe dery" IV, ii; pp. 43, 69 n.

Eyre's cheerful employees sing at their work.

The Weakest Goeth to the Wall

"King Richard's gone to Walsingham" B2r to B2v; pp. 62 n., 111 n.

"John Dory bought him an ambling nag" B2v; pp. 62 n., 111 n.

"For early up and never the near" (?) B3r; pp. 62 n., 111 n.

Bunch the botcher sings at his work, oblivious of danger, only to have his spirits dashed when he learns of the approach of the army of Anjou. Cf. Babulo in *Patient Grissill.*

"Ick love myne Lyverkin heye" D4v; p. 74 n.

Jacob sings in tipsiness and in amorous anticipation.

The Welsh Ambassador

"Three merry men, and three merry men"* v, ii

This catch is a cap to an extraneous comic scene and covers the exit of the comedians.

Westward Ho

Blank singing II, i; p. 111 n.

The 'prentice Boniface enters singing as he brushes his master's cloak and cap.

Blank song IV, ii; pp. 72 n., 76 n.

The Earl provides a seduction song as part of his assault on the chastity of a person whom he takes to be Mrs. Justiniano, but who is actually her husband in disguise. The song covers dumb show which saves Dekker from writing a formal seduction scene, as he has already done in II, ii.

Blank song v, ii; p. 77 n.

Gozlin Gloworme, drunk, forces the bawd Birdlime to sing. There is comedy in the song, presumably; in the situation (Birdlime is in a desperate hurry to warn three city wives that their husbands are approaching); and in the comic irony that the wives have retired alone and so need no warning.

"Three merry men, and three merry men"* v, iii

Monopoly sings this snatch, probably in mockery of the three worried citizens, or possibly in ironic mockery of himself and his two luckless companions.

"Oars, oars, oars, oars" After v; pp. 71 n., 111 n.

A singing epilogue, adapted to the conclusion of the play.

The Whore of Babylon

Singing in Latin   Prelusive dumb show

The dumb show represents the funeral of Queen Mary Tudor; the singing, therefore, is a ritualistic dirge.

The Wonder of a Kingdom

Possible blank song IV, iii

Trebatio provides for Alphonsina a serenade which should, and may, include song; Alphonsina rejects his suit at the moment but accepts him later.

DENHAM, JOHN

The Sophy

"Somnus, the humble god, that dwells" v, iii

A curative lullaby performed for the Prince, blinded, imprisoned, and now dying of poison.

DRUE, THOMAS

The Duchess of Suffolk

Blank singing II, ii; p. 42 n.

Dr. Sands, fleeing for his life from Cluny, makes good his escape by disguising as a tiler; he sings as he pretends to work.

FIELD, NATHAN

Amends for Ladies

"Rise, lady mistress, rise" IV, i

Subtle, an evil suitor to Lady Perfect, provides an *aubade*-serenade which he first reads and then has sung by a boy; this song has a very minor plot function.

"If this be true, thou little boy Bold" IV, ii

Lord Feesimple sings in half-incredulous elation when told by Bold that Lady Bright wants to marry him. Cf. Beaumont and Fletcher, *Monsieur Thomas*, IV, ii.

A Woman Is a Weathercock

"They that for worldly wealth do wed" II, i

A wedding song covering the processional entrance of the wedding party of Bellafront and Count Frederick.

Probable blank song After v; p. 53 n.

The concluding speech calls for a song by a boy; Collier suggested that a hymeneal song was intended to serve as an epilogue or to clear the stage.

FISHER, JASPER

Fuimus Troes

"At the spring" I, v

"Thus spend we time in laughter" I, v

"Ancient bards have sung" II, viii

"Thou nurse of champions, O thou spring" II, viii

"Rejoice, O Britanie" III, ix

"Gang ye lads and lasses" III, ix

"Alecto rising from the lakes" IV, vi

"Nor is Landora's loss" IV, vi

"Come, fellow bards, and sing with cheer" v, vii

"The sky is glad that stars above" v, vii

The final scene of each act of this play is given over to two songs by a chorus of bards; these songs apparently are meant to combine the idea of the classic chorus with intermission entertainment.

"Turnus may conceal his name" III, vii

A dirge accompanying the funeral procession of Nennius.

"The Roman eagle threatening woe" III, vii

Part of a masque in celebration of the British victory over the Romans.

"So the silver-feathered swan" v, iii; p. 5 n.

Eulinus, brokenhearted, sings this "swan song," speaks a long soliloquy, and kills himself.

FLETCHER, PHINEAS

Sicelides

"Go, go, thy country's joy and jewel" i, ii

A pagan ritual song and a dirge for a doomed heroine, this song is sung by the procession leading Olinda to be sacrificed to the Orc.

"Olinda, if thou yield not now" ii, v

Atyches has killed the Orc, thus saving Olinda and winning her as his bride; this is the ritualistic chorus of rejoicing of the people returning from the rock. It contains a hymeneal element.

Wordless singing iii, i, vi

Perindus, in love with Glaucilla but afraid to marry her because of an ominous oracle, sings in feigned indifference—Glaucilla calls it "forced mirth."

Blank song v, ii

Olinda is reported dead; Atyches, worn out from grief, goes to sleep beside a huge rock. During this song the rock opens; Glaucus and Circe bring Olinda out and leave her. Rawlinson Poetical MSS 214 might be interpreted to indicate that the song is sung by Circe; at any event, it covers this action.

"Hymen, Hymen, come, saffron Hymen" v, vi

All marriages performed, the wedding parties enter to this joyful wedding song for the tying-up of the comic subplot.

FORD, JOHN

The Broken Heart

"Can you paint a thought, or number" iii, ii; pp. 64 n., 67 n.

This song comes from the bedchamber of Ithocles, suddenly and strangely unwell. Appropriate as a curative song or lullaby, it also covers some minor pantomime, foreshadows the nature of the coming scene, and prepares the audience emotionally for that scene.

"Oh, no more, no more, too late" iv, iii; pp. 64 n., 67 n.

This dirge, coming from her chamber, is explained later as called for by Penthea on her deathbed—a "funerall song" to the strains of which she has died.

"Glories, pleasures, pomps, delights, and ease" v, iii; p. 57

A song fitted by Calantha for her end: she dies of a broken heart during its singing.

The Fancies Chaste and Noble

"And still the urchin would, but could not, do"* i, ii

A snatch by Nitido in ridicule of the supposed eunuch Spadone.

Blank song ii, ii; pp. 82 n., 92 n.

An off-stage wedding song in celebration of the marriage of Secco and Morosa.

"Whoop, do me no harm, good woman"* III, iii
Wordless singing III, iii
 Secco sings, apparently in feigned innocence.
"Crabbed age and youth"* IV, i
"The fit's upon me now"* IV, i
"And still the urchin would, but could not, do"* IV, i
 Spadone sings these snatches in (1) elation, (2) feigned innocence, and (3) revenge for Nitido's snatch in I, ii.
The Lady's Trial
"Pleasures, beauty, youth attend thee" II, iv; pp. 64 n., 67 n.
 Adurni provides this song as part of his attempt to seduce Spinella.
"What ho, we come to be merry" IV, ii; pp. 19 n.
 Fulgoso, a comic suitor who can whistle but not sing, provides a comic lisping serenade appropriate to the lisping lass Amoretta.
The Lover's Melancholy
"They that will learn to drink a health in hell" III, iii
"Hark, did ye not hear a rumbling" III, iii
"Good your honors" III, iii
 These songs are part of the Masque of Melancholy designed to help diagnose the melancholy oppressing the Prince; they are, of course, appropriate to their singers, who represent mad people.
"Fly hence, shadows, that do keep" V, i
 This song is used to wake a patient, on the verge of being cured of madness, from a restorative sleep; cf. *King Lear,* IV, vii.
Love's Sacrifice
Blank choral singing III, iii; pp. 82 n., 92 n.
 A choir sings as part of the ceremonial welcome to Bianca's uncle, the Abbot.
The Sun's Darling p. 118
"Fancies are but streams" I, i
"I will roar and squander" I, i
"Glorious and bright, lo, here we bend" I, i
"What bird so sings, yet so does wail" II, i; pp. *105–6* t
"Hay-makers, rakers, reapers, and mowers" III, iii
"Cast away care; he that loves sorrow" IV, i
"See, the elements conspire" V, i
 The Sun's Darling is a masque rather than a play, but its songs conform to the dramatic patterns. Thus the first is explained as to waken Raybright; the second is a self-characterizing song by Folly; the third is a pagan ritual hymn to the sun; the fourth is a part of Raybright's entertainment by Delight in the court of Spring; the fifth is a part of country sports; the sixth is a drinking song; and the seventh is part of a masque.
'Tis Pity She's a Whore
"Che morte pluis dolce che morire per amore"* IV, iii
"Morendo in gratia Lei morire senza dolora"* IV, iii
 Annabella sings these snatches after her exposure, in defiance of Soranzo.

The Witch of Edmonton
  "And have I met thee, sweet Kate ?"* III, i
  "Tarry and kiss me, sweet nymph, stay"* III, i
  These snatches are probably sung by Cuddy Banks in amorous anticipation as he pursues a spirit in the shape of his mistress Katherine.
  Wordless singing IV, i
  Ann Ratcliffe, driven mad by witchcraft, apparently sings as part of her four incoherent speeches.

FREEMAN, RALPH
  Imperiale
  "Come, Hymen, light thy full-branch'd pine" IV, iv
  Part of a slightly premature hymeneal masque.

GLAPTHORNE, HENRY
  Argalus and Parthenia
  "Love's a child, and ought to be" I, ii; p. 47
  This song is a part of country sports presented in an attempt to pacify Demagoras, angry at Parthenia's indifference to his suit; Demagoras' scornful response to the music helps to characterize him as savage and brutish.
  Blank song II, ii; pp. 24 n., 26 n.
  Parthenia sings a love complaint off stage; Demagoras follows the sound to find her and work his cruel vengeance for her indifference to him.
  "Great Pan, to thee we do confine" II, iii; p. 61
  This song for Pan's feast combines pagan ritual and country sports; a Fletcher reversal is achieved a moment later when Parthenia enters, veiled in black, to report her disfigurement.
  Blank song IV, i
  A song and dance by shepherds celebrates the wedding of Argalus and Parthenia; Glapthorne then achieves a Fletcher reversal by having Argalus proceed to tell his bride that he has been appointed to fight Amphialus.
  The Hollander
  Blank song IV, i; p. 56
  A mock-ritual song forms part of the initiation of the Dutch gull Sconce into the "Knights of the Twibill." This is also a drinking song.
  The Ladies' Privilege
  "Triumph appear, Hymen invites" v, i
  Doria, condemned to death, has just been saved under an old law permitting a condemned man to be begged in marriage by a virgin; this song is the "hymn after nuptials." Under the circumstances it is ironic, though the audience may not yet realize that the "virgin" who has saved Doria is his page in disguise.
  The Lady Mother
  Blank song II, i; pp. *92–3* t
  The town waits, with a singing boy, provide entertainment for a drinking party.
  The Revenge for Honor
  Blank song Between II, i, and II, ii

This inter-scene song is probably either a drinking song to carry on the suggestion of the concluding lines of ii, i, or a seduction song to prepare the audience for the discovery in the opening lines of ii, ii, that Caropia has decided to yield to Abilqualit and that her seduction is, in everything but the act itself, a *fait accompli*.

Blank song ("The Soldier's Joy") iii, ii; p. 89

A soldier sings to provide entertainment at a drinking party; the song develops a mild reversal in that it is followed almost immediately by the arrival of dire news about the soldiers' favorite Abilqualit.

Wallenstein

Blank song iv, iii

A page sings a curative lullaby to Wallenstein, weighted down by cares; an independent Fletcher reversal occurs a moment later when the page has to arouse Wallenstein and the latter, starting out of bad dreams, kills the boy before waking fully.

Blank song v, ii; pp. 56, 61

The traitorous officers have a drinking party for Wallenstein's loyal followers; during it, all join in a catch. A Fletcher reversal follows when, shortly afterward, the loyal officers are murdered in cold blood.

Wit in a Constable

Blank song iii, iii; pp. 19, 46

A page sings a serenade to Covet's daughter on behalf of her ridiculous suitor Sir Timothy Shallow-wit.

"Sing and rejoice, the day is gone" v, ii; p. 74 n.

A fiddler's boy sings a satiric song in praise of constables to entertain Busy and the watch as they drink in a tavern.

GOFFE, THOMAS

The Careless Shepherdess

"Grieve not, fond man, nor let one tear" i, i; p. 15

"Blind Cupid lay aside thy bow" i, i; p. 15

The play opens with these conventional love complaints, sung by a boy for and to the unhappy lover Philaritus.

"Come, shepherds, come, impale your brows" ii, i

"On, shepherds, on, we'll sacrifice" ii, i

This song (or these songs) by Sylvia is a combination of country sports and pagan ritual; but the entire scene is nonessential to the main action, apparently being intended to furnish an entertaining interlude and to create a pastoral mood.

"Now fie on love, it ill befits" ii, iii

This "sung soliloquy" by Arismena states her "carelessness" (i.e., indifference to love) and so is part of the characterization of her and the dramatic statement of the obstacle confronting her suitor Philaritus.

"We to thy harp, Apollo, sing" ii, vi

This song by two sibyls combines the ideas of supernatural singing and pagan ritual; it opens and sets the mood for an oracle scene.

"I am in love and cannot woo" iii, x

The comic servant Graculus, intimidated by satyrs into agreeing to lure Arismena into the forest where they can kidnap her, is keeping his promise; in the process he sings a mock complaint for her entertainment. The song is suspensive and is followed by a reversal.

"Sigh, shepherds, sigh" v, xiii

A dirge announcing the murder by satyrs of Arismena and Castarina, this song gives a last emotional fillip before the revelation that the girls are alive and the subsequent happy denouement.

The Courageous Turk

"Gaze, you mortals, gaze you still" I, iv

This song by Cupid, though an entrance rather than a hymeneal song, forms part of a hymeneal masque celebrating the marriage of Amurath and Eumorphe.

"Drop golden showers, gentle sleep" II, ii; p. 66 n.

A foreshadowing lullaby, sung apparently by supernatural singers, to Eumorphe when she retires on her fatal bridal night. See Reed, *Songs from the British Drama,* p. 302, for a conjecture concerning the odd stage direction.

"Thine, O Hymen, thine is she" IV, ii; p. 52 n.

A hymeneal song symbolizing the actual marriage ceremony of Bajazet and Hatum.

"Horror, dismal cries, and yells" v, iii; p. 66 n.

A song by four fiends, a direct supernatural warning to Amurath of his imminent doom.

The Raging Turk

"Then, thou sweet muse, from whence there flows" v, vii

Corcutus sings this soliloquy of grief, thus putting himself to sleep; during his sleep two murderers enter and kill him.

The Tragedy of Orestes

"Lullaby, lullaby, baby" IV, i

One of the rare genuine lullabies to infants, this is sung by a nurse to the child of Clytemnestra and Aegisthus; to an audience at all familiar with the Orestes story, the effect would be one of powerful tragic irony.

"Weep, weep, you Argonauts" v, v

A dirge, apparently by the Argive people over the murders of Clytemnestra and Aegisthus and the madness of Orestes.

GOMERSALL, ROBERT

The Tragedy of Sforza

"Io, Io, gladly sing" II, vi; p. 68 n.

A song of ritualistic rejoicing, part of the secular celebration of Sforza's victory which halts the first French invasion.

"How I laugh at their fond wish" IV, i

Sforza, as fortune begins to turn against him, has his boy sing a soothing song. This scene, according to Pearn, is patterned after *Julius Caesar,* IV, iii.

GOUGH, JOHN

The Strange Discovery

"O Nereus, god in surging seas" II, vii

A pagan ritual song, representing part of the ceremonies of the quad-
rennial sacrifice at the tomb of Pyrrhus.

HABINGTON, WILLIAM
The Queen of Aragon
"Not the phoenix in his death" II, i

Though essentially extraneous, this song is described as a courtship
song presented to Cleantha; it is sung to calm the Queen, troubled by bad
news; and it may be mildly suspensive.

"Fine young folly, though you were" IV, i

Essentially extraneous, this song is sung ostensibly to calm and entertain Sanmartino, impatient.

HARDING, SAMUEL
Sicily and Naples
"Noblest bodies are but gilded clay" III, ii; p. 61

Calantha, returning from the church where she has just been married
to Ferrando, pauses at the tomb of her father (killed in battle by Ferrando)
and hears this dirge; under the circumstances it is ironic and foreshadows
unhappiness.

"My heart is big with grief, my womb with lust" III, v

This complaint by a forsaken lover (Felecia) is overheard; as a result, Felecia's disguise is penetrated, her story is discovered, and half of the
catastrophe is motivated.

HAUSTED, PETER
The Rival Friends
"Drowsy Phoebus, come away" Induction

This play has an elaborate operatic induction designed for its performance before the King and Queen on their visit to Cambridge.

"Cupid, if a god thou art" After I
"To the ladies, joy, delight" After II
"But why" After III
"Have you a desire to see" After IV

These four songs have the dual purpose of complimenting the royal
visitors and providing inter-act entertainment; they do not have any dramatic function.

"Have pity, grief, I cannot pay" I, iii; p. 5

This is the conventional complaint of an unhappy lover (Lucius),
sung by his page or musician; its performance is comic in that the anti-
Platonic music-hater Anteros, in concealment, is tortured by having to
listen.

Wordless singing II, i, ii

Ursely, a feeble-minded girl, sings wordlessly on two occasions; the
first is an entrance snatch.

"Newly from a poach'd trade, and"* v, v
"Be'st thou ruder than was e'er"* v, v

Snatches by a "Bedlam" masquerading as Oberon. Their function,
of course, is principally comedy.

HAWKINS, WILLIAM
Apollo Shroving

"Come away, come away" I, v

Though there is no stage direction to indicate singing, the meter and italics suggest that this is an entrance song by Lauriger and Drudo.

"To thee, renowned Lauriger" II, vi

"Hedone, Queen Hedone, sweet Hedone" III, vi

These two passages, printed in italics, are either declaimed or sung by Siren; the dialogue refers to both passages as "song." Song would be appropriate to Siren, both mythologically and psychologically (as a provocative, fitting for a temptation).

HEMING, WILLIAM
The Fatal Contract

"Come, blest virgins, come and bring" III, ii, by Q division; actually III, iii

A dirge for a girl about to be executed, this song helps to develop a double reversal.

"Wisdom bids us shun the court" IV, iii

This provocative song sets the mood for a scene in the love nest of Queen Fredigond and her paramour Landrey.

The Jews' Tragedy

"See those buildings where once thy glory lived in" IV, viii

This choral song in the temple is one of religious ritual—as Hebrew ritual, it is in effect a link between the songs of pagan and those of Christian ritual. It helps to establish a religious mood which, by a Fletcher reversal, makes the subsequent murder of the high priest Ananias seem particularly shocking and sacrilegious.

"Weep, O weep, mine eyes, a flood of tears" IV, ix

The Lady Miriam's soliloquy of grief sung during the famine makes Jehochanan's subsequent theft of her little wallet of food seem particularly outrageous.

"From the infernal kingdom we" IV, x; p. 66 n.

A direct warning by Persephone and three Furies to Eleazar of his imminent doom.

"There were three fiddlers at a fray"* v, v

Eleazar, mad, apparently sings a snatch in joy when told by Zareck that Conscience has been bound for three days.

HEYWOOD, THOMAS; *see also* Anonymous *and* Webster
The Captives p. 85

"O Charity, where art thou fled" II, i

Palestra and Scribonia, shipwrecked, sing for charity outside a monastery and are rudely answered from within by Friar John in a dialogue song.

"Te tuosque semper, O semper beamus"* II, i

Heywood seems to intend a burst of choral music from within the church to give an atmosphere of Christian ritual as the Lord de Averne and his party enter for matins.

"Help, help, O aid a wretched maid" III, ii

This dialogue song is unique in describing, and so representing, vigorous off-stage action: two villains drag the two girls from the sanctuary of the monastery—a deed which, if shown on stage, might offend an audience.

"Let each man speak as he's possessed" IV, i

Gripus, a comic fisherman, sings a relatively extraneous song in praise of poverty.

A Challenge for Beauty

Blank song III, ii; pp. 41, 72 n.

Helena, in the bliss of a new love, demands a modest, yet wanton, yet chaste song; sung by her maid Rosara, it covers some essential stage business—the stealing of Helena's ring while she washes.

"The Spaniard loves his ancient slop" v, ii; pp. *66, 82*

Manhurst sings to the clown while the audience are kept in suspense whether Helena will learn of Bonavida's plight in time to save him. This song appears also in *The Rape of Lucrece,* III, v.

The Fair Maid of the Exchange

"Why, then, attend, you hills and dales"* II, 30

Fiddle the clown may sing to create suspense in a "gag" he plays upon Master Berry.

"Ye gods of love that sit above" II, 32–4

Frank's "sung soliloquy" of his love for Phillis.

Blank singing II, 71

Bowdler capers and sings in joy at having, as he thinks, won Moll.

The Golden Age

"Hail, beauteous Dian, queen of shades" II, iv; p. 98 n.

"Thou, Trivia, dost alone excel" II, iv; p. 98 n.

A song by six satyrs is part of country sports performed before Diana in welcoming Calisto to her train of nymphs; the second song probably closes the same scene.

"Whether they be awake or sleep" IV, v; pp. 66 n., *97–8* t

This song discovered by Bullen in Eg. MS. 1,994 seems to be the lullaby demanded by Danae on her retiring.

If You Know Not Me, Part I

"Let bells ring, and children sing"* I, 243

The Clown may sing this snatch in joy at the death of Mary Tudor.

If You Know Not Me, Part II

"Pins, points, and laces"* I, 285, 287

On two occasions Tawneycoat the peddler breaks into rhyme suggesting that he may sing his cry-song, after the manner of Autolycus.

King Edward IV, Part I

"Oh, Captain Spicing, thy vain enticing" I, 38

The rebel Chub, having betrayed his former leader, leads him off stage to hanging with a jingle, the form of which suggests that Chub may sing it.

"Agencourt, Agencourt! Know we not Agencourt?" I, 52; pp. 8 n., 89 n.

Hobs and his men sing this three-man song (printed only in part) to entertain their guest Edward IV, incognito.

The Late Lancashire Witches

"There was a deft lad and a lass fell in love" I, ii; p. 74 n.

The Seely family is represented as upset by witchcraft, and normal authority overturned; the daughter Winny, having worked herself into palpitations by scolding her mother, makes the mother sing this smutty song for its therapeutic effect.

"Come, Mawsy, come, Puckling" II, i; pp. *109–11* t

A supernatural song, by which the witches summon their familiars. The text of the song is appended to the play.

Blank song IV, i.

A song and dance form part of a witches' sabbath, thus combining the ideas of song for supernatural creatures and "party" music.

Love's Mistress

Possible blank song I, iv

The dialogue seems to demand a song while, at Cupid's command, Zephyrus carries off Psyche from the top of the hill.

"Phoebus, unto thee we sing" III, ii

"Thou that art called the bright Hyperion" III, ii

These songs are those of the contest between Apollo and Pan, who are represented, according to Heywood, by their respective champions.

A Maidenhead Well Lost

Blank song II, ii; p. 6 n.

Lauretta, destitute, sings a song to "end her passions," thus demonstrating her steadfastness in face of misfortune; her voice attracts the Prince, who thus finds her and falls in love with her.

"Hence with passion, sighs, and tears" v, ii; p. 66 n.

This song is clumsily introduced, but there are several possible explanations for it: it may be a therapeutic lullaby for Lauretta, it may be suspensive, or it may foreshadow the imminent denouement.

The Rape of Lucrece pp. 84, *103* t, 116 n., 118

"When Tarquin first in court began" II, i; p. 4 n.

"Let humour change and spare not" II, i

"Now what is love I will thee tell" II, i

"Lament, ladies, lament" II, i

"Why, since we soldiers cannot prove" II, i

After the usurpation of the throne by Tarquin, Valerius puts on a protective humor of song, which is exhibited at length in this scene.

"She that denies me, I would have" Q5 only; II, iii

"Shall I woo the lovely Molly" II, iii; p. 74 n.

Valerius again.

"The gentry to the King's Head" QQ4–5 only; II, iv

"Though the weather jangles" Q5 only; II, iv

"Pompey, I will show thee the way to know" II, iv; p. 74 n.

Valerius again.

"John for the King has been in many ballads"* II, iv

The Clown sings this snatch in requesting Valerius to do the third song immediately above.

"O mork giff men ein man" III, iii; p. 74 n.

Valerius sings a "Dutch Tassaker" to entertain the other young officers during a revel in Sextus' tent.

"O yes, room for the crier" Q5 only; III, iv; p. 72
Valerius.

"There was a young man and a maid fell in love" III, v; pp. 72, 74 n.

"The Spaniard loves his ancient slop" QQ4–5 only; III, v; p. 72

These songs by Valerius are represented as sung to while away the tedium of the night ride from the city back to the camp at Ardea. Cf. *A Challenge for Beauty*, v, ii, and *The Late Lancashire Witches*, I, ii.

"Pack clouds away, and welcome day" QQ4–5 only; IV, vi.

"On two white columns arched she stands" Q5 only; IV, vi; p. 74 n.

"Come, list and hark" QQ4–5 only; IV, vi

"I'd think myself as proud in shackles" Q5 only; IV, vi

Valerius; the first is an *aubade*, the third a mock dirge inspired by Sextus' grumpiness on his return.

"Did he take fair Lucrece by the toe, man" IV, vi; pp. 67 n., 74 n.

A catch, in which the Clown *sings* the news of Lucrece's rape which he has sworn not to *tell*.

"Thus go the cries in Rome's fair town" (appended) pp. 68 n., 108, 109

"Arise, arise, my juggy, my puggy" (appended) pp. 75 n., 108, 109

These two songs are appended to all editions of the play with the explanation that they were sung by a stranger who had acted the part of Valerius.

The Silver Age

"With fair Ceres, queen of grain" III, iv

A combination of harvest song and pagan ritual, sung by swains and wenches in honor of Ceres just before the rape of Proserpine.

Thomas Lord Cromwell

Blank song III, ii; pp. 66 n., 72 n.

The Earl of Bedford escapes capture in a Bononian hotel by exchanging clothing with Cromwell's man Hodge. After the Earl leaves unchallenged, Hodge waits to face the Bononians, writing a letter and singing a song to amuse himself. The song is suspensive; it indicates the passage of time; and there is comedy in that the Bononian Governor overhears Hodge and presumably is puzzled by the incongruity of a clownish song to the supposed singer, the Earl.

HOLYDAY, BARTEN

Technogamia

Solmization I, v

Wordless singing III, iv

Musica sings, probably as a normal attribute, though others comment on her being "pleasant" and "merry." These include entrance and exit snatches.

Solmization I, vii

Poeta sings in reviewing a conversation with Musica.

"Tobacco's a musician" II, iii

A nondramatic smoking song by Phlegmatico.

"O happy state" III, v

A sociable song for entertainment during Ethicus' party to make peace among the arts.

"Fill up my bowl to the brim-a" III, v

"The black Jack" III, v

After Astronomia has been taken sick at the party, Poeta, Geometres, and Geographus proceed to get drunk and sing these two songs in the process.

JONSON, BEN

Bartholomew Fair

"Hey, now the fair's a filling" II, ii; p. 68 n.

"Hear for your love, and buy for your money" II, iv; p. 68 n.

If sung, these are cry-songs of Nightingale, the ballad-singer.

"Behold, man, and see what a worthy man am ee!"* III, ii

If sung, this snatch by Captain Whit, with its blend of braggadocio and good humor, helps to characterize the roarer.

"My masters and friends, and good people, draw near" III, v; pp. 68 nn., 77, 80

Wordless singing III, v

Nightingale sings his "caveat against cut-purses" to the delight of the gull Cokes, who listens eagerly and even joins in; during the song Nightingale's accomplice Edgeworth cuts Cokes's purse. This is a superb comic scene; at the same time it apparently is a realistic portrayal of an actual Elizabethan skin game.

The Case Is Altered

"You woeful wights, give ear a while"* I, i; pp. 69 n., 70 n., 101 n., 117

Literally a curtain raiser; the Dekkerian singing cobbler Juniper is "discovered" sitting at work and singing; the efforts of his friend Onion to interrupt his song and impart some news provide immediate comedy.

Wordless singing III, i

Angelo sings or hums in feigned nonchalance and unconcern.

Blank singing IV, v; pp. 69 n., 70 n.

Juniper is again revealed singing in his shop and is again interrupted by Onion.

Catiline

The first four acts of this play are followed by "choruses," but there is no indication that these are intended to be sung. Herford and Simpson, however, suggest the possibility in *Ben Jonson,* II, 115; p. 116

Cynthia's Revels pp. 117, 127

"Slow, slow, fresh fount, keep time with my salt tears" I, ii

In what amounts to an induction to the play, Echo is permitted by Mercury to "sing some mourning strain" over the fountain of Narcissus; the song is a dirge-complaint.

"Come follow me, my wags, and say as I say" II, v

Prosaites, Gelaia, and Cos, sent to fetch water from the Fountain of Self-Love, march away to this "beggar's rhyme," a sort of patter song.

Wordless singing III, v; p. 37

Asotus sings and possibly dances while rehearsing "courtship" under Amorphus; Jonson seems to consider such singing typical of the empty court conversation he is satirizing.

"Oh, that joy so soon should waste" IV, iii; p. 74 n.

"Thou more than most sweet glove" IV, iii; p. 74 n.

Philarchus and then Amorphus sing to while away the time at court, to please the ladies, and (at least in Amorphus' case) to show off. The triviality of their songs is satirical. Cf. *The Poetaster* for a similar but more pointed situation.

"Queen and huntress chaste and fair" v, vi; p. 117

This hymn to Cynthia combines pagan ritual and pageantry. Cynthia has been the center of the play but has not appeared until now, in Act v; her entrance, so long delayed, needs all the pomp Jonson can give it.

"From Spanish shrugs, French faces . . ." Conclusion; pp. 71 n., 72

"Now each one dry his weeping eyes" Conclusion; pp. 71 n., 72

The palinode, a burlesque of Christian ritual, reviews the sort of thing Jonson has been satirizing; the other lyric is another summary and an exit song, followed only by the epilogue.

The Devil Is an Ass

Blank song II, vi

"Do but look on her eyes, they do light" II, vi

Exactly what happens in this scene is not wholly clear. Manly definitely sings to attract Mrs. Fitzdottrel to her window, where she is wooed by Wittipol; Wittipol later is assigned the lyric cited, which he may either sing or declaim. Manly's song is not given *in situ.*

Epicoene

"Still to be neat, still to be dressed" I, i; p. 74 n.

This song, composed by Clerimont and sung by his page, helps to set the tone of the play and may have characterizing values in regard to Clerimont, Truewit, and the Ladies Collegiate.

Every Man Out of His Humour

Wordless singing v, v

Carlo Buffone dances and sings his own accompaniment, chiefly as an expression of his exuberance at the downfall of four gulls but also partly as a result of some heavy drinking.

The New Inn

"And a lady gay"* IV, ii

Hodge Huffle sings snatches in a combination of drunkenness and, probably, amorousness.

"It was a beauty that I saw" IV, iv, and conclusion; pp. 53 n., 117

Lovel, in Act IV, reads a love song which he has written for his second hour of conversation with the Lady; it is not sung at this point but seems to be the song performed as an epithalamium and exit song at the very end of the play.

The Poetaster p. 117

"If I freely may discover" ii, ii; pp. 77, 85

"She should be allowed her passions" ii, ii; pp. 77, 85

The pushing Crispinus and the musician Hermogenes sing stanzas to entertain a fashionable company; this is another of Jonson's fine musical-comic scenes.

"Love is blind, and a wanton" iv, iii

Crispinus sings to the company again; this scene is part of Jonson's general satirical plan.

"Wake, our mirth begins to die" iv, v; p. 85

"Then in a free and loft strain" iv, v; p. 85

Drinking songs, performed to liven up a party which has begun to drag. Mallory points out indebtedness to the *Iliad*, 1.

"Blush, folly, blush; here's none that fears" Conclusion; pp. 71 n., 72–3

A kind of epilogue song, summarizing the author's intended moral.

The Sad Shepherd

"Though I am young and cannot tell" i, v; p. 117

Karolin sings to soothe the madness of Aeglamour, distracted by the supposed death of his love Earine.

Intended song Argument of the third act; pp. 68 n., 117 n.

Jonson intended to make Earine sing during her imprisonment in a tree and to make the overhearing of her song by Clarion and Aeglamour a factor in subsequent plot manipulation.

Sejanus

A "chorus of musicians" is called for after each of the first four acts, but there is no clear indication of the nature of these choruses.

The Staple of News

"Good morning to my joy, my jolly Peniboy" i, iii

Peniboy Canter, in his disguise as a merry old beggar, sings this song on his first entrance and is answered "in tune" by Peniboy Junior, joyful at coming of age and receiving his inheritance.

"As bright as is the sun her sire" iv, ii; pp. 74 n., 117

"She makes good cheer, she keeps full boards" iv, ii; pp. 74 n., 117

These songs composed by the poetaster Madrigal in praise of the Lady Pecunia are read by him, and one at least is then sung by a boy. There is apparently a satiric treatment of the serenade motif here.

Volpone

"Fools, they are the only nation" i, ii; p. 73

Part of the entertainment provided for Volpone by his servants, this song has probably both a characterizing function and a philosophical one.

"Had old Hippocrates or Galen" ii, ii

"You that would last long, list to my song" ii, ii

These two songs, probably by Nano, are part of Volpone's masquerade as a mountebank; as such, they seem to reflect the practice of genuine mountebanks.

"Come, my Celia, let us prove" iii, vii; pp. 82–3, 124

This apparently is intended as a seduction song, sung by Volpone himself directly to Celia.

JORDAN, THOMAS

The Walks of Islington and Hogsdon

"My mistress hath a rosy cheek"* I, i

This drinking snatch by Flylove develops a mild reversal, since it covers the entrance of a drawer who brings news which dashes Flylove's spirits.

"I have been a fiddler these fifteen year"* II, i

An exit snatch by Trimwell, elated at the immediate prospect of surprising his wife and her lover together. Incidentally, he is about to disguise as the bass viol player with a party of fiddlers.

"We come to be merry"* II, ii

A snatch by Flylove in high spirits inspired by the combination of wine and women.

"From selling or from mortgaging of lands" v, ii

This mock dirge is sung at the sham funeral for Mercurio as a part of Flylove's plot to save Mercurio from Nice's prosecution for debt; a Fletcher reversal is achieved when, the plot having succeeded, the "corpse" revives.

KILLIGREW, HENRY

The Conspiracy

"While Morpheus thus doth gently lay" II, v; p. 66 n.

This song, apparently supernatural, accompanies the "discovery" of Cleander, asleep; it explains to the audience and so in a sense represents a prophetic dream which Cleander is supposed to be having and which he describes when he wakens. The song foreshadows the course of the plot.

KILLIGREW, THOMAS

Claricilla

Blank song v, x

This is described as an epithalamium; it also serves as an exit song and a finale, the few lines which follow it amounting to an epilogue.

The Parson's Wedding

Possible blank song I, ii

The dialogue opening this scene suggests that it has been preceded by a serenade (possibly instrumental, though the dialogue suggests a song) to Mistress Pleasant.

"Happy only is that family that shows"* II, iii

This couplet is either sung or recited twice by Wanton in a combination of wantonness and impudence. If she sings it, Wanton joins the ranks of the singing courtesans.

Blank catches IV, iv

Young Wild and his friends are having a party, with a country-dance, catches, and healths.

The Princess

Blank singing IV, iv

Tullius, whose friends are attempting not to delay his natural death, sings twice in what seems to be a combination of real joy at the prospect of getting some food and feigned joy or contentment to try to conceal his eagerness from his tormentors.

"To Bacchus bow, to Bacchus sing" v, ii, iv

The Lieutenant, working up his soldiers to a point where they will be ready to join him in a mutiny, has them join in a drinking song (and drinking scene) which he dresses up with an element of the pseudosupernatural. He and his men then leave the stage singing this same song; in v, iv, they re-enter, still singing it.

The Prisoners

"Fond Pausanes, let not thy love aspire" ii, iii

Pausanes is characterized by his singing in prison; his song is a love complaint which, overheard by Lysimella, is partly responsible for her falling in love with the singer.

KIRKE, JOHN

The Seven Champions of Christendom

"I have a love, as white as a raven" v, iii

Suckabus the Clown sings a completely extraneous and rather repulsive mock love song.

"Three whitings they cockle, and set in their luddle"* v, viii

Suckabus sings a nonsensical snatch, probably in joy at the prospect that his life will be spared.

KNEVET, RALPH

Rhodon and Iris

"Upon the black rock of despair" i, iii; p. 6 n.

Eglantine, deserted by Rhodon, sings the conventional complaint of a lady abandoned by her lover.

MARKHAM, GERVASE, AND SAMPSON, WILLIAM

Herod and Antipater

"Come, will you buy, for I have here" i, iv

"Come, buy, you lusty gallants" iii, i

The comico-villainous mountebank Achitophel sings his sales talk, apparently after the fashion of real mountebanks.

MARMION, SHACKERLEY

The Antiquary

Blank song ii, i; pp. *19–20*

Aurelio provides a serenade for Lucretia; though eventually he wins her, her immediate response to the song is anything but encouraging.

The Soddered Citizen

"The merry old pock one time"* i, v; p. 121

"What's pleasure but a mere conceit" i, v; p. 121

"The scrivener writes" iii, vii; p. 121

"Round about to the coal fire"* iii, vii; p. 121

"He that is poor" v, iv; p. 121

Brainsick is presented as a singing character, debauched and customarily drunk; his songs fall into no conventional pattern except that of drunken singing, but they contain as well elements of comedy and occasionally characterization and/or satire.

"March on, thou merry man" IV, vii

"What you have wished and sought is now" IV, vii; p. 102 n.

These are both wedding songs, the first sung by Brainsick and the second by his boy, as Brainsick and Miniona return from the church; both are sexual in tone, rather than hymeneal or religious.

MARSTON, JOHN

Antonio and Mellida p. 129 nn.

Blank song II, i

Two pages and a serving wench join in a song climaxing a purely extraneous Lylyan comic scene.

Blank singing II, i

As part of a little procession pointing up the extravagance and folly of the court, Castilio enters "singing fantastically."

Blank song III, i; p. 5 n.

Andrugio, lamenting his defeat by Piero and other griefs, has his boy sing a song (in which he may possibly join) as an expression of and solace in his grief and possibly also in defiance of fate.

Blank song III, ii

Castilio sings a morning song for his mistress' benefit, though she has no part in the scene; this song is probably done for comic effect.

"And was not good King Solomon"* III, ii

Feliche sings in amusement and exhilaration at his share in outwitting Piero by helping Antonio and Mellida to escape.

Blank song IV, i; pp. 5 n., *26* n., *62*

Antonio, thinking he has lost Mellida, makes his boy sing a song of grief; the scene is one of comic irony, since Mellida herself is watching from concealment.

Three blank songs V, i; p. *65*

Two pages and Balurdo compete in a singing contest which is part of a prenuptial celebration of Mellida's impending forced marriage to Galeatzo; the contest immediately precedes the catastrophe and so provides both suspense and Sophoclean irony.

Antonio's Revenge p. 129 n.

Blank song I, ii; p. 21

At Antonio's request, Castilio sings to waken the slumbering bride-to-be Mellida; after some other action, her curtains are drawn to reveal the butchered body of Feliche. The song, then, is suspensive and probably ironic.

Blank song II, ii; p. 5

Piero commands a song to "augment despair" in Antonio, who is mourning the murders of his father Andrugio and his friend Feliche and the imprisonment of his love Mellida.

Blank song III, ii

Balurdo sings a (probably comic) lullaby to the distraught Maria; immediately after his departure she is visited by the ghost of Andrugio, so that the song develops a reversal.

Blank song v, i; p. 43 n.

Balurdo sings in prison, apparently in comic parody of the traditional prisoner's song.

Blank song v, ii; pp. 41, 65

A song as Piero carouses to the health of his dead enemies immediately precedes the entrance of masquers who proceed to murder Piero. This song thus combines drinking, elation, suspense, and Sophoclean irony.

Blank song Conclusion; p. 71 n.

This song, coming after the concluding speech of the play, apparently is a dirge for Mellida and is intended to emphasize the tragic mood of the denouement.

The Dutch Courtezan

"The dark is my delight" i, ii; pp. 31, 43

Franceschina, another musically trained courtesan, sings for two visitors; her song affords a pretext for the visit of Malheureux which gets the plot under way.

Blank song ii, i; p. 19 n.

Freevill himself serenades Beatrice, his fiancee; this serenade is unusual in that it leads into a romantic love scene.

Blank singing ("Cantat Gallice") ii, ii

"Mine mettre sing non oder song"* ii, ii; p. 75 n.

Franceschina sings in feigned carefreeness and wantonness, and because song is part of her business.

Blank song or singing ii, iii

Cocledemoy apparently is intended to sing in triumph at filling Mulligrub's eyes with soapsuds and so leaving himself free to steal Mulligrub's money.

"Purest lips, soft banks of blisses" iii, i

Beatrice either reads or sings this song, sent to her by Freevill. It is printed only in part.

"The night grows old" iv, v

Cocledemoy sings this smutty parody of a cry-song in his disguise as a bellman; the intended effect is a blend of comedy and realism. Cf. Chapman, *May-Day,* iii, i.

Blank singing v, i

Franceschina, feigning a natural and innocent air as she prepares to betray Malheureux, "cantat saltatque cum cithera."

"O love, how strangely sweet" v, ii

Beatrice mourns the supposed death of Freevill; he himself returns in disguise and sings a song "to make sweet her grief" before discovering himself.

Eastward Ho p. 64 n.

"Thus whilst she sleeps I sorrow for her sake"* i, i; p. 69 n.

"And ever she cried 'Shout home' "* i, i; p. 69 n.

"And ever and anon she doubled in her song"* i, i; p. 69 n.

"And if she will not go to bed"* i, i; p. 69 n.

Gertrude, dressing for her fiance Sir Petronell Flash, talks wildly and sings these snatches; they are part of her characterization, here suggesting the lightness and discourtesy which she thinks ladylike.

"When Samson was a tall young man" ii, iii

Quicksilver is apt, especially when drunk, to spout tags from old plays; here he is apparently doing the same thing with a ballad.

"But a little higher"* iii, ii

"His head as white as milk"* iii, ii

More snatches by Gertrude, whose singing is part of her character. The first is from Campion and Rosseter, *Book of Airs*, No. 16.

"Now, O now, I must depart"* iii, ii

"What a grief 'tis to depart"* iii, ii

Tags by Quicksilver as Gertrude tries to part from Sir Petronell. For the first, see Dowland, *First Book of Songs or Airs*.

"O hone, hone, O no nera"* v, i

"Fond fables tell of old" v, i

A dying flicker of Gertrude's old humor of singing as, disillusioned and hungry, she remains too stubborn to humble herself to her father; the song is the climax to a bit of wishful thinking.

"In Cheapside, famous for gold and plate" v, v; pp. 77, 80

A long, elaborate, and comic "ballad of repentance," or "last farewell," by Quicksilver.

"O Master Touchstone" v, v; p. 77

Security's ballad of repentance is a comic anticlimax to that of Quicksilver, which it follows almost immediately. These two ballads bring about the final reconciliations necessary to the happy denouement.

The Fawn (Parasitaster)

Wordless singing ii, i; p. 32 n.

Donna Zoya, feigning wantonness for the benefit of her jealous husband, sings to accompany her own dancing.

Histrio-Mastix pp. 46, 64 n., 129 n.

"The nut-brown ale, the nut-brown ale" i, ii

The players make their first entrance to this drinking song.

"Holyday, O blessed morn" i, iv

A song by harvest folk, sung in the presence of Plutus, Ceres, and Bacchus; at the end of the song Peace announces that she is supplanted by her daughter Plenty.

Blank ballad ii, ii; pp. 68 n., 90

Apparently for realistic atmosphere in a market-place scene, a ballad-singer enters and sings a ballad.

"Brave lads, come forth and chant it" ii, iv; p. 8

The players sing for their supper and in praise of Mavortius before they are summoned to present their play for the guests.

"Some up and some down, there's players in the town" ii, v

The players' entrance song as they enter the hall to perform their play.

"Give your scholar degrees, and your lawyer his fees" ii, v; p. 75 n.

After the play fails to please Mavortius' guests, Post-Haste the Poet attempts to salvage the evening by singing an extemporaneous song on a theme given him. Cf. Brome, *The Weeding of Covent Garden,* III, i.

"With laurel shall our altars flame" VI, vi; p. 71n.

"Religion, arts, and merchandise" VI, vi; p. 71 n.

These songs form part of the triumphant climax of the play, during which Peace and Astraea return and tribute is paid to Queen Elizabeth.

The Insatiate Countess

Probable blank song III, i

The dialogue requires a song as a serenade provided by Mendoza for Lady Lentulus; a love scene follows, culminating in a reversal when Mendoza falls from a rope ladder. Mendoza is by implication, though not by statement, successful eventually.

Blank song III, iv; pp. *28–9, 72*

"Some short song" is demanded by Isabella and Gniaca as a sexual stimulant, and symbolizes their off-stage intercourse.

Jack Drum's Entertainment p. 129 n.

"Skip it and trip it, nimbly, nimbly" I, i

Members of a Whitsuntide morris sing and dance in honor of Sir Edward Fortune; the episode is a springboard to the development of the characters of Mammon, Sir Edward, and Katherine.

"Delicious beauty that doth lie" II, i; p. 19 n.

"Chunk, chunk, chunk, chunk, his bags do ring" II, i; pp. 19 n., *21*

Serenades sung to Katherine by pages for their respective masters Puffe and Mammon, both ridiculous and unsuccessful suitors. The songs are appropriate to the characters of their respective sponsors—particularly the second, in which Mammon, a miser, tries to win his love by boasting of his wealth.

Wordless singing II, ii; p. *62*

"Grand sot Mammon . . ."* ("John for the king"?) II, ii

Mammon sings in evil glee at the supposed murder of Pasquil, only to have the supposed corpse rise up and strike him; a moment later M. John fo de King enters singing in amused ridicule of Mammon.

Wordless singing (two instances) III, i; pp. 6, 33 n.

Jack Drum sings in drunkenness; M. John fo de King sings in uncontrollable exultation based on amorous anticipation.

"Now dally, sport, and play, this merry month of May" III, ii; p. *23*

This love song, possibly a love duet, is virtually the only dramatic statement of the love affair of Camelia and Ellis.

"By gor den me must needs now sing" IV, iv; p. 33 n.

M. John fo de King sings in excitement and amorous anticipation.

Blank song IV, v; p. 21 n.

Camelia sings a love song to Planet in the hope of stirring his affections but is unsuccessful.

"Give us once a drink, for an the black bowl" V, i; p. 74 n.

Ellis entertains the guests at a picnic with a "high Dutch" (actually English) drinking song—an interminable cumulative game song, on the "Schnitzelbank" order.

The Malcontent

Blank song I, i

A song, possibly discordant and out of tune, precedes Malevole's first entrance on the main stage; Moore, *JEGP, 28,* 195, interprets it as "indicative of his eccentric character."

"When Arthur first in court began"* II, ii

In this snatch Malevole seems to be at once taunting Pietro with being a *cornuto* and reminding Pietro that he (Malevole) is a malcontent and so has much the same privilege as a court fool.

Blank song II, iii; pp. 29 n., 65

During the Duchess' assignation with Ferneze, a song is sung; immediately after it Ferneze is frightened from her chamber and received, according to plan, on Mendoza's sword. Reed cites this as a suspensive song; surely it also symbolizes the off-stage adulterous act.

Blank song III, ii; p. *47*

Pietro interrupts a hunt to chat with three pages and ends by having one of them sing to him; the scene seems meant to prepare the audience for Pietro's conversion to more sympathetic conduct very soon afterward.

"The Dutchman for a drunkard"* v, ii

This entrance snatch by Malevole and Maquarelle, an old bawd, leads into an attack on the latter's morals by Malevole.

Blank song v, iii; p. *65*

A "song to the cornets" covers the entrance of masquers who proceed to murder Mendoza; this is one of Marston's structural songs of suspense and Sophoclean irony.

Sophonisba

"A modest silence though't be thought" I, ii; pp. 52 n., *60–1*

Whether all or only part of this oratorio-like scene is actually sung, it is an elaborate hymeneal song used to achieve a reversal when, as it ends, a messenger enters to announce that Rome is attacking Carthage and that the bridegroom must leave immediately for the wars.

Blank song III, i

Sophonisba stalls off the unwelcome advances of Syphax by performing a sacrifice for her supposedly dead husband Massanissa; a pagan ritual song is preparatory to this sacrifice and forms part of her delaying tactics.

Blank (?) song IV, i

Though the text is somewhat obscure, instrumental music and at least one song are provided infernally by Erichtho, to whom Syphax has appealed for aid in winning Sophonisba; the music is intended as a sexual stimulant, for Erichtho herself now enters to Syphax in the shape of Sophonisba.

Possible blank song v, iv

When Massanissa, in accordance with his oath, presents the body of Sophonisba to Scipio, the act is represented in dumb show to music which may be vocal but on the other hand may be performed by instruments in unison.

What You Will

Blank song I, i

Iacomo brings his page to serenade the supposedly widowed Celia; when she throws him a willow garland, he is ready to fall in with a plot to thwart the proposed marriage of Celia to another suitor, Laverdure.

Wordless singing (?) II, i

Laverdure occasionally breaks out, in conversation, with the phrase "La la ly ro," which seems intended as a distinguishing trait and which may or may not be sung.

Blank song II, i

Laverdure makes his page Bydet sing and dance to entertain his guests.

Blank song II, ii

When the four friends visit a schoolroom, the schoolmaster has one tiny boy sing for them; Simplicius has already been attracted by the child and eventually takes him along to be his page. This and the preceding song are essentially extraneous.

Blank song III, iii; p. 78

A song climaxing a scene of extraneous comedy by Lylyan pages.

Blank song v, i; p. 71 n.

This act begins with the discovery of a banquet scene; a song is sung, and during it a page whispers with one of the characters. The song seems a combination of elements: the "party" song, inter-act entertainment, and Marston's own trick of opening an act with the equivalent of a little dumb show.

MASON, JOHN

Mulleasses the Turk

Blank song IV, i

Amada provides a song to cheer and console Julia, depressed over the treatment given her by her guardian Borgias. This song may be intended partly as preparation for a sham-supernatural scene which follows immediately, or for an indirect reversal.

MASSINGER, PHILIP

Believe as You List

Blank song IV, ii; pp. 27–8

The Romans try torture, starvation, and finally the blandishments of a courtesan in their effort to make Antiochus confess himself an impostor. The entrance of the courtesan is prepared for by a song, obviously in the seduction pattern.

The City Madam

Probable blank song v, iii; pp. 99–100 t

A long-overlooked marginal note indicates the presence of a song somewhere in this play; the most appropriate place for it is as an entertainment during the sham-supernatural banquet provided for Luke by Sir John.

The Duke of Milan

Probable blank song I, iii; pp. 21 n., 37, 66 n., 67 n., 95, 122

During the annual banquet celebrating the birthday of the Duchess Marcelia, the Duke commands the singing of a song he has composed in praise of his wife. There is little but this song to create a festive mood; the mood is immediately shattered by the arrival of a messenger (a Fletcher reversal); and the situation characterizes the Duke as dangerously uxorious.

Blank song II, i; p. 87 n.

During the Duke's absence his mother and sister, jealous of Marcelia, avenge their having been forced to celebrate her birthday by insulting her in her sadness with a mock serenade—"a scurvy ditty, to a scurvy tune." The song has a plot function in that Francisco, left as regent, unexpectedly takes Marcelia's part, punishes the offenders, and uses the incident as an opportunity for pleading his own love to Marcelia.

The Emperor of the East

"Why art thou slow, thou rest of trouble, Death?" v, iii; p. 5 n.

Eudocia, falsely accused of adultery and banished from the emperor's presence, sings what she calls a swan song of grief; it prepares the mood for the emotional, in fact, spiritual, scene which follows.

The Fatal Dowry   In regard to all these songs, see pp. 108–9

"Fie, cease to wonder" II, i

Represented as a dirge during the funeral procession of Charalois Senior.

"Set, Phoebus, set, a fairer sun doth rise" II, ii; p. 67 n.

This song, actually a duet, is introduced as a serenade sung by Aymer to Beaumelle for her worthless but successful suitor Novall Junior. If the text represents the original song, it may foreshadow Beaumelle's base yielding to Novall after her marriage to Charalois.

"Courtier, if thou needs wilt wive" IV, ii; pp. 29 n., 66 n.

"Poor citizen, if thou wilt be" IV, ii; pp. 29 n., 66 n.

These songs are provided by Aymer partly to enhance the adulterous pleasure of Beaumelle and Novall, partly to stall off Charalois and Beaumont and to prevent them from discovering this adultery. The songs are thus suspensive, and the second, if it is the original text, provides dramatic irony in that it describes a situation very similar to what is actually going on.

The Guardian

"Enter a maid, but made a bride" IV, ii; p. 66

Adorio's tenants provide a hymeneal song to welcome him and his bride home after their elopement. Since the audience know—but Adorio does not—that he has eloped with the wrong girl, the song provides genuine comic irony, together with suspense as to when Adorio will discover the truth and what he will do then.

"Welcome, thrice welcome to this shady green" v, i; p. 109

When Severino, the bandit chief, brings his wife to the forest, his men welcome her with this song, which is on the country-sports order and characterizes the men as amiable outlaws.

The Picture

Blank song ("in praise of war") II, ii

Song covering the ceremonial entrance of Ladislaus and his victorious officers, evidently as a combination of court ceremony and compliment to the military heroes.

"Though we contemplate to express" II, ii; p. 66 n.

This lyric is either sung or declaimed during a court masque; lines 4–6 seem to be a definite foreshadowing of the trial to which Mathias is almost immediately to be subjected.

"The blushing rose and purple flower" III, v

A fine example of the seduction song, provided by Honoria as a part of her trial of Mathias' virtue.

The Renegado

Blank song II, iv; pp. 27, 71 n., *122–3*

Donusa, having decided to try to seduce Vitelli, sends for him and provides this seduction song to be sung as he enters. This is one of the very few seduction songs that are successful in their purpose.

The Roman Actor

Blank song II, i; p. 85

Domitian, having stolen Lamia's wife Domitia (Augusta), tortures the bereaved husband by having Domitia sing to him and then commanding him to fall down and worship her. The whole situation, of course, helps to characterize both Domitian and Domitia.

Blank song v, i; p. 68 n.

Domitian, very tired, demands a lullaby, which puts him to sleep so that his table-book can be stolen (as is necessary to the plot) and so that he can see ominous apparitions warning of his impending doom.

The Unnatural Combat

Blank song ("The Soldier's Delight") III, iii; p. 89

During a drinking party, Beaufort Senior, like a good host, steers the conversation away from dangerous ground by calling for this song. It is followed by the unexpected appearance of Belgarde in a minor reversal.

A Very Woman

Blank song III, i; p. 68 n.

A slave merchant has one of his slaves sing a song in the market. From his point of view, the song is to stir up business; from Massinger's, it suggests the color and bustle of the market place.

Blank singing III, v

Borachia, set to keep Pedro away from Leonora, is made drunk by Antonio, who then proceeds to give the girl a letter from Pedro; Borachia sings in her cups.

Blank song IV, ii

A sham-supernatural song between people personifying a good and an evil genius is part of the physician Paulo's elaborate treatment of Cardenes' melancholy-madness; it is the final touch of the treatment and accomplishes the cure.

MAY, THOMAS

The Old Couple

"This is not the Elysian grove" II, ii

Matilda goes to the woods to sing a complaint about the supposed death of her lover Scudmore. She is a minor but relatively clear-cut figure, thanks almost entirely to this song.

The Tragedy of Cleopatra

"Not he that knows how to acquire" I, ii; pp. 72, 116 n.

This hedonistic banquet song is part of a scene the function of which is to demonstrate the sort of life which has Antony's officers shaking their heads sadly.

MAYNE, JASPER
The Amorous War

"Time is the feathered thing" IV, v; p. *29* n.

The context calls this song a lullaby; actually it is stimulative music furnished by the supposed Amazons Orithya and Thalaestris who, unrecognized, are entertaining their own husbands. The song clearly symbolizes off-stage intercourse.

"Behold these hallowed tapers, and here see" v, ix; p. 52 n.

A hymeneal song symbolizing the actual wedding ceremony joining Archidamas and Roxane at the end of the play.

The City Match

"We show no monstrous crocodile" III, ii

Some gay blades play a joke on Timothy by getting him drunk, dressing him up as a strange fish, and charging admission to see him. This song forms a sort of dividend to the paying customers.

MEAD, ROBERT
The Combat of Love and Friendship

"Two-topped Parnassus I defy" v, iv

This is a ludicrous serenade, sung under particularly low-comedy circumstances by a boy for his master Pisistratus, a blustering captain and a ridiculous and unsuccessful suitor.

MIDDLETON, THOMAS
Anything for a Quiet Life

Speaking at a given pitch v, ii

The apprentice George will not allow Mrs. Water-Camlet to speak above the key "sol."

Blurt, Master-Constable

"What meat eats the Spaniard?" I, ii; p. 78

A comic song by three pages, sung as a cap to a Lylyan comic scene. Since it ends the act, the song may actually represent inter-act music worked into the fabric of the scene proper.

Wordless singing II, ii; p. 32 n.

"In a fair woman what thing is best?" II, ii; pp. 32 n., 76

The courtesan Imperia, in a restless, wanton mood, sings to her own dancing; then she demands this song, which is sung by two of her women. It contains intrinsic comedy and is also productive of the comedy of incongruity, in that its subject is not what one would expect to find under the circumstances.

"Love is like a lamb, and love is like a lion" II, ii; pp. 74 n., 83 n.

This song is performed for entertainment either for or by a party of masquers visiting Imperia's house.

"Pity, pity, pity!" III, i

A serenade performed by musicians for Camillo, who, though not a ridiculous lover, is definitely an unsuccessful one; the serenade brings forth only a tongue-lashing from its recipient Violetta.

"Go from my window, go"* IV, i; p. 75 n.

Simperina sings this snatch in amused derision of Curvetto, an unwelcome suitor whom she has just drenched with water.

"Midnight's bell goes ting, ting, ting, ting, ting" IV, ii

Imperia has sent the comic Lazarillo to wait for her in a "haunted" chamber; this sham-supernatural song is only one of the alarming adventures which befall him there.

"Mapew, la, la, la, &c"* v, ii

Imperia apparently sings this snatch in conversation with Fontinelle, either for the sake of some now lost allusion or merely as part of her erotic-musical character. Cf. Chapman, *The Gentleman Usher,* v, i.

"Love for such a cherry lip" v, ii; p. 29 n.

Imperia sings to Violetta's bridegroom Fontinelle; her song is probably a practical device to symbolize more passionate love-making. It is interrupted violently in a Fletcher reversal.

Wordless singing (the refrain to the preceding song?) v, ii

After hiding Fontinelle, Imperia goes to meet the supposed intruders, singing in nonchalance which may be feigned but is more probably genuine.

The Changeling

"Sweet love, pity me"* III, iii

Franciscus, a gentleman feigning madness in order to gain access to Isabella, pretty wife of the madhouse keeper, sings this snatch as part of his pretense but incidentally hints to Isabella at his real purpose.

Wordless singing IV, iii

Antonio, also feigning madness, is made to sing an accompaniment to his own dancing in a rehearsal for a masque of madmen to be presented at a wedding.

Wordless singing IV, iii

Franciscus again sings in feigned madness, this time upon an entrance.

A Chaste Maid in Cheapside

Wordless singing I, ii

Allwit, a contented wittol, sings cheerfully in contemplation of his complete freedom from care.

"Cupid is Venus' only joy" IV, i

Possible blank song IV, i

A supposed Welsh heiress (actually a courtesan) sings to Tim Yellowhammer in a comic courtship scene; Dyce and Bullen feel that Tim may sing in turn to show off his talents to his bride-elect.

"Weep eyes, break heart" v, ii; pp. 5 n., 6 n.

Urged by her mother to sing to "revive her spirits," Moll, whose love for Touchwood Junior now seems hopeless, sings this complaint, which her father recognizes as in effect a swan song.

Blank song v, iv

"A sad song" accompanies the entrance of the funeral processions of

Moll and Touchwood, both of whom are soon afterward discovered to be alive, not dead.

A Fair Quarrel

"Then here thou shalt resign" IV, iv; pp. *102* t, 107

Chough and his servant Trimtram, fresh from "roaring school," encounter the bawd Meg and the prostitute Priss, and force them to sing. This is a comic scene, apparently interpolated after the first printing of the play.

"Take heed in time, O man, unto thy head" v, i; p. 67 n.

Chough and Trimtram *sing* a secret they have sworn not to *tell*. The song has a plot function in helping to bring about the final complete victory of Fitzallen and Jane over the latter's miserly father.

The Family of Love

"Now, if I list, will I love no more" I, ii

"Let every man his humour have" I, iii

These short songs by Lipsalve characterize him by stating his irreverent attitude toward women; the second also covers an entrance.

A Game at Chess

"Wonder work some strange delight" v, i

The Black House provides a lavish welcome, including this song, to the visiting White Duke and White Knight, in the hope of impressing them and perhaps proselyting them.

A Mad World, My Masters

Blank song After II, i; p. 71 n.

Blank song After II, vii; p. 71 n.

These two songs are clearly inter-scene or inter-act entertainment; they are, however, given a remote but rather skillfully worked out relationship to the plot. They also seem intended to indicate the passage of time.

Wordless singing IV, i; p. 28

A succubus in the shape of Mrs. Harebrain, attempting to seduce Penitent Brothel, sings and dances in the process.

"O for a bowl of fat canary" After v, ii; pp. *102* t, 105, 108, 109

This drinking song, appended to the play with the comment that it is sung by Sir Bounteous to his guests in the fifth act, is almost certainly a late interpolation.

The Mayor of Queenborough p. *99* t

"Boast not of high birth or blood" I, i; p. 36

The processional song of a group of monks, among them Constantius, whom the song in effect characterizes. The procession is halted by Vortiger, who calls on Constantius to accept the crown.

"If in music were a power" IV, ii

A welcoming or "party" song provided by Hengist in honor of Vortiger and Castiza, his guests in his newly built Thong Castle.

More Dissemblers besides Women

"To be chaste is woman's glory" I, i

The play opens with this song, which elicits in the dialogue a characterization of the Duchess, to be a major figure; links the two plots; and draws an ironic contrast between the behavior of the Duchess and that of Lactantio and Aurelia, who overhear the song.

"Laurel is a victor's due" i, iii
"I am a little conqueror too" i, iii
"Welcome, welcome, son of fame" i, iii

These songs (or this song), in a masque of welcome for the triumphant general Andrugio, cover some dumb show which results in a Fletcher reversal shortly afterward. The scene, moreover, affords time for the Duchess to see and fall in love with Andrugio.

"Cupid is Venus' only joy" i, iv

Lactantio's page, actually his mistress in disguise, persuades the lumpish servant Dondolo to do her heavy work by singing for him; this song is the cap to a Lylyan scene of essentially extraneous comedy. Cf. *A Chaste Maid in Cheapside*, iv, i.

"Come, my dainty doxies" iv, i
"Our wealth swells high, my boys" iv, i

Entrance and exit songs, respectively, of a band of gypsies—genuine gypsies, as the words make clear. The first song is mentioned also in *The Widow*, iii, i.

Solmization v, i; pp. 7, 77 n.
Blank prick-song v, i; pp. 77 n., 129
Blank song v, i; p. 77 n.
Solmization as accompaniment to dancing v, i; p. 77 n.

All this music is part of a comic scene based on singing and dancing lessons being given to the supposed page.

The Roaring Girl

"I dream there is a mistress" iv, i
"Here comes a wench will brave ye" iv, i

Moll, the Roaring Girl, sings both these songs for no particular reason other than to reiterate the idea that Moll is fond of pointing out: that there is a great difference between reputation and actuality, particularly as applied to her own good character and questionable reputation.

"A gage of ben rom-bouse" v, i; p. 74 n.
"A rich cup of wine" v, i; p. 74 n.

The first song is an outgrowth of a conversation on rogues' cant; the second is a translation of the first.

The Spanish Gypsy

"O that I were a bee to sing" ii, i

A comic serenade sung by the foolish gentleman Sancho to the pretty little gypsy girl Constanza.

Partial scale iii, i

Sancho apparently sings part of the scale in conversation, as a roundabout way of saying, "We are singers."

"Trip it, gypsies, trip it fine" iii, i

Sancho (or the whole gypsy band) sings this song as the group march off to give a performance at the house of Francisco. Their singing throughout, of course, characterizes them as amiable outlaws.

"Come, follow your leader, follow" III, ii; p. 70 n.

"Now that from the hive" III, ii; p. 70 n.

Both these songs form part of the gypsies' act at Francisco's house; the first is their entrance or overture song, the second their begging song.

"Thy best hand lay on this turf of grass" IV, i

"Brave Don, cast your eyes" IV, i

The first of these lyrics is long and elaborate; whether sung or declaimed (or both in combination), it represents the ceremonies of John's induction into the gypsy band and his betrothal to Constanza. The second is Sancho's instructions to the new initiate, a reiteration of the harmless way of life of this particular gypsy band.

"Hence merrily fine to get money" IV, i

Another song by Sancho covers the exit of the group and affords further group characterization.

A Trick to Catch the Old One

"Let the usurer cram him, in interest that excel" IV, v

A traverse-drawing song, sung by the maidservant Audrey as she sits and spins beside the bed of the sick usurer Dampit. The song is a grotesque travesty of both the spinning song and the lullaby.

The Widow

"Kuck before and kuck behind"* III, i; pp. 68 n., 77 n.

"Come, my dainty doxies"* (title only) III, i; pp. 68 n., 77 n.

"I keep my horse, I keep my whore" III, i; pp. 68 n., 77 n.

The singing highwayman Latrocinio disarms his victims by falling in with them on the road, charming them with his gay singing, and finally demanding their purses in song. Martia, disguised as a youth, is his victim here.

Blank song III, i; p. 77 n.

Remembering that she has a pistol, Martia recovers her purse, takes Latrocinio prisoner, and in revenge forces him to "sing all his songs for nothing."

"How round the world goes, and everything that's in it" III, i; p. 77 n.

Another thief enters, posing as a sympathetic servingman; Martia confides that her pistol is not loaded; so the tables are immediately reversed again, and Latrocinio and his entire gang sing this song of triumph. All their singing characterizes them as amiable outlaws.

"If in this question I propound to thee" III, ii; p. 68 n.

Philippa, disappointed when Francisco fails to keep an assignation, consoles herself by having her maid Violetta join her in this duet, which is essentially extraneous.

"Give me fortune, give me health" IV, ii; p. 78 n.

Latrocinio and his crew sing this exit song after reckoning up their booty from another good haul.

The Witch

"In a maiden-time professed" II, i; p. 41

Isabella sings to cover up her internal disquiet after her loveless bridal night with Antonio. Cf. Amintor's suggestion of a catch under similar circumstances in Beaumont and Fletcher, *The Maid's Tragedy*, III, i.

"Come away, come away" III, iii

A supernatural song: witches, companions of Hecate, summon her to a night's frolic.

"Black spirits and white, red spirits and grey" v, ii

Hecate and the witches sing this charm-song over their cauldron as they brew an evil potion.

Women Beware Women

Blank song I, iii

A variety of music and song is part of the state religious procession during which the Duke first sees Bianca and falls in love with her.

"What harder chance can fall to woman" III, ii; p. 53 n.

At Livia's banquet, Isabella shows off her accomplishments by singing and later dancing. There is dramatic irony, pointed out by the Duke, in this demonstration of her grace and talents in the fact that she is to be married to the clownish and completely unappreciative Ward.

"Juno, nuptial goddess" v, i

Part of a hymeneal masque presented ostensibly to celebrate the Duke's marriage to Bianca, but designed actually as a means of achieving vengeance, and resulting in general catastrophe.

Your Five Gallants

Blank song II, i; p. 31

Primero keeps a bawdy house under the pretense that it is a music school for young ladies; this song is, accordingly, presented as appropriate entertainment to guests and serves as a cover under which Primero's boy steals a jewel from one of these guests, Fitzgrave. The whole scene is comic in effect.

"O, the parting of us twain"* II, i

Tailby sings this snatch, probably to express regret at the departure of a novice courtesan.

"Cousin, cousin, did call, coz?"* IV, vii

Bungler is trying to call a supposed cousin without rousing suspicion, and probably is bubbling over with inward amusement at what he thinks is a joke.

"Sound lute, bandora, gittern" v, ii; p. 68 n.

This "hymn" seems intended as an induction to the masque in which the five gallants plan to present their cases to Katherine.

MONTAGUE, WALTER

The Shepherds' Paradise

"Press me no more, kind love, I will confess" v, i

This lyric passage is either sung or recited by Bellesa as a soliloquy of love which puts the singer to sleep in preparation for a minor plot twist which depends on her being discovered sleeping. Other lyrics in the play are apparently read or declaimed.

MOUNTFORT, WALTER

The Launching of the Mary

"My father's high constable, and I his own son"* III, iv

An entrance snatch by Trunnell, who has been eavesdropping and is now ready to make his presence known.

NABBES, THOMAS
The Bride
Blank singing III, iv

Kickshaw, a comic French cook, demands a wench at a tavern, but a group of "blades" pick a quarrel with him, bind him, and rob him; then they sing and dance around him in derision, perhaps also in a burlesque of sex music.

Hannibal and Scipio p. 116 n.
"March on, my merry mates" I, iii; p. 72 n.

This song, praising Venus' wars in comparison with Mars', is the third statement of the soft and lascivious life lived by Hannibal's army at Capua, with emphasis on the contrast between this life and an honorable one. Hannibal is characterized by his reaction to the song.

"Beauty, no more the subject be" II, v

Hannibal, trying to outbid Scipio for the allegiance of Syphax, offers Sophonisba to the young king in marriage. She is first presented to him in a masque-like entrance including a dance and this song, which implies some reliance on the stimulative power of music.

"On bravely, on; the foe is met" IV, v; p. 72 n.

Scipio's followers celebrate his final victory with a martial dance and song which contrast with the song for the Carthaginians in Act I.

Microcosmos
This is a masque rather than a play, and the songs are not essentially dramatic.

"Hence, confusion and dissension" I

A "discovery" song during which Love reduces the four warring elements to order.

"Descend, thou fairest of all creatures" II

Love and Nature descend from the second scene and present Bellanima to Physander as his bride.

"Flow, flow, delight" III

The third scene is discovered and Sensuality revealed to Physander.

"Welcome, welcome, happy pair" v

Love and the Virtues lead Bellanima and Physander to the throne at the finale.

Tottenham Court
"What a dainty life the milkmaid leads" I, iii; p. 7

Bellamie, separated from Worthgood in the darkness, is frightened when she hears singing but is reassured by the nature of the song; it is sung by Ciceley, whom it helps to characterize.

NEALE, THOMAS
The Ward
"I would I were a carter" II, iv; p. 36

This "sung soliloquy" by Thomaso helps to establish him, immediately upon his first appearance, as a sympathetic little lad.

"Now that the cold and hoary frosts" iii, ii

Will Scatterbrain sings this drinking song during a drinking scene.

PEAPS, WILLIAM

Love in Its Ecstasy

"Let amorous lovers take delight" iii, iv

Actually the complaint of a steadfast but unappreciated lover, Desdonella, this song is mistaken by Bermudo as supernatural music; it has some plot function.

"Swell, swell, my thoughts, and let my breast" v, i; p. 5 n.

This is a "swan song" by Constantina, who, with Thesbia, has been sentenced to die for violating the edict against love; in addition, the song has a soporific effect on both girls.

PERCY, WILLIAM

None of Percy's songs are truly dramatic; they are frequently used to end a scene when the next scene supposes a change of place.

The Cuckquean's and Cuckold's Errand

"With a whist and with a hush" i, iii

A scene-closing song by Shift and possibly Nim, reaffirming their resolution to steal Dr. Pearl's bowl.

"All laud and praise be giv'n to God" ii, vi

This is a rather sacrilegious song of joy and thanksgiving at the successful theft of the bowl; it also is a scene-closing song.

"Sorrow, sorrow, make haste with speedy wing" iii, ii

A scene-ending song, a complaint sung by the servant girl Janekin for her mistress Arvania, an abandoned wife.

"When men once grow weary of love" iv, i

Doucebella and Arvania, both deserted by their husbands, join forces; they celebrate their alliance by joining in this scene-ending song.

"Hercules, Hercules along" v, vii

Two comic servants, Rook and Rafe, try to find courage in a song, which probably indicates a lapse of time covering off-stage action.

"Along, along, gallants, along" v, ix

This song follows the epilogue, with no spoken introduction.

The Fairy Pastoral

"I see the squirrel in the tree" i, ii

A hunting song closing a Lylyan pattering scene by the elfin pages Hylas and Atys and the keeper Christophel. Incidentally, Christophel says, but does not sing, a snatch of "Three Merry Men."

"On a day" ii, ii

Another Lylyan scene-ending song.

"Forward hie we with pace and trot" iii, ii

This song closes a passionate but extraneous love scene between the huntsman Sylvius and his leman Sylvia; ostensibly a hunting song, it makes considerable use of *double-entendre*.

"In the month of May" iii, iii

Another Lylyan scene-ending song.

"The time hath been that a tawdry lace" iv, iii

Picus, masquerading as Sapho, sings as a sewing song this lyric borrowed from Sir Philip Sidney.

"We have found a witch down the Leye" iv, iii

Picus sings this song, too, while waiting for Camilla to enter. The song is reminiscent of the prank played on Sir David.

"Right pepper is black" iv, x

Another Lylyan song, this one ending the act.

"With solemn oath and humble vow" v, v

The entire cast joins in song as part of the ceremony of the coronation of Orion as king of the fairies.

QUARLES, FRANCIS

The Virgin Widow

"How blest are they that waste their weary hours" iii, i ; p. 108

Queen Augusta, her heart "oppressed with melancholy" (she is plotting the murder of Kettreena), has her maid sing her a soothing song. This song, incidentally, is prefixed to a later edition of Brome's *The Queen and Concubine.*

"Is any sick? Is any sore" iv, i

Most of Act iv is a vaudeville turn—a take-off on the routine of a mountebank ; this song by a boy is part of the "pitch."

RANDOLPH, THOMAS

Amyntas

"Nos beata Fauni proles" iii, iv; p. 74 n.

Dorylas, masquerading as Oberon, enters attended by "fairies" (small boys with an eye on the apples in Iocastus' orchard). The fairies sing in Latin at intervals through the scene, thus helping to convince Iocastus of their genuineness and making possible a ridiculous comic scene.

"Ceres, to whom we owe that yet" v, v

Claius is about to be sacrificed to Ceres to satisfy her oracle, and Damon is to die for shedding blood in the Sacred Valley ; this pagan ritual song by the priest develops genuine suspense.

Blank singing v, v

Amyntas expounds the oracle in such a way as to save the lives of the doomed men, and all go off singing in joy and thanksgiving.

Blank singing After v, viii ; p. 71 n.

All "exeunt cantantes" after the epilogue—a final exit song worked in, like the preceding one, as a sort of ritual of rejoicing at the happy outcome of the action.

Aristippus

"Slaves are they that heap up mountains"

"What ails thee, thou musing man"*

"But come, you lads that love Canary"*

"Aristippus is better in every letter" p. 74

"We care not for money, riches, or wealth"

These are all drinking songs, with no particular dramatic function ; but note that the fourth is a "patter" song.

The Conceited Peddler
"I am a peddler, and I sell my ware"

A self-characterizing "sung soliloquy." Though this work is a mono-drama or "show" and not a legitimate play, it is interesting in providing another example of the genus of singing peddler, which also includes Auto-lycus, Tawneycoat, and Thornton.

The Drinking Academy
"Madam and why" ii, i

Simple, delivering a love letter for his master, decides to read it; not impressed, he apparently proceeds to sing it to a ballad tune. If he does so, the end is pure comedy, enhanced by the ludicrous contrast between Simple's performance and the concept of a genuine love song.

"Though it may seem rude for me to intrude" iii, ii; p. 77 n.

This scene is a direct imitation of Jonson's in *Bartholomew Fair*, iii, v. The ballad itself, with four additional stanzas (totaling ten), is sung in Jonson's *Masque of Augurs*.

"Break from the east, my brighter day" v, iii; p. 19 n.

Knowlittle, a ridiculous suitor, is persuaded to sing a serenade to Lady Pecunia and so lays himself open to abuse by a band of cheaters. The song provides comic suspense by delaying the denouement, which the audi-ence suspect and are eagerly anticipating.

The Jealous Lovers
Blank song and blank singing v, vi, ix (actually the same scene)

A pagan ritual song accompanies a sacrifice to Hymen on behalf of two proposed marriages; Hymen forbids these marriages, whereupon the two romantic couples are reassorted properly, two comic couples are matched, other threads are tied up, and the play closes with the direction *"Exeunt cum choro cantantium in laud. Hym."*

The Muses' Looking-Glass
"Say, in a dance how shall we go" i, iv; p. 46

The play demonstrates the efficacy of the stage as a scourge of folly; Roscius, the presenter, begins with a song and dance, presumably discordant and grotesque, by the seven deadly sins.

Probable blank song ii, iv

The dialogue indicates a song as intermission entertainment between Acts ii and iii.

Blank song v, i, ii; p. 46

The contrasted extremes (the vices—e.g., cowardice and foolhardi-ness), ashamed of their ugliness as reflected in the looking glass of the drama, have reformed and combined into the golden means which are vir-tues (e.g., courage). The virtues then present a song and dance which, by its contrast with that of the vices in Act i, restates the moral lesson of the play. Afterward, the virtues go off singing.

RAWLINS, THOMAS

The Rebellion
" 'Tis a merry life we live" iv, vi; p. 69 n.

A work song by three tailors, similar in effect to the shoemakers' songs in Dekker and elsewhere.

RICHARDS, NATHANAEL
Messallina

"From those blue flames burning dim" II, ii

This lyric is either sung or chanted by three furies who appear to Messallina in her sleep and encourage her in her evil course. Skemp, in his edition of the play, assumes that the passage is sung.

Wordless singing IV, iii

Valens sings to accompany his own dancing during a discussion of a masque to be presented before the empress; Valens' conduct represents the cheerful assurance that goes before a fall.

"Helpless wretch, despair, despair" V, iv; pp. 66 n., 100–1, 125 n., 128 n.

This song of despair by two spirits tells Messallina of her imminent doom. Richards notes that this song "was left out of the Play in regard there was none could sing in Parts."

RIDER, WILLIAM
The Twins

Blank singing III, iii

A wood nymph sings to Carolo in his sleep; the song seems non-functional unless it symbolizes the power of sleep; it does not represent a dream or vision.

ROWLEY, SAMUEL
When You See Me, You Know Me

Wordless singing iii

Patch, Wolsey's fool, sings wordlessly.

Blank song viii (ed. Elze, p. 53); p. 46

A song is part of the music lesson of the young Prince of Wales; the passage in general stresses the spiritual and philosophical values of musical training for a prince.

ROWLEY, WILLIAM
All's Lost by Lust

Wordless snatch I, iii

The clownish Jaques sings a brief exit snatch, apparently in joy that his sister is to marry the noble Antonio.

Blank song III, i; p. 68 n.

Lothario, tired and troubled, has his page Cob sing him a soothing song to "fetch out" whatever it is that troubles his brain. The song has a plot function in that it puts Lothario to sleep and so makes possible Jacinta's escape from his custody.

"There was a nobleman of Spain"* III, iii; p. 67 n.

Jaques, sent to deliver a letter to Antonio and warned not to approach the latter discourteously, is neglected by Antonio until he indicates, by an ambiguous snatch of song, that his mission is important. Antonio's bride Dionysia wonders what is going on but is satisfied by the explanation that Jaques is a merry doctor who can cure Antonio's strange melancholy.

A Match at Midnight

"Did her not see her true love"* I, iii; pp. 42, 70 n.

"Her loved her once, her loved her no more"* II, i; pp. 42, 70 n.

"When high King Henry Second ruled this land"* III, i; pp. 42, 70 n.

"Farewell, widows prave, her shall no Randalls have"* IV, ii; pp. 42, 70 n.

"If Randall false to Marys prove"* IV, vii; pp. 42, 70 n.

"And Marys now was won, and all her pusiness done"* V, iv; pp. 42, 70 n.

"Will hear a noble Priton, how her gull an English flag"* V, iv; pp. 42, 70 n.

"Her wail in woe, her plunge in pain"* V, iv; pp. 42, 70 n.

Randall is developed throughout the play as a comic singing character; his snatches are from ballads and familiar songs, sung in Welsh accent and selected for their appropriateness to the occasion or adapted to fit it. Five of the eight are entrance snatches (nearly all of Randall's entrances are singing ones); the others arise out of the dialogue.

A Shoemaker a Gentleman

Blank singing I, ii; pp. 7 n., 69 n.

Christian shoemakers at their work "sing away sorrow" at the necessity of hiding their religion; their song covers the entrance of Crispinus and Crispianus, who interpret it as expressing peace of soul and therefore ask the shoemaker for work.

RUTTER, JOSEPH

The Shepherds' Holiday

"Shall I because my love is gone" I, i

Thyrsis, mourning over the inexplicable disappearance of his love Sylvia, has his boy sing the conventional complaint of a bereaved lover.

"He that mourns for a misteris [mistress]" II, i

Mirtillus sings a witty anti-Platonic song which characterizes the singer and may also be an attempt to cheer Thyrsis by light music, since sad music has brought no relief.

"Tell me what you think on earth" III, i

Our first sight of the missing Sylvia shows her, forlorn without her lover, singing a duet complaint with Delia.

"Come, lovely boy, unto my court" III, iii

An anti-Platonic song, performed as part of a country-sports masque which Mirtillus is rehearsing to be presented before the king. It develops a Fletcher reversal, being followed immediately by a messenger's announcement that Nerina is dying.

"Hymen, god of marriage bed" V, iv

Mirtillus sings a hymeneal song to celebrate the marriage of Thyrsis and Sylvia.

SAMPSON, WILLIAM

The Vow-Breaker

"When from the wars I do return" V, i

Joshua, the comic Puritan soldier, drinks too much and sings a satiric song about war (there is no stage direction that he sing, but Reed considers the passage a song and there is no reason to think it anything else).

"You dainty dames, so finely decked"* v, ii

A rude serenade (staves from the ballad of "Bateman's Tragedy") sung by Miles, a ridiculous suitor to Ursula; it results in his being beaten away by her uncle.

SHARPE, LEWIS
The Noble Stranger

"Tell me, Jove, should she disdain" ii, i; p. 19 n.

An *aubade* sung by a boy for Honorio, who is here in the apparently hopeless position of a subject in love with his princess; but the princess returns his love at this point, and the song leads into a genuine love scene.

"Charm, oh, charm, thou god of sleep" v, ii

A curative-consolatory lullaby sung by a lady to the princess Dulcimenta, whose love for Honorio seems hopeless.

SHARPHAM, EDWARD
Cupid's Whirligig

"Venus lay where Mars had found her" iii, i

An entrance song by young Lord Nonsuch, appropriate to the military nature of his temporary disguise as a begging soldier and to the amorous nature of his real character.

"They marched out manly by three and by three"* iv, iv

"Will you hear of a Spanish lady"* iv, iv

Entrance snatches by Nuecome, a frivolous, empty-headed, and empty-pursed courtier.

The Fleire

"His man's red hose were the color of his nose" ii, i; p. 74 n.

Felecia and Florida have set up as courtesans; this is an entrance snatch by Felecia in a particularly light or wanton mood.

SHIRLEY, HENRY
The Martyred Soldier

"What are earthly honors" iii, ii

This song covers the visit of an angel to Eugenius, a Christian bishop imprisoned by the pagan vandals. Angelic singing is traditional, according to Moore; this song also covers some action in dumb show.

"Fly, darkness, fly in spite of caves" v, i

"Go, fools, and let your fears" v, i

"She comes, she comes, she comes" v, i

"Come, oh come, oh come away" v, i

"Victory, victory! hell is beaten down" v, i

These five songs are sung by two angels who descend to free Victoria and Bellizarius from their martyrdom and to manifest God's power through other miracles.

SHIRLEY, JAMES
The Arcadia

Blank song ii, i; pp. *24*, 85 n., 87–8

Pyrocles, disguised as Zelmane, sings a love complaint "within."

"Which being done, blithely to work I fall"* iii, ii

"Art thou poor, and wouldst thou be" iii, ii

Dametas, digging for buried gold, sings in joyful anticipation; his spirits are dashed in a comic reversal when he discovers something very different from the treasure he expects.

Blank song v, i; p. 43

Pyrocles and Musidorus sing in prison; though essentially extraneous, their song shows them to be steadfast and unmoved in face of misfortune.

The Bird in a Cage

Blank song iii, iii; p. 68 n.

Eugenia and her attendant ladies try to relieve the boredom of a life without men by a song, a dance, and even amateur theatricals.

"What other is the world than a ball" iv, i

"Oh, yes, they are the best gamesters of all" iv, i

"There was an invisible fox, by chance" iv, i

A plot element in the play is the conversion of the rather foolish Morello into a keenly satiric court jester; these songs by him are a result of the humor of singing which accompanies his metamorphosis. They also have intrinsic comic and satiric values.

"Among all sorts of people" v, i

This song by Morello is a summary of his lecture on the power of the court fool.

Captain Underwit (The Country Captain)

"The juice of Spanish squeezed grapes is it" iv, i; p. 102 n.

A song performed by professional musicians as entertainment for the members of a drinking party in a tavern.

Wordless singing iv, iii

Device, exhilarated at having tricked Courtwell, runs off stage singing.

The Cardinal

"Come, my Daphne, come away" v, iii

The Cardinal seeks revenge on Rosaura by seducing her or raping her; as a preliminary, he provides this song—which, since she is mad, he apparently disguises as curative music. The first part of this action takes place off stage, and the song is therefore suspensive.

The Changes (Love in a Maze)

"Melancholy, hence! go get" iv, i; pp. 6 n., 10

Eugenia, apparently deserted by Thornay, has her maid sing her this soothing consolatory song.

"If Love his arrows shoot so fast" v, iii

Gerard, who has suddenly lost the love of both Goldsworth girls and has been rendered deeply melancholy by the loss, has his servant sing him this complaint, which has a soothing and in fact a soporific effect.

The Constant Maid

Wordless singing ii, i

Startup, a clownish country heir, sings to accompany his own dancing. Since he is showing off his accomplishments, the whole passage characterizes him as foolish and without breeding.

"An old man with a bed full of bones"* ii, ii

"With ding dong bell"* ii, ii

Hornet's Niece is so delighted at the prospect of escaping from her uncle and eloping with Playfair that she cannot conceal her joy; it bubbles forth in song. The lovers' accomplice, posing as a doctor, quiets Hornet's suspicions by telling him that the girl is mad.

Blank song iii, ii; pp. 68 n., 71 n.

Part of the elopement depends on an elaborate plan to keep Hornet busy by persuading him that he has been brought to court to be knighted; this song is part of the masquerade.

Blank song iv, iii

Hornet is further persuaded that he has been put in charge of the king's masques; a masque is presented forthwith, of which this song forms a part.

The Court Secret

"What help of tongue need they require" i, i; p. 24 n.

Manuel, a successful and eventually happy suitor, sings directly to his lady at the end of a long love conversation.

The Duke's Mistress

Blank song i, i

The Duke, infatuated with Ardelia, demands a song to quicken the minutes of her absence. This song is essentially extraneous.

Blank song ii, ii

This scene begins with a "song in dialogue," during which the people of the court enter; it may be designed for verisimilitude of court life, or possibly it is one aspect of the Duke's wooing of Ardelia.

Blank song iv, i

Horatio, courting the hideously ugly Fiametta, provides a song for her; this entire passage is a low-comedy burlesque of an ordinary romantic courtship.

The Example

"Welcome, welcome again to thy wits" v, iii

Sir Solitary Plot has regained his sanity and become a jovial person; in this rather improbable dialogue song he and his lady celebrate his recovery.

The Gamester

Wordless singing iii, i; p. 32 n.

Penelope, feigning wantonness, sings and dances to her own singing.

The Gentleman of Venice

Blank song iii, iv

Rosabella, a courtesan, sings to entertain the wild companions of Thomazo, worthless son of the Duke of Venice, who are meeting and drinking at her house.

Honoria and Mammon

Blank song (in praise of a courtier) ii, ii; p. 68 n.

Blank song (in praise of a soldier) ii, ii; p. 68 n.

These are partly suspensive songs; they are part of the unnecessarily theatrical way in which Honoria announces her choice among her suitors.

Blank song III, v

Allworth, chosen by Honoria, becomes ill with joy; this song is provided in an attempt to help him to sleep and so to recover.

The Humourous Courtier

Wordless singing III, i

Volterre, a vain courtier, dances to the accompaniment of his own singing.

Wordless singing IV, ii

Crispino dances to his own singing in imitation of Volterre.

Hyde Park

"Come, Muses all, that dwell nigh the fountain" IV, iii; p. 93

Venture, a semiridiculous suitor to Carol, sings a long "ballad" of famous race horses to entertain a group of his friends during a stroll; Shirley utilizes this incident, itself relatively extraneous, in a later plot complication.

The Imposture

"You virgins that did late despair" I, ii

Leonato, who has just saved Mantua from invasion, is welcomed into the city to this ceremonial chorus of rejoicing—which is, incidentally, part of the build-up of the Duke of Mantua to the imposture he plans to practice upon Leonato.

"Oh, fly, my soul! What hangs upon" II, iii

This song by nuns establishes the scene as a convent, covers the entrance of major characters, and establishes a mood of religious peace to contrast with Leonato's subsequent kidnaping of Juliana from this nunnery.

Wordless singing v, i

Bertoldi, a comic character, sings in anticipation as he joins friends who are drinking in a tavern.

Love's Cruelty

Blank song III, iii

This song begins the scene; it would seem to cover pantomimic action by the Duke and Eubella, whom he hopes to seduce. Cf. the songs in *The Duke's Mistress,* I, i, and II, ii.

"Courtier, hey! Courtier, ho!"* IV, i; p. 32 n.

"For he did but kiss her"* IV, i; pp. 32 n., 75 n.

Clariana and Hippolito have just committed adultery; he feels conscientious pangs mixed with twinges of fear, but Clariana feels neither and sings in ridicule of him and in wantonness and self-confidence. A moment later her wronged husband bursts into the room.

Love Tricks

"God of war, to Cupid yield" II, i

The senile amorist Rufaldo has "made a ditty" for his mistress Selina; in this scene his musician rehearses the song.

"When cannons are roaring and bullets are flying"* II, i; p. 46

"Oh music, the life of the soul"* II, i; p. 46

The rich gull Bubulcus is unmoved by Rufaldo's song; he prefers ballads and apparently sings a snatch in illustration of his tastes, whereupon Rufaldo sings a line in praise of music.

"Phyllis fair, do not disdain"* IV, v

The cunning servant Gorgon sings this snatch to demonstrate his readiness to join Gasparo in the latter's pastoral project.

Blank song v, i; pp. 24 n., 56

Gorgon, masquerading as a lovelorn shepherdess, sings what is probably a burlesque complaint. The situation is comic; the song is part of Gorgon's and Gasparo's little act to start a conversation with other supposed shepherds; and it affords time for Gasparo to recognize Felice.

"Woodmen, shepherds, come away" v, iii

Part of a play-within-a-play, a combination of country sports and masque.

The Maid's Revenge

Blank song v, iii; pp. 6 n., 68 n.

Castabella, disguised as a page, sings in an attempt to bring relief to Sebastiano, who is grieving over having killed Antonio in a duel. The song lulls Sebastiano to sleep (a plot device), and a Fletcher reversal follows when Berinthia enters almost immediately to avenge her brother by stabbing Sebastiano.

The Opportunity

Blank song II, iii; pp. 26 n., 68 n.

Cornelia, a lovelorn lady, sings a complaint at the Duchess' window; her song attracts the attention of two men outside and leads directly into some complicated comedy of mistaken identities.

The Politician

Blank catch III, ii; p. 53 n.

Two parasites of Gotharus are trying, by means of a drinking party, to debauch the character of Haraldus; when Haraldus wants to leave them, they suggest this catch to persuade him to stay.

St. Patrick for Ireland

"Post maris saevi fremitus Iërnae" I, i

Patrick and the other Christian priests sing this hymn at their first processional entrance on their arrival in Ireland.

"Come away, oh, come away" II, ii

A pagan ritual song, part of a sacrifice to Jupiter.

"Have you never seen in the air" III, i

"Oh, the queen, and the king, and the royal offspring" III, i

"Love is a bog, a deep bog, a wide bog" III, i

"Patrick, welcome to this isle" III, i

"Come, we will drink a cup, boy, but of better brewing" III, i

All these are sung by the Bard, a singing character presumably intended to combine comedy and local color, whose normal conversation frequently turns into song.

" 'Tis long of men that maids are sad" IV, i; pp. 30 n., 62, 74 n.

"A poor wench was sighing and weeping amain" IV, i; pp. 30 n., 62, 74 n.

Emeria has been raped by Corybreus and is naturally melancholy;

her brutish father Milcho sends the Bard to try to cheer her up and incidentally to enflame her thoughts to make her responsive to the courtship of
Corybreus. The Bard accordingly sings two ribald, salacious songs, the second of which is bitterly ironic in that the Bard attempts to amuse Emeria by
describing, unwittingly, a situation very like her own.

"Look down, great Jove, and god of war" IV, ii

Another pagan ritual song, accompanying a sacrifice to Jupiter and
Mars.

"I neither will lend nor borrow" V, i

The Bard's farewell, a "sung soliloquy" explaining his preference
for pleasure as opposed to the self-sacrifice demanded by Christianity.

"Down from the skies" V, iii

"Patrick, sleep; oh, sleep a while" V, iii

These two songs are part of an apparition to Patrick of his guardian
angel Victor and other angels, preparatory to and foreshadowing the grand
climax and feature attraction of the play, the approach and repulse of the
reptiles.

The Sisters

"Beauty and the various graces" III, i

An entrance song by Frapolo and his gang of thieves, who, disguised as "mathematicians," have been admitted to Paulina's castle. The
song, of course, helps to establish them as amiable outlaws.

Possible blank song III, ii; p. 30 n.

Antonio has urged the waiting woman Francescina to attempt to
stimulate his niece Angellina to more responsiveness to the wooing of Con-
tarini; at the end of this act Francescina offers to sing to Angellina of Venus
and Adonis, or of Calisto.

The Witty Fair One

"Back, back again! fond man, forbear" IV, iii; p. 68 n.

"Love, a thousand sweets distilling" IV, iii; p. 68 n.

These contrasted songs (the first a warning to repent, the second a
conventional seduction song) are elements in Penelope's elaborate trick to
expose Fowler in all his lechery and so to reform him.

SUCKLING, JOHN

Aglaura

"Why so pale and wan, fond lover" IV, ii; p. 29 n.

The scene seems to be mainly a setting for the anti-Platonic song;
but the song may possibly symbolize off-stage adultery.

"No, no, fair heretic, it needs must be" IV, iv

Aglaura is virtually imprisoned, and her love for Thersames seems
hopeless; she has her boy sing this sad song, a complaint intended to be
soothing and consolatory.

Brennoralt

"Come, let the state stay" II, ii

A drinking song in a drinking scene involving five cavaliers; it is
preceded in the same scene by four other lyrics which seem intended to be
recited rather than sung.

The Goblins

"Bring them, bring them, bring them in" I, iii

The thieves, who masquerade as goblins, are bringing captives before their chief; this quatrain, if sung, must be part of their sham-supernatural masquerade.

"And for the blue"* I, iii

One of the captives, a drunken poet, hiccoughs out snatches of a drinking song.

Blank song II, i

Musicians serenade Sabrina for the Prince, an unsuccessful suitor; but the music has an additional purpose—it is intended to cover the entrance into Sabrina's house of men searching for her lover Samorat, supposed a murderer.

"Welcome, welcome, mortal wight" III, i

Another sham-supernatural song by the "goblins," whose singing of course helps to identify them as amiable outlaws.

"Some drink! what, boy, some drink" III, ii

"Around, around, around"* III, ii

"A health to the nut-brown lass" III, ii

These two songs and fragment are sung by several cavaliers who, helping in a prison break, calmly sit drinking and singing while they keep an eye on the captured gaoler. This song and scene are similar in spirit to *Brennoralt,* II, ii.

The Sad One

"Hast thou seen the down i' th' air" IV, iii

Florelio, who has just learned that his wife is unfaithful, has his boy sing him this song in a combination of purposes: it is an attempt to relieve his melancholy and simultaneously a proxy-sung lyric soliloquy of Florelio's bitterness.

"Come, come away to the tavern, I say" IV, iv

Multecarni (representing Jonson) goes off to dine at the Mermaid singing this anticipatory drinking snatch.

TAILOR, ROBERT

The Hog Hath Lost His Pearl

"And you that delight in trulls and minions"* I, i

Haddit and a player are dickering over the acceptability of a jig which Haddit has written; the player objects to the meter and sings a couple of lines to emphasize his point. This is realistic comedy.

TATHAM, JOHN

Love Crowns the End

"I will follow through yon grove" vi

Cloe, going mad for love of Lysander, suddenly breaks into song; this is the first indication of her madness and suggests the cause of that madness.

"Hey down a down derry" viii

"When love did act a woman's part" viii

Mad songs by Cloe.

"Love cannot choose but pity yield" viii

Nymphs sing this song to soothe Cloe as they lead her away to be cured.

"Sit, while I do gather flowers" ix; p. 23 n.

This love duet by Gloriana and Lysander apparently is Tatham's method of condensing a major romance into his pocket-sized play; incidentally, the song puts both lovers to sleep.

"Sleep on, sleep on" ix; p. 66 n.

"Rise, rise, Lysander, to prevent" ix; p. 66 n.

Both these songs are by supernatural visitants; they foreshadow coming events but have no practical value as warnings to Lysander.

"I know Lysander's dead" xii

"Do you see where he doth stand" xii

Mad songs by Gloriana, distracted by fear and by the supposed death of Lysander. Like Cloe's, they suggest the cause of her madness.

TOMKIS, THOMAS

Albumazar

"Bear up thy learned brow, Albumazar" i, i

Furbo enters and later goes out singing in triumph at having spied out the secrets of Pandolfo in preparation for the latter's fleecing by Albumazar. Furbo is an amiable outlaw.

"Sing sweetly, that our notes may cause" i, iii

Ronca entertains Pandolfo by showing him an "otacousticon," through which Pandolfo supposedly hears the interact song at a university play far away; presumably either Ronca or Furbo actually sings the song.

"Flow streams of liquid salt from my sad eyes" iii, viii

As part of a deception being practiced on Trincalo, the courtesan Bevilona poses as a rich lady mourning Antonio, and as part of the stage setting Furbo sings for her this complaint of a bereaved lover.

"My heart in flames doth fry" ("Alcoch Dolash") iii, viii; p. 74 n.

Trincalo, fully deceived, serenades Bevilona with this "shaped" lyric. The dialogue indicates that before he sings it in English, he performs it in gibberish supposed to represent Moorish.

Lingua

Wordless singing i, vii

Tactus sings in joy at having found a crown and robe and having kept Olfactus from suspecting his discovery.

TOURNEUR, CYRIL

The Atheist's Tragedy

Solmization iv, i

Cataplasma, another musical bawd, sings in giving a lesson on the lute to Sebastian while he waits for Levidulcia to arrive for an assignation.

WEBSTER, JOHN

Appius and Virginia

Two blank songs ii, i

Appius sends Clodius to woo Virginia for him with two serenades, which of course are ineffective.

The Devil's Law-Case

"All the flowers of the spring" v, iv

Romelio, facing a trial by combat, either sings or declaims this dirge in octosyllabics. Cf. the similar dirges in Webster's other plays.

The Duchess of Malfi

"Arms and honors deck thy story" iii, iv; p. 89

This ritualistic ditty, the authorship of which is disclaimed by Webster, covers the dumb show in which the Cardinal surrenders his hat for a helmet and then banishes Antonio and the Duchess.

"Oh let us howl some heavy note" iv, ii; p. 38 n.

A part of the masque of madmen sent the Duchess by Ferdinand, ostensibly to cure her melancholy but actually to torment her before her murder. Lucas considers this masque a "half-comic interlude."

"Hark, now everything is still" iv, ii

Bosola may sing, but more probably chants, this dirge before murdering the Duchess.

The White Devil

Blank song v, iv; p. 70 n.

Flamineo draws the traverse to reveal Cornelia and other ladies singing a dirge as they wind the corpse of the murdered Marcello.

"Call for the robin redbreast and the wren" v, iv

"Let holy Church receive him duly" v, iv

This dirge and couplet are either declaimed or sung by Cornelia, mad. The scene as a whole seems imitative of Ophelia's madness.

WILD, ROBERT

The Benefice

"Mnemosyne no more shall be" i, i

A song in praise of Ceres forming a sort of overture to the play proper, which is set within a framework or induction to which Act i is wholly devoted.

"How shall he sing, whose throat is hoarse with care"* iv, i

"God prosper long our noble king" iv, i

"I am confirmed, a scholar can" iv, i

Snatches by Bookworm—the first in depression, the others as part of his disguise as a ballad-seller.

"When Alexander crossed the seas" iv, i; p. 42 n.

"There is good liquor" iv, i; p. 42 n.

The songs of a tinker, the first covering his entrance. Drinking songs seem characteristic of tinkers.

"I have been a jovial rambler" After iv; p. 74 n.

A satirical song by Furor Poeticus, evidently intended as inter-act entertainment.

"Come on and let's be merry"* v, i

"First begin with the horn-book"* v, i

"But still she replies, good sir, let it be"* v, i

Drunken snatches by Hob.

"Lullaby, lullaby baby, lullaby" v, i

A gypsy woman sings this lullaby to her child.

"Good people all, give ear a while to me" v, i; p. 77 n.

As the conclusion to some absurd comedy, Hob puts a rope about his neck and sings a "hanging ballad" of repentance.

WILSON, ARTHUR

The Inconstant Lady

"If the power of art can draw" ii, iv; p. 68 n.

Cloris sings to lull Aramant to sleep as the first step in the cure of his madness.

"If I were a wanton lover" iii, iv

Romilia, a bawd, has the wench Mela sing as entertainment for Busiro, a patron of her brothel.

The Swisser

"So doth the early lark salute the day" iii, i

Alcidonus has his boy sing this serenade to Selina to summon her to an interview. The serenade is unconventional in that it is provided by a husband for the wife to whom he is secretly married; it is conventional in that it has unexpected results.

"He's a cabinet of treasure" v, iii; pp. *32–3*

Panopia, feigning an absolutely uncontrolled passion for Arioldus amounting to distraction, sings this song to him.

BIBLIOGRAPHY

1. Texts of the Plays

This study is based on an examination of 479 plays. For purposes of economy, individual titles are listed below only when they have been read in separate volumes; in a large canon like the Beaumont and Fletcher one, for example, I name the collected editions used and state the number of plays read. The following abbreviations are used:

Apocrypha C. F. Tucker Brooke, ed. *The Shakespeare Apocrypha*. Oxford, Clarendon Press, 1918.

Bullen A. H. Bullen, ed. *A Collection of Old English Plays*. London, Wyman & Sons, 1883. 4 vols.

Dodsley Robert Dodsley, ed. *A Select Collection of Old Plays*. "A new edition." London, Septimus Prowett, 1825. 12 vols.

Materialien W. Bang. *Materialien zur Kunde des älteren Englischen Dramas*. Louvain, A. Uystpruyst; Leipzig, O. Harrassowitz; and London, David Nutt. Volume and date listed separately for each item cited.

Materials Henry de Vocht, ed. *Materials for the Study of the Old English Drama*. Louvain, A. Uystpruyst (Librairie Universitaire). Volume and date listed separately for each item cited. A continuation of *Materialien*.

MSR Malone Society reprints. Oxford, Oxford University Press. Date listed separately for each item cited.

TFT The Tudor Facsimile Texts. Amersham, Tudor Facsimile Text Society. Date listed separately for each item cited.

Seventeenth-century editions are listed only as printed in London, with the date; for fuller information on them, see *The Cambridge Bibliography of English Literature*.

This is not a complete bibliography of editions consulted in the preparation of this study; it is merely a check list of the texts used for quotation or for scene division.

Alexander, Sir William. "The Dramatic Works," *The Poetical Works of Sir William Alexander Earl of Stirling,* I. Ed. L. E. Kastner and H. B. Charlton. Manchester, Manchester University Press and Longmans, Green, 1921. 4 plays.

Anonymous. *Alphonsus, Emperor of Germany*. Read in the Pearson reprint of Chapman, *q.v.*

Andromana, or The Merchant's Wife. Reprinted in *A Select Collection of Old Plays,* XI. London, printed for R. Dodsley in Pall-Mall, 1744.

The Bloody Banquet. TFT, 1914.

Caesar and Pompey. TFT, 1913.

Claudius Tiberius Nero. TFT, 1913.

The Costly Whore. Reprinted in *A Collection of Old English Plays,* iv. Ed. A. H. Bullen. London, Wyman & Sons, 1885. 4 vols.

The Country Girl. London, 1647.

Every Woman in Her Humour. TFT, 1913.

Exchange Ware at the Second Hand, Viz. Band, Ruff, and Cuff. London, 1615. Dialogue.

The Fair Maid of Bristow. TFT, 1912.

The Faithful Friends. Read in the Dyce edition of Beaumont and Fletcher, *q.v.*

The Ghost, or The Woman Wears the Breeches. London, 1653.

The Honest Lawyer. TFT, 1914.

How a Man May Choose a Good Wife from a Bad. Ed. A. E. H. Swaen. *Materialien,* LIII (1912).

Jeronimo, The First Part of. Dodsley, III.

The Knave in Grain, New Vamped. London, 1640.

The London Prodigal. Apocrypha.

Look about You. TFT, 1912.

The Merry Devil of Edmonton. Apocrypha.

Narcissus. Ed. Margaret L. Lee. London, David Nutt, 1893

Nero. London, 1624.

Nobody and Somebody. TFT, 1911.

The Partial Law. Ed. Bertram Dobell. London, Ballantyne, 1908.

Pathomachia, or The Battle of Affections. Reprinted in *Collectanea Adamantaea,* xxii. Edinburgh, privately printed, 1887.

Philotus. Reprinted from the edition of Robert Charteris. Edinburgh, Ballantyne, 1835.

The Pilgrimage to Parnassus with the Two Parts of the Return from Parnassus. Ed. W. D. Macray. Oxford, Clarendon Press, 1886. 3 plays.

The Second Maiden's Tragedy. MSR, 1909.

Swetnam the Woman-Hater. TFT, 1914.

The Two Merry Milk-Maids. TFT, 1914.

The Two Noble Ladies. MSR, 1930.

Two Wise Men and All the Rest Fools. TFT, 1913.

The Valiant Scot. London, 1637.

The Wit of a Woman. MSR, 1913.

Work for Cutlers, or A Merry Dialogue between Sword, Rapier, and Dagger. Q 1615 reprinted and edited by Albert F. Sieveking. London, C. J. Clay & Sons, 1904. Dialogue.

A Yorkshire Tragedy. Apocrypha.

Armin, Robert. *The Two Maids of More-Clacke.* TFT, 1913.

(?) *The Valiant Welshman.* TFT, 1913.

Barnes, Barnabe. *The Devil's Charter.* TFT, 1913.

Barrie, Lodowick. *Ram-Alley.* TFT, 1913.

Baylie, Simon. *The Wizard.* Ed. Henry de Vocht. *Materials, 4* (1930).

Beaumont, Francis, and Fletcher, John. *Beaumont and Fletcher.* Ed. Arnold Glover and A. R. Waller. Cambridge, Cambridge University Press, 1905–12. 10 vols., 50 plays (counting *The Coronation* as J. Shirley's).

Four Plays in One. In *The Works of Beaumont and Fletcher.* Ed. Alexander Dyce. London, Moxon, 1843–46. 11 vols. Scene division follows this edition.

    The Tragedy of Sir John van Olden Barnavelt. Ed. Wilhelmina P. Frijlinck. Amsterdam, H. G. van Dorssen, 1922.

Berkeley, William. *The Lost Lady.* London, 1639.

Brewer, Anthony. *The Love-sick King.* Ed. A. E. H. Swaen. *Materialien, 18* (1907).

Brome, Alexander. *The Cunning Lovers.* London, 1654.

Brome, Richard. *The Dramatic Works of Richard Brome.* London, John Pearson, 1873. 3 vols., 15 plays.

Carlell, Lodowick. 1 and 2 *Arviragus and Philicia.* London, 1639.

    The Deserving Favorite. Ed. Charles H. Gray. Chicago, University of Chicago Press, 1905.

    The Fool Would Be a Favorite. Reprinted by Allardyce Nicoll. Waltham Saint Lawrence, Golden Cockerel Press, 1926.

    1 and 2 *The Passionate Lovers.* London, 1655.

    Osmond the Great Turk. Reprinted by Allardyce Nicoll. Waltham Saint Lawrence, Golden Cockerel Press, 1926.

Cartwright, William. *Comedies, Tragi-Comedies, with Other Poems.* London, 1651. 4 plays.

Cary, Elizabeth (Viscountess Falkland). *The Tragedy of Mariam.* London, 1651.

Chamberlain, Robert. *The Swaggering Damsel.* London, 1640.

Chapman, George. *The Comedies and Tragedies of George Chapman.* London, John Pearson, 1873. 3 vols. 12 plays (counting *Alphonsus* as anonymous).

    Chabot, Admiral of France. Read in the Gifford and Dyce edition of J. Shirley, *q.v.*

    Charlemagne, or The Distracted Emperor. MSR, 1938.

    Sir Giles Goosecap, Knight. TFT, 1912.

    Scene division follows *The Plays and Poems of George Chapman.* Ed. Thomas Marc Parrott. New York, E. P. Dutton, 1910. 3 vols.

Chettle, Henry. *The Tragedy of Hoffman, or A Revenge for a Father.* TFT, 1913.

Cokayne, Aston. *The Obstinate Lady.* London, 1657.

    Trappolin Supposed a Prince. In *Small Poems of Divers Sorts.* London, 1658.

    Scene division follows *The Dramatic Works of Sir Aston Cokain.* Ed. James Maidment and W. H. Logan. Edinburgh, William Paterson, and London, H. Sotheran, 1874.

Cooke, Jo[shua?]. *Greene's Tu Quoque.* TFT, 1913.

Cowley, Abraham. *Essays, Plays and Sundry Verses.* Ed. A. R. Waller. Cambridge, Cambridge University Press, 1906. 2 plays.

Daborne, Robert. *A Christian Turned Turk.* Reprinted by A. E. H. Swaen in *Anglia, 20* (1898), 153–256. Text begins on p. 188.

    The Poor Man's Comfort. Reprinted by A. E. H. Swaen in *Anglia, 21* (1899?), 373–440.

Daniel, Samuel. *The Complete Works in Verse and Prose of Samuel Daniel.* Ed. Alexander B. Grosart. London, privately printed by Hazell, Watson, & Viney, 1885. 5 vols., 4 plays in Vol. III.

D'Avenant, William. *The Platonic Lovers.* London, 1665.
   10 other pre-Civil War plays, first editions.
   Scene division follows *The Dramatic Works of Sir William D'Avenant.* Ed. James Maidment and W. H. Logan. Edinburgh, William Paterson, and London, H. Sotheran, 1872–74. 5 vols.

Davenport, Robert. *The City Nightcap.* London, 1661.
   King John and Matilda. London, 1655.
   A New Trick to Cheat the Devil. Reprinted in "The Works of Robert Davenport," *Old English Plays,* n. s., III. Ed. A. H. Bullen. London and Redhill, Hansard Publishing Union, 1890. 3 vols.

Day, John. *The Works of John Day.* Ed. A. H. Bullen. London, Chiswick Press, 1881. 2 vols., 4 plays. Quotations from *Humour Out of Breath* follow text in *Nero & Other Plays.* Mermaid Series. London, T. Fisher Unwin, and New York, Charles Scribner's Sons, n.d. (1887?).
   The Isle of Gulls. The Shakespeare Association Facsimiles, No. 12. London, Oxford University Press, 1936.

Dekker, Thomas. *The Dramatic Works of Thomas Dekker.* London, John Pearson, 1873. 4 vols., 13 plays (counting *The Roaring Girl* as Middleton's, *The Witch of Edmonton* and *The Sun's Darling* as Ford's).
   (?) *Lust's Dominion.* Ed. J. Le Gay Brereton. *Materials, 5* (1931).
   (?) *The Noble Soldier.* TFT, 1913.
   Patient Grissill. TFT, 1911.
   (?) *The Weakest Goeth to the Wall.* TFT, 1911.
   (?) *The Welsh Ambassador.* MSR, 1920.
   See also Anonymous.

Denham, Sir John. *The Sophy.* London, 1642.

Drue, Thomas. *The Life of the Duchess of Suffolk.* London, 1631.

Fane, Mildmay. *Candy Restored.* Ed. Clifford Leech. *Materials, 15* (1938).

Field, Nathan. *Amends for Ladies.* London, 1618.
   A Woman Is a Weathercock. In *Nero & Other Plays.* Mermaid Series. London, T. Fisher Unwin, and New York, Charles Scribner's Sons, n.d. (1887?).

Fisher, Jasper. *Fuimus Troes (The True Trojans).* London, 1633.

Fletcher, Phineas. *Sicelides.* Reprinted in Giles and Phineas Fletcher, *Poetical Works,* I. Ed. Frederick S. Boas. Cambridge, Cambridge University Press, 1908. 2 vols.

Ford, John. *The Sun's Darling* and *The Witch of Edmonton.* In *The Works of John Ford.* Ed. Alexander Dyce with notes by William Gifford. London, James Toovey, 1869. 3 vols.
   8 other plays. In *Materialien, 13* (1906), *23* (1908); *Materials, 1* (1927).

Freeman, Ralph. *Imperiale.* London, 1655.

Glapthorne, Henry. *The Plays and Poems of Henry Glapthorne.* London, John Pearson, 1874. 2 vols., 6 plays.
   The Lady Mother. Bullen, II.

Goffe, Thomas. *The Careless Shepherdess*. London, 1656.
   Three Excellent Tragedies. London, 1656.
Gomersall, Robert. *The Tragedy of Lodovick Sforza*. Ed. B. R. Pearn. *Materials, 8* (1933).
Gough, John. *The Strange Discovery*. London, 1640.
Habington, William. *The Queen of Arragon*. London, 1640.
Harding, Samuel. *Sicily and Naples, or The Fatal Union*. Oxford, 1640.
Hausted, Peter. *The Rival Friends*. London, 1632.
Hawkins, William. *Apollo Shroving*. Ed. Howard Garrett Rhoads. Philadelphia, press not named; Ph.D. dissertation, University of Pennsylvania, 1936.
Heming, William. *The Fatal Contract*. London, 1653.
   The Jews' Tragedy. Ed. Heinrich A. Cohn. *Materialien, 40* (1913).
Heywood, Thomas. *The Dramatic Works of Thomas Heywood*. London, John Pearson, 1874. 6 vols., 23 plays.
   The Captives. Ed. Alexander Corbin Judson. New Haven, Yale University Press, 1921.
   (?) *Dick of Devonshire*. Reprinted from Bullen by J. Brooking Rowe. In *Devon Notes and Queries*, III, Pt. II. Exeter, James G. Commin, 1905.
   (?) *Thomas Lord Cromwell*. *Apocrypha*.
   See also Anonymous and Webster.
Holyday, Barten. *Technogamia, or The Marriages of the Arts*. Ed. Sister M. Jean Carmel Cavanaugh. Washington, D.C., Catholic University of America Press, 1942. Contains photographic reproduction of Q 1618.
Jonson, Ben. *Ben Jonson*. Ed. C. H. Herford and Percy Simpson. Oxford, Clarendon Press, 1925-47. 8 vols., 16 completed plays, 1 incomplete play, 1 fragment.
Jordan, Thomas. *The Walks of Islington and Hogsdon, with the Humours of Woodstreet-Compter*. London, 1657.
Killigrew, Henry. *The Conspiracy* (*Pallantus and Eudora*). London, 1638.
Killigrew, Thomas. *Comedies, and Tragedies*. London, 1664. 3 plays.
   The Parson's Wedding. Dodsley, XI.
Kirke, John. *The Seven Champions of Christendom*. With introduction and notes by Giles E. Dawson. *Western Reserve University Bulletin*, n. s., XXXII, 16 (September 15, 1929).
Knevet, Ralph. *Rhodon and Iris*. London, 1631.
Lower, William. *The Phoenix in Her Flames*. London, 1639.
Lyly, John. *The Complete Works of John Lyly*. Ed. R. Warwick Bond. Oxford, Clarendon Press, 1902. 3 vols., 8 plays.
Machin, Lewis, and Markham, Gervase. *The Dumb Knight*. London, 1633.
Markham, Gervase, and Sampson, William. *The True Tragedy of Herod and Antipater, with the Death of Fair Mariam*. London, 1622.
Marmion, Shackerley. *The Antiquary*. In *The Dramatic Works of Shackerley Marmion*. Ed. James Maidment and W. H. Logan. Edinburgh, William Paterson, and London, H. Sotheran, 1875.
   A Fine Companion. London, 1633.
   Holland's Leaguer. London, 1632.
   (?) *The Soddered Citizen*. MSR, 1936.

Marston, John. *The Plays of John Marston*. Ed. H. Harvey Wood. Edinburgh and London, Oliver and Boyd, 1934–39. 3 vols., 11 plays. Scene division follows *The Works of John Marston*. Ed. A. H. Bullen. London, John C. Nimmo, 1887. 3 vols.

Mason, John. *The Turk* (*Mulleasses*). Ed. Joseph Q. Adams, Jr. *Materialien, 37* (1913).

Massinger, Philip. *Three New Plays* (*The Bashful Lover, The Guardian, A Very Woman*). London, 1655.

Believe as You List. MSR, 1927.

The Bondman. Ed. Benjamin Townley Spencer. Princeton, Princeton University Press, 1932.

The City Madam. Ed. Rudolf Kirk. Princeton, Princeton University Press, 1934.

The Duke of Milan. Ed. Thomas Whitfield Baldwin. Lancaster, Pa., New Era Printing Co., 1918.

The Fatal Dowry. Ed. Charles Lacy Lockert, Jr. Lancaster, Pa., New Era Printing Co., 1918.

The Great Duke of Florence. Ed. Johanne M. Stochholm. Baltimore, J. H. Furst, 1933.

The Maid of Honor. Ed. Eva A. W. Bryne. London, R. Clay & Sons, 1927.

A New Way to Pay Old Debts. Ed. A. H. Cruickshank. Oxford, Clarendon Press, 1926.

The Parliament of Love. MSR, 1928.

The Roman Actor. Ed. William Lee Sandidge. Princeton, Princeton University Press, 1929.

The Unnatural Combat. Ed. Robert Stockton Telfer. Princeton, Princeton University Press, 1932.

The Emperor of the East, The Picture, and *The Renegado*. In *The Dramatic Works of Massinger and Ford*. Ed. Hartley Coleridge. "New edition." London, Edward Moxon, 1848.

May, Thomas. *The Tragedy of Cleopatra*. London, 1639.

The Heir. London, 1633.

The Tragedy of Julia Agrippina. Ed. F. Ernst Schmid. *Materialien, 43* (1914).

The Old Couple. Ed. Sister M. Simplicia Fitzgibbons. Washington, D.C., Catholic University of America Press, 1943.

Mayne, Jasper. *The Amorous War*. London, 1659.

The City Match. London, 1639.

Mead, Robert. *The Combat of Love and Friendship*. London, 1654.

Middleton, Thomas. *The Works of Thomas Middleton*. Ed. A. H. Bullen. London, John C. Nimmo, 1886. 8 vols., 21 plays.

The Puritan. Apocrypha.

Note that the songs for *Hengist, King of Kent; or The Mayor of Queenborough* occur in only one edition, that of R. C. Bald. New York and London, Charles Scribner's Sons, 1938.

Montague, Walter. *The Shepherds' Paradise*. London, 1659.

Mountfort, Walter. *The Launching of the Mary*. MSR, 1933.

Nabbes, Thomas. *The Bride*. London, 1640.
    Covent Garden. London, 1638.
    Hannibal and Scipio. London, 1637.
    Microcosmos. Dodsley, IX.
    Tottenham Court. London, 1639.
    The Unfortunate Mother. London, 1640.
Neale, Thomas. *The Ward*. Ed. John Arthur Mitchell. Philadelphia, press not named; Ph.D. dissertation, University of Pennsylvania, 1937.
Peaps, William. *Love in Its Ecstasy, or The Large Prerogative*. London, 1649.
Percy, William. *The Cuckquean's and Cuckold's Errand* and *The Faery Pastoral*. Printed from manuscript, London, Shakspeare Press, by William Nicol, 1824. 2 plays.
Quarles, Francis. *The Complete Works in Prose and Verse of Francis Quarles*. Ed. Alexander B. Grosart. Edinburgh, Edinburgh University Press, 1881. 3 vols, 1 play (*The Virgin Widow*).
Randolph, Thomas. *Amyntas*. In *The Poems and Amyntas of Thomas Randolph*. Ed. John Jay Parry. New Haven, Yale University Press, 1917.
    Aristippus ("show") and *The Conceited Peddler* (monodrama). In *Poetical and Dramatic Works of Thomas Randolph*. Ed. W. Carew Hazlitt. London, Reeves & Turner, 1875. 2 vols.
    The Drinking Academy. Ed. Samuel A. Tannenbaum and Hyder E. Rollins. Cambridge, Mass., Harvard University Press, 1930.
    The Jealous Lovers. Cambridge, 1632.
    The Muses' Looking-Glass. In *Poems, with the Muses' Looking-Glass and Amyntas*. London, 1638.
Rawlins, Thomas. *The Rebellion*. London, 1640.
Richards, Nathanael. *The Tragedy of Messallina*. Ed. A. R. Skemp. *Materialien, 30* (1910).
Rider, William. *The Twins*. London, 1655.
Rowley, Samuel. *When You See Me, You Know Me*. Ed. Karl Elze. Dessau, Emil Barth, 1874.
Rowley, William. *All's Lost by Lust* and *A Shoemaker a Gentleman*. Ed. Charles Wharton Stork. Philadelphia, John C. Winston, 1910.
    The Birth of Merlin. TFT, 1910.
    A Match at Midnight. London, 1633.
    A New Wonder, a Woman Never Vexed. London, 1632.
Rutter, Joseph. *The Shepherds' Holiday*. London, 1635.
Sampson, William. *The Vow-Breaker*. Ed. Hans Wallrath. *Materialien, 42* (1914).
Shakespeare, William. *The Complete Works of William Shakespeare*. Ed. W. J. Craig. London, New York, and Toronto, Oxford University Press, 1945 (first published 1904). 1 vol., 37 plays.
Sharpe, Lewis. *The Noble Stranger*. London, 1640.
Sharpham, Edward. *Cupid's Whirligig*. Ed. Allardyce Nicoll. Waltham Saint Lawrence, Golden Cockerel Press, 1926.
    The Fleire. Ed. Hunold Hibbe. *Materialien, 36* (1912).
Shirley, Henry. *The Martyred Soldier*. Bullen, 1.

Shirley, James. *The Dramatic Works and Poems of James Shirley.* Ed. William Gifford and Alexander Dyce. London, John Murray, 1833. 6 vols., 32 plays.

Shirley, James, and Cavendish, W. *The Country Captain (Captain Underwit).* Bullen, II.

Smith, Wentworth. *The Hector of Germany.* Ed. Leonidas Warren Payne, Jr. Philadelphia, John C. Winston, 1906.

Suckling, John. *Fragmenta Aurea.* London, 1646. 3 plays.
    Scene division follows *The Works of Sir John Suckling.* Ed. A. Hamilton Thompson. New York, E. P. Dutton, 1910. The fragmentary *The Sad One* was read in this volume.

Tailor, Robert. *The Hog Hath Lost His Pearl.* London, 1614.

Tatham, John. *The Dramatic Works of John Tatham.* Ed. James Maidment and W. H. Logan. Edinburgh, William Paterson, and London, H. Sotheran, 1879. 2 plays.

Tomkis, Thomas. *Albumazar.* Q 1615 reprinted and edited by Hugh G. Dick. Berkeley and Los Angeles, University of California Press, 1944.
    Lingua, or The Combat of the Tongue and the Five Senses for Superiority. Dodsley, v.

Tourneur, Cyril. *The Plays and Poems of Cyril Tourneur.* Ed. John Churton Collins. London, Chatto & Windus, 1878. 2 vols., 2 plays.

Webster, John. *Appius and Virginia, A Cure for a Cuckold, The Devil's Law-Case, The Duchess of Malfi,* and *The White Devil.* In *The Complete Works of John Webster.* Ed. F. L. Lucas. New York, Oxford University Press, 1937. 4 vols.

Wild, Robert. *The Benefice.* London, 1689.

Wilkins, George. *The Miseries of Enforced Marriage.* TFT, 1913.

Wilson, Arthur. *The Inconstant Lady.* Oxford, S. Collingwood, 1814.
    The Swisser. Ed. Albert Feuillerat. Paris, Librairie Fischbacher, 1904.

2. Analytical Works

Although one is likely to discover, in any edition of any Stuart play or in any work dealing even remotely with the Stuart drama, a word of comment on or appreciation of the songs, the literature concerned with the actual function of the dramatic lyric is very slight, Shakespeare's songs alone having received much attention. The following titles form at once a selective bibliography of the subject and a list of the works most frequently cited in the notes to this study.

It does not seem necessary to list all the general works—Bentley, Chambers, Harbage, and the rest—which are indispensable to any student of the Tudor and Stuart drama.

Anonymous. "Song and Drama," *TLS,* March 25, 1926, pp. 225–6. Leading article and review of E. B. Reed, *Songs from the British Drama.*

Boyd, M. C. *Elizabethan Music and Musical Criticism.* Philadelphia, University of Pennsylvania Press, 1940.

Cowling, G. H. *Music on the Shakespearian Stage.* Cambridge, Cambridge University Press, 1913.

Evans, Willa McClung. *Ben Jonson and Elizabethan Music*. Lancaster, Pa., Lancaster Press, 1929.

Lathrop, H. B. "Shakespeare's Dramatic Use of Songs," *MLN, 23* (January, 1908), 1–5.

Moore, John Robert. "The Function of the Songs in Shakespeare's Plays," *Shakespeare Studies by Members of the Department of English of the University of Wisconsin*, pp. 78–102. Madison, University of Wisconsin Press, 1916.

"The Song in the English Drama to 1642." Ph.D. dissertation, Harvard University, 1917.

"The Songs of the Public Theaters in the Time of Shakespeare," *JEGP, 28* (April, 1929), 166–202.

Noble, Richmond. "Shakespeare's Songs and Stage," in *Shakespeare and the Theatre*, a Series of Papers by members of the Shakespeare Association, pp. 120–33. London, Humphrey Milford, 1927.

Shakespeare's Use of Song. London, Humphrey Milford, 1923.

Reed, Edward Bliss. *Songs from the British Drama*. New Haven, Yale University Press, 1925.

Symonds, John Addington. "The Lyrism of the English Romantic Drama" and "Lyrics from Elizabethan Song-Books," *In the Key of Blue and Other Prose Essays*, pp. 241–302. New York, Macmillan, 1893.

Walker, Andrew Jackson. "Popular Songs and Broadside Ballads in the English Drama, 1559–1642." Ph.D. dissertation, Harvard University, 1934.

Wood, Warren Welles. "A Comparison between Shakespeare and His Contemporaries in Their Use of Music and Sound Effects." Ph.D. dissertation, Northwestern University, 1944.

Wright, Louis B. "Extraneous Song in Elizabethan Drama after the Advent of Shakespeare," *Studies in Philology, 24* (April, 1927), 261–74.